Best Outdoor Adventures
Chattanooga

Best Outdoor Adventures
CHATTANOOGA

A Guide to the Area's Greatest
Hiking, Paddling, and Cycling

JOHNNY MOLLOY

GUILFORD, CONNECTICUT

FALCONGUIDES®

An imprint of The Rowman & Littlefield Publishing Group, Inc.
4501 Forbes Blvd., Ste. 200
Lanham, MD 20706
www.rowman.com
Falcon and FalconGuides are registered trademarks and Make Adventure Your Story is a trademark of The Rowman & Littlefield Publishing Group, Inc.

Distributed by NATIONAL BOOK NETWORK

Photos by Johnny Molloy
Maps by Melissa Baker

Printed in the United States of America

British Library Cataloguing-in-Publication Information available

Library of Congress Cataloging-in-Publication Data available

ISBN 978-1-4930-4144-2 (paperback)
ISBN 978-1-4930-4145-9 (e-book)

∞™ The paper used in this publication meets the minimum requirements of American National Standard for Information Sciences—Permanence of Paper for Printed Library Materials, ANSI/NISO Z39.48-1992.

This book is for the adventurers—those willing to head out into new places to hike, bike, paddle, camp, and climb, making outdoor memories along the way.

The upper falls in
Rock Creek Gorge
Scenic Area

Acknowledgments

Thanks to my wife, Keri Anne, for her help. Thanks to Peter Williams for floating many a river. Also, thanks to Kelty for their fine tents, sleeping bags, and other camping gear I used while adventuring around greater Chattanooga.

Moments like this are part of Chattanooga's outdoor adventures.

Contents

Overview

Bluffs along the Bluff Trail

Introduction

Chattanooga, Tennessee, and surrounding environs have deservingly gained a reputation as an outdoor haven, with opportunities to hike, pedal, and paddle found right in town and stretching outward from the Cumberland Plateau to the west to the Appalachians to the east to the Valley and Ridge Province country to the south. It's one thing to have a beautiful landscape—after all, Chattanooga is known as the Scenic City—yet another altogether to have attractive lands under public domain preserved as parks and forests, overlain with hiking trails, biking trails, and boat landings, as well as places to camp or climb, destinations where we can execute outdoor adventures. Greater Chattanooga is blessed with parks aplenty in town—from the celebrated Riverwalk to Greenway Farms to South Chickamauga Greenway. Radiating outward, Prentice Cooper State Forest, South Cumberland State Park, and lands of the Cumberland Trail present adventure opportunities atop the Cumberland Plateau. Easterly, the Cherokee National Forest houses half a million acres of waters and mountains to ply your kayak or canoe, mountain bike a mountainside, or hike in the wilderness. The Chatta-hoochee National Forest in Georgia also offers adventure and lands to explore, as does Alabama's Desoto State Park.

All this spells paradise for the outdoor adventurer. Let's start with hiking—the most accessible of activities. In this guide you can find hiking adventures representing a mosaic of opportunities found in these parts. You can make a rugged, rocky trek along the Grand Canyon of the Tennessee River to Edwards Point or walk the rolling shores of Chickamauga Lake at Harrison Bay State Park. Perhaps you prefer an in-town hike to view the rock quarry and designated small wild area at Greenway Farms Park. You could enjoy a historic hike at Point Park or Chickamauga Battlefield. Waterfalls are found all around the Chattanooga sphere: View the tall shower of Keown Falls down Georgia way, stair-stepping Benton Falls atop Chilhowee Mountain in the Appalachians, powerful Foster Falls on the Fiery Gizzard Trail, or remote Imodium Falls up by Soddy-Daisy. Perhaps instead you want to grab a first-rate panorama at Cloudland Canyon State Park or North Chickamauga Creek Gorge.

Mountain bikers and greenway riders can also find a variety of rewarding adventures within easy striking distance of the Scenic City. You can tackle the challenging and rocky trails up on TVA's Raccoon Mountain or ride the speedy in-town course at Stinger's Ridge. Enterprise South Nature Park presents a stellar set of dedicated mountain biking trails that will scratch your pedaling itch. Sometimes we just want to roll down a greenway or cruise with our family. In that case, Chattanooga has got you covered. Roll down the famed Riverwalk along the Tennessee River right into downtown, crossing the celebrated Walnut Street bridge, or cruise the South Chickamauga Creek Greenway. Ride through history on the quiet roads of Chickamauga Battlefield. Still more mountain biking trails await you at White Oak Mountain, Chilhowee Mountain, Cloudland Canyon, and Tanasi.

The paddling opportunities are varied and rewarding as well. Tackle narrow and fun West Chickamauga Creek, or stroke down the mighty Tennessee River, landing in downtown Chattanooga. Or perhaps you are looking for a little whitewater on the gorgeous, fun, and mountain-rimmed Hiwassee River. If you are in the mood for a quieter river experience, float the Sequatchie through one of the world's most beautiful valleys. Make a relaxed rural paddle on the Oostanaula River, or wind your way through the gravelly shallows and pools of the Conasauga River. Yet there are times when we are looking for a flatwater paddle; this guide offers several paddling adventures of that sort. Take a trip around formerly inhabited Patten Island from Harrison Bay State Park on Chickamauga Lake, or paddle mountain-rimmed Parksville Lake, exploring quiet, slender coves fed by mountain streams. Make the beautiful yet strange water trip to the graves of Nickajack Lake, standing above the waters of Mullens Cove.

This guide also includes a section on car camping and rock climbing adventures. The camping section details five nearby car camping destinations where you can not only camp for the sake of camping and relaxing but also enjoy many of the hiking, paddling, and bicycling adventures detailed in this guide. In fact, I stayed at every one of these campgrounds while assimilating information for *Best Outdoor Adventures Chattanooga*. The campground information includes an overview of the locale, when to go, and what activities are available.

Chattanooga is a nationally renowned rock climbing area—often dubbed the best rock climbing area east of the Mississippi or, alternatively, the best rock climbing in the entire country near an urban area—including such places as Sunset Rock and the famed Tennessee Wall. This narrative will inform you of rock climbing opportunities, helping you get started in that sport. However, rock climbing is something you only engage in with experienced people leading the way.

No matter what activity you choose, the important thing is to get out there, have some adventures, and make some memories. May this guide help you reach that goal.

Weather

Located along the Tennessee River, with the Cumberland Plateau rising to the west and the Appalachians forming a wall to the east, the city of Chattanooga experiences all four seasons in their glory. The city can get downright hot in summer, but area residents can head to the Appalachians, the Cumberland Plateau, or their favorite body of water for a cooler experience. If hiking or biking, try to go in the morning for cooler conditions and to avoid common afternoon thunderstorms. An outdoor adventurer's pulse quickens when autumn's leaves turn colors and fresh air sweeps across the land. It is a time of cool mornings and warm afternoons and reliably dry weather. This accommodating period gives way to winter, but the cold season in Chattanooga is not bad. Although you will experience all-day rains, subfreezing temperatures, and snow in the adjacent high country, outdoor enthusiasts will also enjoy plenty of mild days fine for camping, climbing, hiking, and biking, even paddling. Springtime in Chattanooga is a roller-coaster ride. Mild sunny days are followed by cold, wet, and windy ones. However, the same thing applies to spring as it does winter—you will have plenty of nice days each month during which to adventure, and the second half of spring in Chattanooga can simply be a delight. Revel in it.

The chart below provides Chattanooga's monthly weather averages to help you know what to expect. (**Note:** Be prepared for cooler temperatures and more precipitation on the Cumberland Plateau and the Appalachians.)

Month	Average High (°F)	Average Low (°F)	Precipitation (inches)
January	50	31	4.9
February	55	34	5.0
March	64	41	5.0
April	73	48	4.0
May	80	57	4.1
June	87	66	4.1
July	90	70	4.9
August	90	69	3.5
September	83	62	4.0
October	73	50	3.3
November	62	40	5.0
December	52	33	4.9

Flora and Fauna

The landscape of greater Chattanooga varies greatly—from the deep valley of the Tennessee River to the rising Cumberland Plateau, forming a 1,000-foot-high wall capped with sandstone cliffs and seemingly endless forests, to the rolling hills of the Tennessee River Valley, from which rise the magnificent Southern Appalachian Mountains, to the long narrow ridges separated by slender parallel valleys south of town. Widespread public lands within these areas create large swaths for wildlife to roam.

At the top of the food chain stands the black bear. You can run into one anywhere in the region and on any adventure outside the city limits (and occasionally within the city limits) included in this guide. Although attacks by black bears are very rare, they have happened in the Southern Appalachians. Seeing a bear is an exciting yet potentially scary experience. If you meet a bear, stay calm and don't run. Make loud noises to scare off the bear and back away slowly. Remain aware and alert.

A wide variety of wildlife in addition to bruins calls these landscapes home. Deer are the land animal you are most likely to see hiking area trails. They can be found throughout the greater Chattanooga region. A quiet hiker may also spy turkeys, raccoons, even a coyote.

Paddlers will see more birdlife, from waterfowl such as ducks to raptors, including bald eagles. Bicyclers, especially mountain bikers, have a tougher time seeing wildlife due to the speed and concentration needed to tackle trails. Greenway pedalers may have better luck. For all types of adventures, simply follow this rule of thumb: If you feel uncomfortable when encountering any critter, keep your distance and they will generally keep theirs.

Overhead, many raptors ply the skies for food, including hawks, falcons, and owls. Depending on your location, you may spot kingfishers or woodpeckers. Songbirds are abundant during the warm season, no matter the habitat.

The flora offers as much variety as you would expect with such elevational and habitat range. In the mountains and atop the Cumberland Plateau, moisture-dependent forests are found along the streams and waterways, places where rhododendron creates immense thickets below black birch, tulip trees, and maple. Here grow incredible displays of wildflowers reflecting a cornucopia of color—purple dwarf crest iris, white trillium, pink phlox, and red cardinal flower. Drier slopes support hickory, oak, and mountain laurel. Cedars and pines thrive on rocky, sun-burnished hillsides. In the Appalachians east of town, northern hardwood forests of yellow birch, beech, and cherry appear as you head to higher elevations. It all adds up to vegetational variety that can be seen and experienced as spring climbs the mountains and fall descends back to the valleys.

Wilderness Restrictions/Regulations

The best outdoor adventures near Chattanooga take place on Tennessee state forest and park lands, federal lands of the Cherokee and Chattahoochee National Forests as well as Chickamauga & Chattanooga National Military Park, and, to a lesser extent, Chattanooga city parks, and Georgia and Alabama state parks. Entrance to these areas is mostly free except for Point Park and Cloudland Canyon State Park. Boat ramps are generally managed by the state in which they lie. Lake paddlers may see Tennessee Wildlife Resources Agency officers checking for life vests and such. Hikers, paddlers, and mountain bikers are expected to monitor their own behavior, though you may see park rangers in the battlefield park units as well as urban parks. Developed recreation areas with campgrounds and trails will also be supervised.

Looking out from the top of the quarry toward Walden Mountain

Getting Around

AREA CODES

The greater Chattanooga area code in East Tennessee is 423, the area code in northwest Georgia is 762, and the area code in northeast Alabama is 256.

BY ROAD

For the purposes of this guide, the best outdoor adventures near Chattanooga are confined to a 1-hour drive from downtown, which includes north and west up the Cumberland Plateau, east to the Appalachians near the North Carolina state line, south into Georgia down to Calhoun, and southwest into a sliver of northeast Alabama.

Three major interstates converge in the greater Chattanooga region. Directions to trailheads are given from these arteries. They include interstates I-75, I-24, and I-59. Other major roads are US 27, US 64, and TN 153.

BY AIR

Chattanooga Metropolitan Airport (CHA), also known as Lovell Field, is located about 5 miles east of downtown Chattanooga near I-75. To book reservations online, check your favorite airline's website or search one of the following travel sites for the best price: cheaptickets.com, expedia.com, orbitz.com, priceline .com, travelocity.com, or trip.com—just to name a few.

BY BUS

Chattanooga Area Regional Transportation Authority (known as CARTA) operates bus service throughout greater Chattanooga, though many of the outdoor adventures in this guide are in areas not served by mass transit. Visit gocarta .org or call (423) 629-1473. Greyhound serves many towns in the region; visit greyhound.com for more information.

VISITOR INFORMATION

For general information on greater Chattanooga, visit the city's official tourism website: chattanoogafun.com or call (800) 322-3344. The website provides an overview of things to do, where to stay, restaurants, and other Scenic City attractions.

How to Use This Guide

This guide contains just about everything you will ever need to choose, plan for, enjoy, and survive an outdoor adventure near Chattanooga. Stuffed with useful area information, *Best Outdoor Adventures Chattanooga* features forty mapped and cued outdoor adventures: twenty hikes, ten bicycle rides, and ten paddles, as well as informative narratives on car camping and rock climbing. The adventures are grouped by activity.

Each section begins with an introduction to the hiking, bicycling, or paddling adventure in which you are given a sweeping look of what lies ahead. Each adventure narrative starts with a short **summary** of the adventure's highlights. These quick overviews give you a taste of the adventure to follow.

Following the overview you will find the **specs** relevant to the activity: quick, nitty-gritty details of the route. Most are self-explanatory, but here are some details:

Distance: This is the total distance of the recommended route—one-way for loop trips, the round-trip for an out-and-back or lollipop, point-to-point for a shuttle.

Time: The average time it will take to cover the route. It is based on the total distance, elevation gain, and condition and difficulty of the trail; also condition and difficulty of the water surface for paddles. Your fitness level will also affect your time.

Difficulty: Each adventure has been assigned a level of difficulty. The rating system was developed from several sources and personal experience. These levels are meant to be a guideline only, and an adventure may prove easier or harder for different people depending on ability and physical fitness.

Trail surface: General information about what to expect underfoot.

Seasons: The best time of year for the activity.

Other trail users: Others you may encounter along the route, from equestrians to mountain bikers to motorboaters, depending on the activity.

Canine compatibility: Know the trail regulations before you take your dog with you.

Land status: National park, national forest, state forest, city park, etc.

Fees and permits: You may need to carry money with you for park entrance fees and permits.

The Upper Truck Trail makes
for easy scenic hiking

Maps: A list of other maps to supplement the maps in this book. US Geological Survey (USGS) maps are the best source for accurate topographical information, but the local park map may show more-recent trails. Use both.

Trail contacts: The location, phone number, and website URL for the local land and water managers in charge of all selected routes. Before you head out, get trail access information; contact the land and/or water manager after your visit if you see damage or misuse.

Other considerations: Additional information to enhance your adventure.

Finding the trailhead gives you dependable driving directions to where you will want to park.

The Hike, The Ride, or The Paddle. The meat of the chapter, this is a detailed and honest, carefully researched impression of the route. It often includes area history, both natural and human.

Miles and Directions (hikes and rides only): The mileage cues identify all turns and trail name changes, as well as points of interest along the given route.

Paddling entries use additional, more-relevant criteria, such as river/lake type, current, boats used, and the like.

Do not feel restricted to the routes mapped here. Be adventurous; use this guide as a platform to discover new routes for yourself. One of the simplest ways to begin is to tackle the route in reverse (though this may be difficult when paddling a river!). This way you get two adventures on one map. For your own purposes, you may wish to photograph the pages from this guide on your device then take it with you on your adventure, or just take the book along. The important thing is to get out there on outdoor adventures and make some memories of your own.

How to Use the Maps

Overview map: This map shows the location of each route in the area by route number.

   Route map: This is your primary guide to each hike, pedal, or paddle. It shows all accessible roads and trails, points of interest, water, landmarks, and geographical features. It also distinguishes trails from roads, paved roads from unpaved roads, or the proper water route from other creeks, channels, or parts of a given lake. The selected route is highlighted, and directional arrows point the way.

An alluring gravel bar
on the Sequatchie

Map Legend

Municipal

≡(75)≡ Interstate Highway

≡(41)≡ US Highway

≡(136)≡ State Road

≡(55)≡ County/Local Road

═══ Featured Local Road

═ ═ ═ Featured Unpaved Road

= = = = Unpaved Road

├──┼──┤ Railroad

·· — ·· — State Boundary

•—•—•— Power Line

Trails

▬▬▬▬ Featured Trail

------ Trail

- - - - - Paddle Route

Water Features

⬭ Body of Water

〜 River/Creek

〜 〜 Intermittent Stream

≋ Waterfall

∥ Rapid

♂ Spring

Symbols

∩ Arch/Natural Bridge

▭ Bench

▥ Boardwalk

➤ Boat Ramp

≍ Bridge

■ Building/Point of Interest

⛰ Campground

▲ Campsite

⬥ Gate

1 Mileage

▲ Peak

🅿 Parking

⊞ Picnic Area

◣ Put-in/Takeout

▣ Ranger Station

▥ Restrooms

o Town

① Trailhead

❓ Visitor/Information Center

Land Management

☐ National Park

☐ State / County / City Park or Forest

☐ State Natural Area / WMA

North Chickamauga Creek is one of the prettiest creeks around greater Chattanooga.

HIKING

Of all the adventures presented in this guide, hiking is the most easily executed by the most people. It can be as simple as putting on your shoes and then putting one foot in front of the other. Making it to the trailhead of your choice is another matter; though no matter where you live in greater Chattanooga, you can find a hiking adventure close by.

Here we present a collection of the best hikes from the greater Chattanooga region—a mosaic of foot-oriented adventures that vary in distance, difficulty, terrain, and highlights so you can sample the assortment of trail trekking experiences available in and around the Scenic City. Grab a first-rate view from Point Park. Walk the nearby wildlands of Prentice Cooper State Forest or the more remote Savage Gulf State Natural Area. Check out the waterfalls of Sitton Sitton's Gulch in north Georgia. Try new and different places—for these are the spices in the entree of hiking.

This waterfall is created at the spillway draining Rainbow Lake.

Looking north from Sunset Rock

1 Point Park Hike

This dramatic hike combines one of Chattanooga's best vistas along with Civil War history atop iconic Lookout Mountain. Start at Point Park and enjoy continuous panoramas to reach the actual point of Lookout Mountain, then loop past spectacular clifflines to view-laden Sunset Rock. Circle past rifle pits used 150 years ago and view the historic Cravens House. Finally, climb back to the superlative overlooks atop Point Park.

Start: Point Park

Distance: 4.6-mile lollipop

Hiking time: About 2.3 hours

Difficulty: Moderate; 600-foot climb

Trail surface: Natural

Best season: Year-round

Other trail users: Civil War buffs

Canine compatibility: Leashed dogs allowed

Land status: National military park

Fees and permits: Entrance fee

Schedule: Daily, 8:30 a.m. to sunset

Maps: USGS Chattanooga; Lookout Mountain Battlefield

Trail contacts: Chickamauga & Chattanooga National Military Park, 3370 Lafayette Rd., Fort Oglethorpe, GA 30742; (706) 866-9241; nps.gov/chch

Overlooking Moccasin Bend and downtown Chattanooga from Point Park

Finding the trailhead: From exit 175 on I-24, west of downtown Chattanooga, take Browns Ferry Road south for 0.4 mile to a traffic light and Cummings Highway, US 41/64/11/72. Turn left on Cummings Highway and follow it for 0.8 mile; turn right on Alford Hill Road. Follow Alford Hill Road and soon reach TN 318/Wauhatchie Pike. Turn left on Wauhatchie Pike and follow it for 1.4 miles to TN 148/Scenic Highway. Turn right on Scenic Highway and follow it for 2.3 miles; veer sharply right on East Brow Road (look for signs to Point Park). Follow East Brow Road for 1.1 miles to Point Park. Parking for the national military park is on your left, just after the road curves left past the stone Point Park entrance, on the right. GPS: N35 0.598' / W85 20.630'

The Hike

Lookout Mountain is one of Chattanooga's signature physical features, rising over the Tennessee River at Moccasin Bend then extending south into Georgia and Alabama. The northern tip of the mountain, overlooking downtown Chattanooga, is home to Point Park, a noble place that presents some of the finest views found anywhere in the region as well as Civil War history. It is claimed that the very name Chattanooga is Cherokee for "Lookout Mountain." After visiting Point Park, it is easy to see how the peak got its name.

Then there's the Civil War history. One of the units of Chickamauga & Chattanooga National Military Park, Point Park, along with other protected lands on Lookout Mountain, contains more than 30 miles of trails to explore. Along with the described hike, you have miles and miles of other pathways to create additional hiking adventures.

This hiking adventure is a good one, full of overlooks, geological sights, history, and plenty of natural beauty, along with some solid elevation change to get your heart pumping. Grab a trail map at the visitor center and be sure to review the exhibits that cover a long period of time here atop Lookout Mountain.

The hike begins after you make your way through the imposing stone entrance to Point Park. A concrete path leads north from the entrance to interpretive information signs and overlooks, while an asphalt trail makes a rough oval along the mountain's brow. Visitors are heading here and there, first-timers meandering about while repeat visitors aim directly for their favorite overlook. Once down at the Ochs Memorial Observatory area, a small museum built on the actual point of Point Park, check out additional exhibits; more importantly, soak in the mother of all panoramas. To your right, the city of Chattanooga extends toward the Appalachians, while the Tennessee River and Moccasin Bend lie below. The greater Cumberland Plateau ranges to the north and west. It is truly a sight to behold.

You will truly begin the hike from the Ochs Memorial Observatory. Thus far it has been more of a meander from one sight to the next. Once on the Bluff Trail (after viewing an inlaid monument on a stone cliff), you will head south along a regal cliffline rising above the path. Spring seeps flow into the trail from above. Dense forest flanks the path, yet the drop-off from the mountain down to Lookout Valley is palpable. The trail in front of you is rugged in places, including one spot where a handrail has been installed, as you work through a narrows with land falling away to your right. This track was laid by the Civilian Conservation Corps (CCC) back in the 1930s. Note where they added short spur trails that work their way into stone clefts. These spurs are no longer maintained but are fun to explore. Ahead you will pass beneath Sunset Rock, one of the premier rock climbing territories in the Southeast. Don't be surprised to see adventurous folk with ropes, harnesses, and carabiners up on the cliff as you hike by.

Be sure to climb the signed side trail up to Sunset Rock. Presenting panoramas to the west and north, it is worth the ascent. Sunset Rock was used to observe troop movements during the Civil War. You're likely to see other visitors at Sunset Rock—it can be reached by a short path from West Brow Road. From Sunset Rock, our hike begins an extended 600-foot downgrade, joining the Gum Spring Trail and passing rocked-in Gum Spring.

The route levels off when you join the Upper Truck Trail, one of a series of paths running along the side slope of the mountain. This wide, easy path makes for a literal walk in the woods. Ahead, view the site of CCC Camp Demory before climbing with the Rifle Pits Trail. Find the stonework of the rifle pits and imagine men perched behind them, waiting for battle during the War between the States.

Then you come to the auto-accessible Cravens House, near where the Battle of the Clouds took place. The home was used by generals on both sides of the Civil War and was eventually burned before Robert Cravens rebuilt the house you see today.

After you've absorbed the interpretive information at Cravens House, the Mountain Beautiful Trail leads you back up to Point Park, reclaiming several hundred feet of elevation lost. On the return you can relish the stellar vistas one more time.

Miles and Directions

0.0 From the Point Park entrance, head north on a concrete path among views and monuments. You can already acquire distant views. After exploring up here, aim for the lower end of the park, taking steps to Ochs Memorial Observatory. Continue down to reach the small stone building surrounded by a stone patio with an unrivaled overlook of greater Chattanooga and surrounding lands to the north.

0.2 Leave the view at Ochs Memorial and walk down metal stairs leading to the base of a vertical cliffline. Pass an inlaid plaque on the cliffline then reach a sign indicating the Bluff Trail. Head south toward Sunset Rock.

0.4 Pass the pipe of Rock Springs, under an alcove in the impressive cliffline. Continue among other stone walls and boulders and immovable rock wonderments.

0.8 Intersect the Cravens House Trail. It leads right, but we keep left here with the Bluff Trail, still walking along the base of remarkable clifflines.

1.4 Take the signed spur leading left, uphill toward Sunset Rock, after passing through a popular rock climbing area. Ascend the spur to reach a large rock slab with an embedded interpretive sign. Enjoy great vistas both north and west, then backtrack to continue south on the Bluff Trail.

1.7 Come to another trail intersection. Turn acutely right and downhill onto the rocky Gum Spring Trail, making a steep descent moderated by switchbacks.

2.2 Look for rocked-in Gum Spring to the right of the trail. Continue downhill along the streambed of Gum Spring.

2.3 Meet the Upper Truck Trail. Turn right (northbound), stepping over the streambed of Gum Springs. Intersect the signed Lower Gum Springs Trail, heading left. Keep straight with the Upper Truck Trail in deep, tall woods.

2.5 Stay right with the Upper Truck Trail as the Guild Trail leaves left.

2.7 Look downhill and left for the stone walls of Camp Demory, a CCC camp whose residents developed much of the park infrastructure.

2.9 Head right on the Rifle Pits Trail. Climb a bit, passing the stone rifle pits ahead.

3.5 Pass the other end of the Cravens House Trail. Keep straight toward Cravens House.

3.6 Reach Cravens House. To return to Point Park, take the singletrack trail leading from the left-hand corner of the homesite as you have your back to the Cravens House. There should be a sign indicating "to Mountain Beautiful Trail." Climb using switchbacks and even a wooden staircase.

Point Park Hike

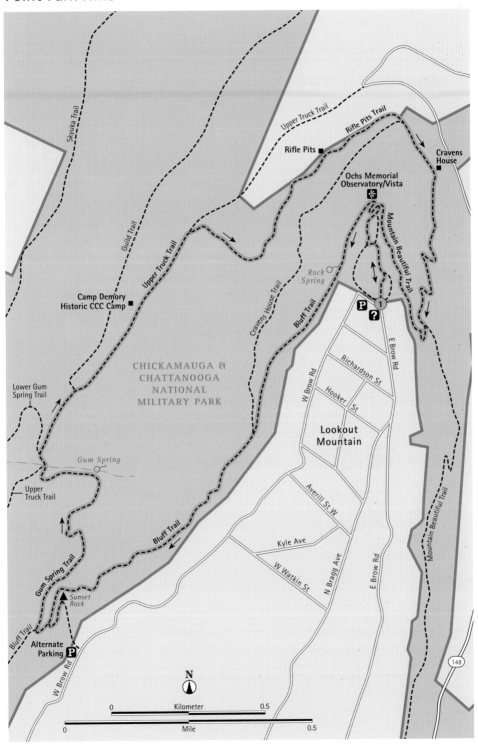

Skyuka Trail

Guild Trail

Upper Truck Trail

Upper Truck Trail

Rifle Pits Trail

Rifle Pits

Cravens House

Ochs Memorial Observatory/Vista

Mountain Beautiful Trail

Rock Spring

Cravens House Trail

Bluff Trail

Camp Demory Historic CCC Camp

CHICKAMAUGA & CHATTANOOGA NATIONAL MILITARY PARK

Lower Gum Spring Trail

Gum Spring

Upper Truck Trail

Gum Spring Trail

Bluff Trail

Sunset Rock

Bluff Trail

Alternate Parking

W Brow Rd

W Brow Rd

Richardson St

E Brow Rd

Hooker St

Lookout Mountain

Averill St W

Kyle Ave

W Watkin St

N Bragg Ave

E Brow Rd

Mountain Beautiful Trail

148

N

0   Kilometer   0.5

0   Mile   0.5

These steps lead to incredible views from Ochs Memorial Observatory

4.1 Meet the Mountain Beautiful Trail, head right and continue climbing; turn north and hike along clifflines.

4.4 Complete the loop portion of the hike. From here, backtrack up past Ochs Memorial Observatory.

4.6 Return to Point Park entrance, completing the hiking adventure.

2 Big Ridge Small Wild Area via Greenway Farms Park

This hiking adventure takes you to and through highlights aplenty. Start at Greenway Farms Park then trek along North Chickamauga Creek, making a big bend, gaining watery views. From there, climb the slope of Big Ridge, gaining land views. Reach TVA's Big Ridge Small Wild Area and make a loop, walking in the shadow of towering hardwoods. Your return route leads you by a rock quarry, a lake, wooded hillsides, and even a park garden.

Start: Greenway Farms Park near Hamill Road

Distance: 6.2-mile triple lollipop

Hiking time: About 3.6 hours

Difficulty: Moderate

Trail surface: Gravel, asphalt, natural

Best season: Year-round; can be hot in summer

Other trail users: Local daily exercisers, bicyclists

Canine compatibility: Leashed dogs allowed

Land status: City park, TVA small wild area

Fees and permits: No fees or permits required

Schedule: Daily, dawn to dusk

Purple asters brighten trailside meadows

The rock quarry at
Greenway Farms Park

Maps: USGS Daisy, East Chattanooga; Greenway Farms—North Chickamauga Creek
Conservancy

Trail Contacts: Greenway Farms Park, 3005 Hamill Rd., Hixson, TN 37343; (423)
643–6311; chattanooga.gov

Finding the trailhead: From exit 4 on I-75, northeast of Chattanooga, take TN
153 North for 7.8 miles, crossing the Tennessee River. Turn right onto Hamill
Road and follow it for 1.6 miles. Turn right into Greenway Farms Park just after
crossing the North Chickamauga Creek bridge; continue just a short distance and
turn right into the first parking area in the park. Here you will pick up the North
Chickamauga Greenway. GPS: N35 7.724' / W85 12.899'

The Hike

This fun, action-packed highlight reel of a hike combines one trail network in two
preserves. You not only see lots of sights but also hike different types of trails—
from the gravel North Chickamauga Greenway, to creekside dirt tracks, to slender singletrack paths scaling hillsides, even asphalt trails. The sights are varied
as well—a creek, wildflower meadows, old cabins, a cemetery, park buildings,
distant ridges, a water-filled quarry, regal tulip trees, and other hardwoods in
excess of a century old. You can easily vary the hike in the network of pathways

that compose Greenway Farms Park, lengthening or shortening the trek to suit your desires.

The story of this hiking destination starts with the construction of Chickamauga Dam back in the late 1930s. What was then backwoods northeast of Chattanooga bustled as the dam was constructed. Limestone was quarried from the base of Big Ridge to build the dam. (The hike actually traces part of the old road connecting the dam to the quarry.) The lands around the dam and quarry became Tennessee Valley Authority (TVA) property. TVA managers saw something special atop Big Ridge, namely regal hardwoods more than a century old. Big Ridge was designated a TVA small wild area, one of twenty-eight such areas, which harbor special or unique plant and animal life. The old-growth woodlands are primarily tulip trees, shagbark hickory, and oaks. The Boy Scout Trail was constructed for hikers to view these woodland giants. The 200-acre property, along with Greenway Farms, also provides an oasis for wildlife, from deer to wild turkeys.

Greenway Farms also has a story. Once the home of dentist Benton Spangler, what is now Greenway Farms Park was bought by the City of Chattanooga in 1990. Parts of the fields were left to regrow in trees, five property ponds were filled in, and the park entrance on Hamill Road was created, among other changes. A working farm most of its existence, the property went through several previous hands before Benton Spangler, even functioning as a dairy farm at one point. Today Greenway Farms Park is a popular destination due to its trails, rental facilities, paddler access to North Chickamauga Creek, plus a wildly popular dog park.

The hike starts along North Chickamauga Creek on the North Chickamauga Greenway, heading south. Grab a view of the creek from the canoe/kayak access you quickly pass. It isn't long before you leave the greenway and join the natural-surface Creek Loop Trail, a level path following an extreme bend of the creek. The stream is always nearby this mostly shaded track. The trail passes occasional small clearings being cultivated for natural prairie wildflowers and vegetation.

Beyond the bend, visit a small creekside cabin before emerging back on the North Chickamauga Greenway. In summer, an adjacent garden will provide an eyeful of color. Ahead, take the short spur to a remote canoe/kayak launch for a water-level view of North Chickamauga Creek. Ahead, enter the "back 40" of Greenway Farms. Here the greenway leads along the lower slope of Big Ridge. Soak in views as you hike past the upper end of the rock quarry, bordered by a fence. The greenway returns to the stream, keeping along the water before eventually finding the TVA's Big Ridge Small Wild Area. Here join the Boy Scout Loop, winding amid big trees to reach the ridgetop before turning downhill, finding still other giants as well as strange sinkholes and huge vines as big around as your leg.

Your return route takes you by the lake at the quarry bottom as well as more remote woods on the Ropes Course Trail—in truth, just a standard hiking path these days. However, you will get in a bit of climbing on it. Finally, join a mostly untrod stretch of greenway, nearing a cemetery from the farm days before backtracking to the trailhead, another hiking adventure in the bag.

Miles and Directions

0.0   Join the gravel North Chickamauga Greenway, heading south into Greenway Farms Park. A paved part of the greenway descends to North Chickamauga Creek and heads north under the Hamill Road bridge.

0.1   Cross a side creek then pass the main park canoe/kayak access.

0.2   Pass a restroom and alternate parking area. Ahead, walk by the park meeting facility. Continue curving with North Chickamauga Creek.

0.3   Reach a trail intersection. Here, split right onto the level natural-surface Creek Loop Trail, popular with joggers.

0.8   A short spur leaves left, shortcutting the Creek Loop Trail. Keep straight, where overhanging trees create an almost tunnel-like effect.

1.3   Pass the other end of the Creek Loop Trail shortcut.

1.4   Walk by an old creekside cabin.

1.5   Stay right as the Creek Loop Trail splits.

1.7   Turn right on the North Chickamauga Greenway. View the gardens.

1.8   Come to a four-way intersection. Head right to the boat ramp to check out the stream, return to the intersection, then continue on the greenway toward the Ropes Course and Boy Scout Trails.

2.0   A closed path heads right. Stay with the greenway as it climbs Big Ridge.

2.2   Stay with the greenway as the north end of the Ropes Course Trail heads left. Next you will walk along the top of the quarry, enjoying views of Walden Ridge to the west. Ahead, walk by the other end of the Ropes Course Trail. Descend to creek level again, still on the greenway, passing the spur trail to the quarry.

Big Ridge Wild Area via Greenway Farms Park

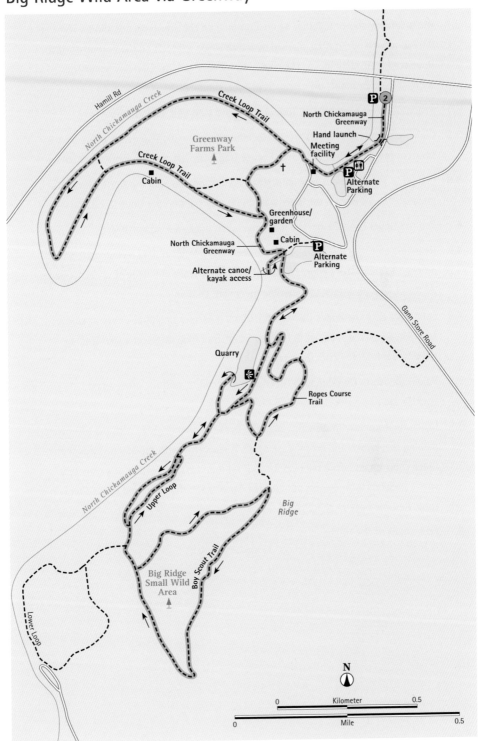

Hamill Rd

North Chickamauga Creek

Creek Loop Trail

Greenway
Farms Park

North Chickamauga
Greenway

Hand launch

Meeting
facility

P 2

P Alternate
Parking

Creek Loop Trail

Cabin

Greenhouse/
garden

North Chickamauga
Greenway

Cabin

P Alternate
Parking

Alternate canoe/
kayak access

Quarry

Ropes Course
Trail

Gann Store Road

North Chickamauga Creek

Upper Loop

Big
Ridge

Boy Scout Trail

Big Ridge
Small Wild
Area

Lower Loop

N

| 0 | Kilometer | 0.5 |
| 0 | Mile | 0.5 |

2.5 The North Chickamauga Greenway splits. Stay with the lower path.

2.7 The greenway comes together again. Continue on the greenway and shortly come to Big Ridge Small Wild Area, marked by a trail kiosk. Split left on the natural-surface Boy Scout Trail, climbing, as the greenway leaves right. The slim Boy Scout Trail soon splits, creating its own loop. Stay right, climbing.

3.1 Reach the crest of Big Ridge. Turn north, rising a bit still. Watch for big trees.

3.5 Come to a trail intersection after descending from the Big Ridge high point. Here a shortcut leaves right to the Ropes Course Trail. Stay left, passing more hefty oaks.

3.9 Complete the Boy Scout Trail loop. Head right, soon rejoining the North Chickamauga Greenway. Ahead, the greenway splits; stay right on the Upper Loop.

4.2 End the Upper Loop. Rejoin the main greenway, backtracking northeast.

4.6 Head left on the gravel road leading to the quarry. Walk around a chain gate and descend to the water's edge. Check out the quarry walls and body of water formed by the quarry. Backtrack to rejoin the greenway, climbing.

4.8 Split right onto the Ropes Course Trail. Climb a narrow singletrack natural-surface trail. Ahead, pass a shortcut to the Boy Scout Trail then intersect a spur leading right to Gann Store Road. Descend.

5.2 Rejoin the North Chickamauga Greenway. Descend toward the creek again, backtracking.

5.5 Reach the four-way intersection near the boat ramp again. Stay with the greenway, passing the garden and greenhouse again. Ahead, stay with the greenway as the Creek Loop leaves left. A hill rises on your right and is the location of a cemetery where previous farm owners are interred. Soon reach the other end of the Creek Loop. Resume backtracking.

6.2 Arrive back at the trailhead.

3   Harrison Bay State Park Hike

Take a walk on the waterside at this Tennessee state park hugging the shores of Chickamauga Lake. The Bay Point Loop Trail is your conduit, leading you beside the waters of the scenic impoundment in woodsy parkland. The circuit hike leads to three separate peninsulas jutting into Chickamauga Lake, offering views nearly the entire way that are eclipsed only by cleared overlooks where you can enjoy an unobstructed panorama of the waters and islands beyond.

Start: Marina parking area

Distance: 4.2-mile lollipop

Hiking time: About 2 hours

Difficulty: Easy to moderate

Trail surface: Pea gravel and natural

Best season: Winter for solitude, autumn for colors

Other trail users: Local daily exercisers, mountain bikers

Canine compatibility: Leashed dogs allowed

Land status: State park

Fees and permits: No fees or permits required

Schedule: Daily dawn to dusk

Maps: USGS Snow Hill; Harrison Bay State Park

Trail contacts: Harrison Bay State Park, 8411 Harrison Bay Rd., Harrison, TN 37341; (423) 344-6214; tnstateparks.com

Author cruises boardwalk on a cloudy morning

Finding the trailhead: From exit 11 on I-75, near Ooltewah, Tennessee, take US 11/ US 64 West for 0.3 mile. Turn left onto Hunter Road and continue for 6.1 miles to TN 58. Turn right on TN 58 and continue 1.5 miles. Turn left onto Harrison Bay Road and follow it for 1.5 miles to the state park. From the park entrance, follow the signs to the marina/boat ramp and the end of the road near the park office. From the ramp area, curve east into a large parking lot. The signed Bay Point Loop trailhead is at the east end of the large parking lot. GPS: N35 10.095' / W85 7.189'

The Hike

Harrison Bay State Park, the setting for this waterside hiking adventure, is Tennessee's oldest state park. The 1,200-acre preserve was set aside in 1937 and offers around 40 miles of shoreline on Chickamauga Lake, a Tennessee Valley Authority (TVA) impoundment, also a product of the 1930s. Once regular meeting grounds of the native Cherokee, the alluring flats beside the once free-flowing Tennessee River became the community of Harrison. When the TVA built Chickamauga Dam, Harrison was inundated and the residents were relocated. The former community of Harrison became Harrison Bay, a large, relatively shallow portion of Chickamauga Lake from which rises several islands, including Patten Island, an integral part of a paddling adventure detailed later in this guide. (See adventure 36: Patten Island Circuit.)

The rising lake also formed a series of peninsulas, low ridges jutting into the water. It is these pine, oak, and hickory covered lands that this hike explores. The park's Bay Point Loop Trail traces the shoreline undulations. Open to both hikers and mountain bikers, the trail is most often used by the walking set, including a surprisingly large number of local residents who ply the loop as part of their daily exercise routine. Mountain biking on this trail is best suited to those seeking a casual woodland pedaling event.

For hikers, the Bay Point Loop Trail makes for an all-around pleasant experience. It is well marked and maintained, not too hard, not too easy, and a shortcut is available if you want to curtail the circuit. I especially enjoy the continual immediate proximity to water. Partial views of the lake and the adjoining islands through the trees can be had at almost any point, while occasional cleared spots present opulent panoramas of Harrison Bay.

The hike takes you by a trailside beach on Chickamauga Lake.

The trailhead has picnic tables and informative signage. You join the Bay Point Loop Trail and have hardly gotten up a head of steam before the trail splits. Our counterclockwise loop begins rolling through sweetgum, sycamore, oaks, and evergreens like cedar and pine. The flatwoods are scattered with ephemeral wetlands that pool in spring then dry out as the year progresses. The path soon leads by a lake cove. Expect to see much more water before this trek is completed. It isn't long before you come to the first official overlook, marked by a covered bench, on the first of three peninsulas the trail explores. The vista points lure you to them, where boaters of all stripes may be seen in season. Other user-created trails lead to small beaches.

It isn't long before you are rolling through a little hillier forest, heavy with fragrant pine, out onto the second peninsula. Views are extensive here, then you journey along a very slender and alluring lake cove. You will see much of this slender cove as the Bay Point Loop takes you along it to the third, longest and largest peninsula. This last peninsula is also the hilliest. Tall pines sway in the breeze overhead in a high-canopied forest. Eventually the Bay Point Loop leaves the water's edge and takes you back to the trailhead.

The state park provides not only hiking and paddling. The marina, immediately adjacent to the trailhead, boasts a restaurant should you hunger before or after your hike. The boat ramp is open 24 hours a day. Canoes, kayaks, and standup paddleboards may be rented here during the warm season. Lakeside picnicking areas abound. Toss a line to fish from the park pier. If Chickamauga Lake doesn't present enough aquatic action, hit the park's swimming pool, open during summer. Back on land, Harrison Bay features a large campground with

Harrison Bay State Park Hike

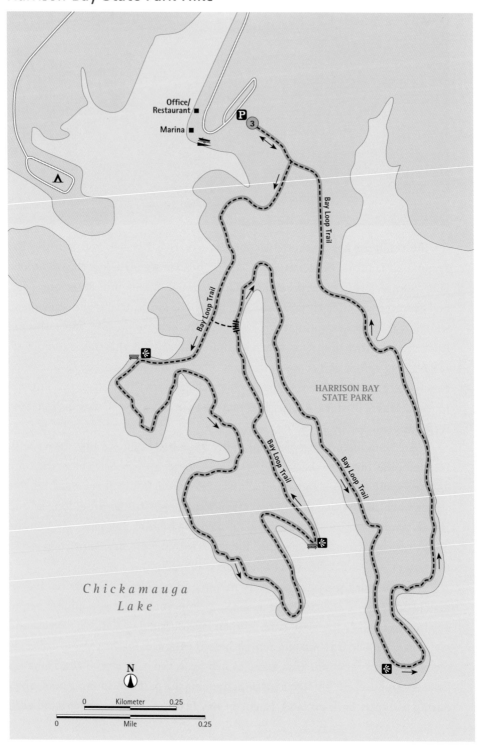

Office/Restaurant

Marina

P
3

Bay Loop Trail

Bay Loop Trail

HARRISON BAY
STATE PARK

Bay Loop Trail

Bay Loop Trail

Chickamauga
Lake

N

| 0 | Kilometer | 0.25 |
| 0 | Mile | 0.25 |

separate sections for tenters and RV campers. The RV sites have water and electricity; the tent sites offer a more primitive experience.

Additional activities at Harrison Bay State Park include golf on a Jack Nicklaus–designed course: the Bear Trace. Birding is also popular here—the melding of land and water attracts shorebirds, raptors, and songbirds to this protected spot on the shores of Chickamauga Lake.

Miles and Directions

0.0   Pick up the Bay Point Loop Trail at the east end of the larger marina parking area at a signed trailhead with picnic tables. Head east into lush flatwoods of both deciduous trees such as sweetgum and oak and evergreens like cedar and pine. The gravel trail stands elevated above low spots.

0.1   Reach a trail intersection where the Bay Point Loop splits. Head right, beginning a counterclockwise loop, still on an elevated path in flatwoods.

0.2   Grab your first views of the lake, passing a cove. Watery vistas are commonplace from here on out. Circle out along the first peninsula. The trail is often rooty—watch your feet.

0.4   An official shortcut leads left to a boardwalk.

0.9   Leave the hike's first peninsula.

1.5   Reach the southern tip of the second peninsula. Turn back north.

1.8   Come to a bench and overlook on a point. Continue north along a narrow lake cove.

2.2   Reach an extended boardwalk through a wooded wetland. A shortcut trail leads left in the middle of the boardwalk.

2.3   Turn south onto the third peninsula. Begin an extended lakeside cruise.

3.1   Reach the southernmost point of the last peninsula and soak in unobstructed lake panoramas. Turn north, traipsing through high-canopied woods dominated by pine.

3.9   Leave the water, aiming for the trailhead as you wander through flatwoods.

4.1   Complete the loop portion of the Bay Point Loop Trail. Backtrack toward the trailhead.

4.2   Arrive back at the trailhead.

4 Edwards Point via Signal Point

This highlight-laden trek starts at Signal Point—southern terminus of the Cumberland Trail—and leads along the Grand Canyon of the Tennessee River as you enjoy views as well as waterfalls and natural arches en route. Culminate your hiking adventure at Edwards Point, offering a first-rate panorama up the Tennessee River toward Chattanooga and beyond.

Start: Signal Point

Distance: 5.6 miles out and back

Hiking time: About 3 hours

Difficulty: Moderate; rocky trail in places

Trail surface: Natural

Best season: Year-round

Other trail users: Backpackers

Canine compatibility: Leashed dogs allowed

Land status: National military park, state forest

Fees and permits: No fees or permits required

Schedule: Daily, dawn to dusk

Maps: USGS Chattanooga, Fairmount, Ketner Gap, Wauhatchie; Prentice Cooper State Forest hiking trail map

Trail contacts: Chickamauga & Chattanooga National Military Park, 3370 Lafayette Rd., Fort Oglethorpe, GA 30742; (706) 866-9241; nps.gov/chch

Finding the trailhead: From exit 178 on I-24 in Chattanooga, take US 27 North for 3.7 miles to US 127. Turn left and take US 127 North for 4.6 miles, then turn left onto Mississippi Avenue at the sign for Justin P. Wilson Cumberland Trail State Park and Signal Point. Continue 0.7 mile; merge into James Boulevard, follow it for 0.1 mile, then veer left onto Signal Point Road. Follow Signal Point Road for 0.3 mile to its end. A hard-surface trail leads from the parking area to Signal Point. The parking area offers restrooms and a picnic shelter. Overnight parking is not allowed. GPS: N35 7.218' / W85 21.996'

The Hike

This greater Chattanooga hiking adventure is a trek of highlights. For starters, it begins at historically significant Signal Point, a view-laden relay station during

the Civil War. Signal Point is also the southern terminus of Tennessee's master path: the Cumberland Trail. What became the town of Signal Mountain was once a vacation retreat, and the views and waterfalls in these parts attest to this locale being worthy of a visit. This hike is good year-round, though summer can be a bit warm and waterfalls may have reduced flows in autumn. This adventure does have its challenges—the hike's beginning traverses a rugged, ultra-rocky boulder garden with a maze of user-created spur trails that may confuse. Other trail segments are rocky too. However, you'll be hard-pressed to find another adventure so rich in highlights on one hike.

The parking lot at Signal Point can fill quickly on nice-weather weekends, so plan to get here early. Also, despite the presence of both legal and illegal backcountry campsites on the route, no overnight parking is allowed at Signal Point. Plan accordingly. The hike follows a concrete and pebble path downhill to an overlook—Signal Point. Federal soldiers used this spot to relay signals between blue-clad companies around Chattanooga after the Confederates sliced local telegraph lines.

While at Signal Point, imagine signaling fellow soldiers while looking up and down the Grand Canyon of the Tennessee River and across to Raccoon Mountain. The hike changes radically from the concrete and pebble path to a steep

Pass this waterfall just before reaching Edwards Point

track of stairs and steps snaking through an incredible cliffline with boulders, tall trees, and outcrops. The segment's nickname is the "Mousetrap," for the decades-old 3-D board game.

Ahead, reach a wide-open outcrop with a stellar view. Known as Julia Falls Overlook, the stone slab allows views across the Middle Creek gorge below to both Julia Falls and Edwards Point. You should be able to hear Julia Falls if not see the long spiller. Leafless times are best for viewing Julia Falls. From there you'll follow the Cumberland Trail into Middle Creek gorge, passing a steep and potentially dangerous user-created trail to Rainbow Falls. Ahead, cross the swinging bridge over Middle Creek in preserved hemlocks. Here you could visit the waterfall-like outflow over the Rainbow Lake Dam. Rainbow Lake was constructed along with the Signal Mountain Inn in 1913. The mineral waters of nearby Burnt Cabin Spring also attracted visitors.

On the far side of the Middle Creek gorge you'll come along a cliffline with small arches above and Lockharts Arch, a smallish rock bridge created when a stream cut a hole in the bluff line. Beyond, the hike reaches the ridge crest, where you wander among pines and partial views. The walking here is easy. Then you turn into a rocky stream, a feeder of Middle Creek, crossing it just above a 10-foot curtain-type waterfall. The Cumberland Trail leads you out to Edwards Point, a first-rate panorama if there ever was one.

The flat rock, framed by evergreens, presents a look up the Grand Canyon of the Tennessee River outlined by Signal Mountain to your left and Raccoon Mountain to your right. The Middle Creek gorge stretches to your left, and a discerning eye can find Julia Falls Overlook across the divide. In the distance, the city of Chattanooga extends into the beyond. Down on the river, you can easily spot teardrop-shaped Williams Island, around which the Tennessee River flows. What a view—and what a start to the Cumberland Trail! This vista should inspire you to explore more of Tennessee's master path.

Miles and Directions

0.0 Start from the parking area and follow a concrete and pebble path downhill to quickly reach Signal Point. After enjoying the view from Signal Point, look right and join the signed southern terminus of the Cumberland Trail. From the trail sign, descend a series of wood and stone steps, working down among the clifflines, boulders, and woods on this steep slope.

0.1 A user-created spur trail descends left to a wet-weather falls then turns back out to a piney overlook of the Tennessee River to rejoin the Cumberland Trail. Stay with the white blazes of the Cumberland Trail as several spurs go to various overlooks and outcrops.

0.5 The trail opens onto Julia Falls Overlook. Views stretch across the Middle Creek gorge to Julia Falls and Edwards Point, while the Grand Canyon of the Tennessee River unfurls downstream. Turn into the Middle Creek gorge.

1.0 An illicit spur drops steeply left to 40-foot Rainbow Falls. Keep on the Cumberland Trail.

1.4 Come to the swinging bridge over Middle Creek. Soak up views of the stream up and down the vale. Here a trail leaves toward Ohio Avenue, part of the loop around Rainbow Lake Wilderness. Cross the swinging bridge then climb and pass the other end of the loop around Rainbow Lake.

1.6 Come along a cliffline and keep an eye peeled for a small arch in the cliff. Find a break in the bluff then reach Lockharts Arch. The rock bridge, 10 feet long, stands beside the trail. From here the Cumberland Trail stays close to the rim and views open.

1.9 Watch carefully as a spur trail leads acutely right to the Lockharts Arch campsite amid ATV trails. Stay straight with the Cumberland Trail, enjoying sporadic views.

Edwards Point via Signal Point

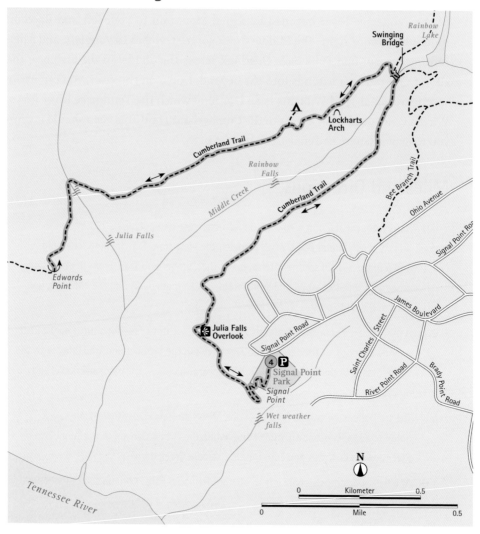

2.6 Cross a creek after turning away from the rim. Look for a 10-foot waterfall after crossing the creek. Return to the rim of the gorge.

2.8 Reach Edwards Point. Here a first-rate vista opens of the Grand Canyon of the Tennessee River, Middle Creek gorge, Chattanooga, Williams Island, and a wealth of woods and clifflines. Soak in the panorama then backtrack, looking for geological wonders you missed on the way in.

5.6 Arrive back at the Signal Point parking area.

5 Lawsons Rock

Follow the Cumberland Trail on this rewarding adventure in Prentice Cooper State Forest. Trek through forest then squeeze between huge boulders to reach Indian Rockhouse. Cruise along the Grand Canyon of the Tennessee River, passing a veil-like waterfall. Grab a warm-up view before turning into the Suck Creek gorge, where you will find Lawsons Rock, forming a natural panoramic platform and worthwhile destination where you can look out over Suck Creek and the Tennessee River racing down their respective chasms.

Start: Cumberland Trail trailhead in Prentice Cooper State Forest

Distance: 6.8 miles out and back

Hiking time: About 3.2 hours

Difficulty: Moderate; rocky trail in places

Trail surface: Natural

Best season: Oct–May

Other trail users: Backpackers

Canine compatibility: Leashed dogs allowed

Land Status: State forest

Fees and permits: No fees or permits required

Schedule: Daily, dawn to dusk

Backpacker peers out from Lawsons Rock

Maps: USGS Ketner Gap; Prentice Cooper State Forest hiking trail map

Trail Contacts: Prentice Cooper State Forest, PO Box 160, Hixson, TN 37343; (423) 658-5551; tennessee.gov/agriculture/forestry

Finding the trailhead: From the junction of US 27 and US 127, northwest of Chattanooga, take US 127 North for 1.6 miles to TN 27 West. Turn left on TN 27 West and follow it for 8 miles to Choctaw Trail and a sign for Prentice Cooper WMA. Turn left on Choctaw Trail and follow it for 0.2 mile to Game Reserve Road. Turn left on Game Reserve Road and enter Prentice Cooper State Forest, where it becomes Tower Road. Keep straight on gravel Tower Road for 2.6 miles to the Cumberland Trail parking area on your right. GPS: N35 7.961' / W85 25.152'

The Hike

The trek to Lawsons Rock is what you want in a hiking adventure—well-maintained singletrack hiker-only trail, highlights aplenty along the way amid everywhere-you-look beauty, plus an option of overnight trailside camping. The adventure takes place in Prentice Cooper State Forest, which restricts forest entry to hunters only during hunt periods. Check their website for hunt dates before you drive here.

I recommend this hike from fall through spring. Summer can be hot, as much of the trek is along the south-facing rim of the Tennessee River Gorge. During autumn you can enjoy the leaf show. In winter the extensive clifflines, stone pillars, and big boulders will stand out. In spring look for wildflowers and photograph the waterfall found en route. On this trail your eyes will need to watch the irregular footing of the well-maintained trail ahead, yet they will be drawn to the gorge falling away to your right, as well as the clifflines rising to your left. Just take your time and try to absorb it all. At least the hike has no steep ups or downs.

The hike's beginning can be confusing. From the parking area you first cross Tower Road near a gas-line clearing. Leave the east side of the road to find the signed path leading toward Lawsons Rock. The singletrack trail gently descends among hardwoods. You are just getting loose when you cross a forest road; then your downgrade intensifies as you near the rim of the Grand Canyon of the Tennessee River, more than 1,000 feet below.

The trail then curves toward some boulders. Coming closer, it becomes evident that the path descends the slender slit between the enormous graybacks. Strategically placed steps ease the tight fit that will test a hiker equipped with a

This slender opening leads to Indian Rockhouse

full backpack. The stone passage leads you down the cliffline to a trail intersection. Here the Cumberland Trail goes left and right. We go left and immediately come under Indian Rockhouse. Even by lofty Cumberland Plateau standards, this is a superlative shelter. The shelter floor is mostly dry and faces southerly, so in winter it receives warming sun yet blocks a north wind—a refuge certainly utilized by aboriginal Tennesseans.

Continue cruising the base of the cliffline, making sure to look up at more remarkable rock formations, big boulders mixed in with a healthy dose of rich woodlands. As you walk along the base of the cliffline, seasonal streams cross

Indian Rockhouse

the pathway. Below the trail these tributaries make their dive for the Tennessee River below, while Raccoon Mountain rises across the water. An unnamed tributary forms a 12-foot curtain-like waterfall, dropping off a cliffline directly beside the trail. If flowing well, this waterfall cannot be missed.

Ahead, you will turn into the Suck Creek gorge, where a view awaits from a downhill outcrop. If you walk down to this off-official-trail outcrop, you will notice a rockhouse beneath the outcrop as well as the confluence of Suck Creek and the Tennessee River below. The name Suck Creek comes from a strange whirl in the river known as "The Suck" dangerous to people floating this stretch. The damming of the river has changed the flow pattern, eliminating the whirl.

Continuing on the Cumberland Trail, look right for narrow rock pillars, pedestal rocks rising like monuments—just another geological wonderment of the Cumberland Plateau. Beyond the pillars, the path is detoured into and out of the desiccated vale of Sulphur Branch. This rocky gorge is a miniature of the rocky gulfs cut by the Tennessee River—clifflines, boulders, towering forests, and moving water. Once out of the grasp of Sulphur Branch, the trail returns to the rock rim above Suck Creek, modestly rising among pines and brambles with the gulf dropping off just a few feet away.

Then you come to the intersection with the short path leading right to Lawsons Rock. Here a flat rock opens to the vale created by Suck Creek dropping off the Cumberland Plateau. The rock walls of the gorge contrast with forest, while in the distance Raccoon Mountain stands across the depths of the canyon of the Tennessee River. This is a place to linger.

If you really want to linger, consider camping out at nearby Poplar Spring campsite. I have stayed here multiple times and found it a fine place to overnight.

Lawsons Rock

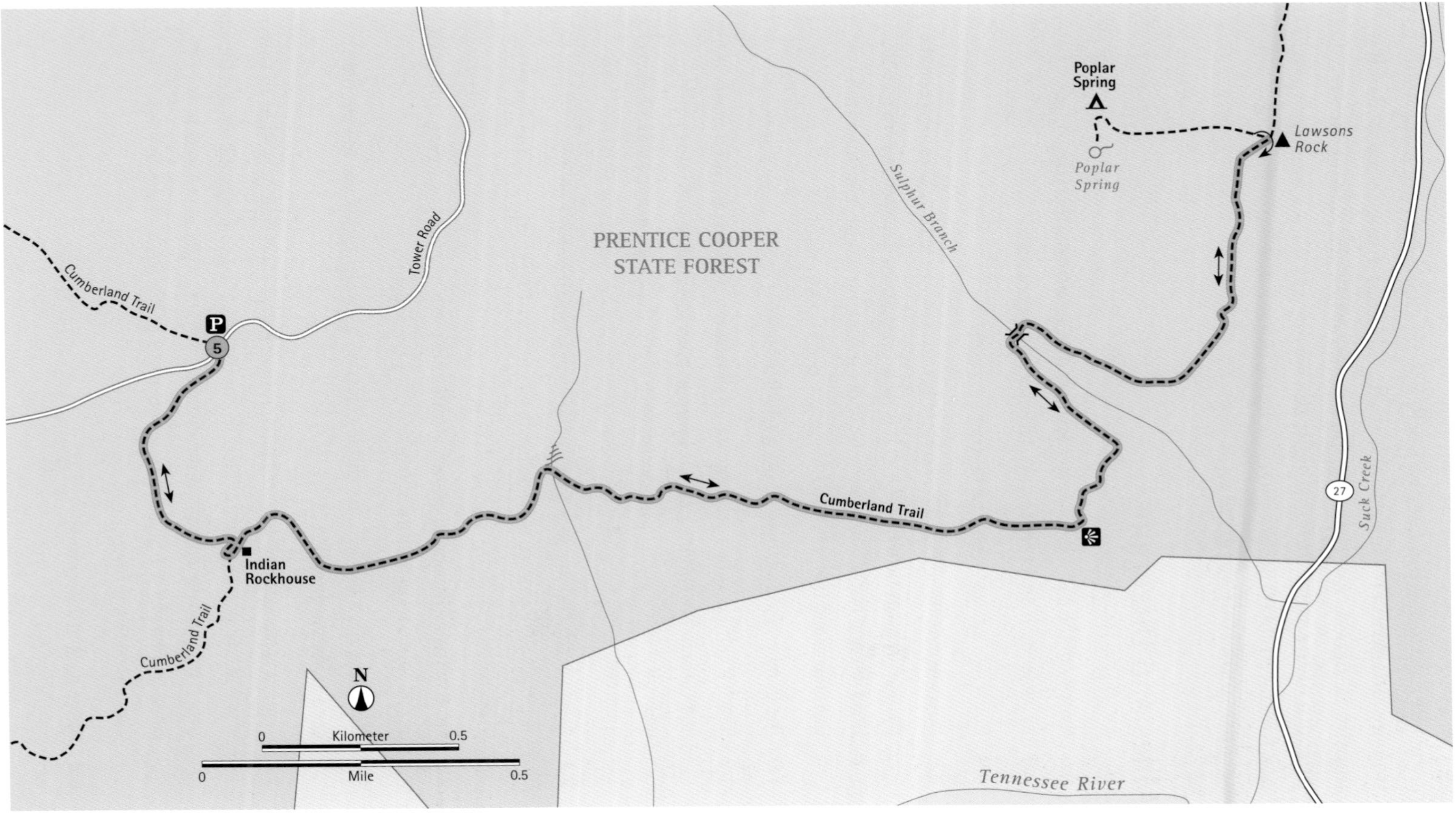

Suck Creek

27

Tennessee River

Lawsons Rock

Poplar Spring

Poplar Spring

Sulphur Branch

PRENTICE COOPER STATE FOREST

Cumberland Trail

Tower Road

Cumberland Trail

P 5

Indian Rockhouse

Cumberland Trail

Cumberland Trail

N

Kilometer 0   0.5
Mile   0   0.5

At the intersection with Lawsons Rock, a somewhat faint path leads uphill to the campsite. The path crosses a forest road and keeps rising to a wooded flat. The campsite is signed. Another sign points toward Poplar Spring, down a hollow just south of the camp. Interestingly, the spring was once a moonshine still site. Look for the circular pit and piled rocks by the modest upwelling, just one more showcase of this fine adventure.

Miles and Directions

0.0   Start from the east side of Tower Road at the Cumberland Trail parking area, joining a slender path under white oaks, hickories, and sourwood.

0.3   Cut across a forest road. The descent increases.

0.5   The path cuts through a slit-like opening between two big boulders. Descend the passage by steps then find a trail intersection. Here the Cumberland Trail splits. Head left and instantaneously walk under Indian Rockhouse, a historic stone shelter. Continue along the rim of the Tennessee River Gorge.

1.0   The Cumberland Trail cuts across a gas-line clearing opening views below.

1.2   Reach a cliffline with a dripping waterfall where a stream pours off a mossy ledge in a curtain. The cliffline extends away on both sides, while rocks and boulders add geological fascination to the scene. Keep along the gorge, gaining views between the trees.

2.1   As you curve into the Suck Creek gorge, a user-created spur trail drops sharply to an outcrop and rewarding view below to where Suck Creek flows into the Tennessee River.

2.5   Cross non-smelly Sulphur Branch after turning into its boulder-strewn, cliff-lined gorge. Turn back out to the rim of the Suck Creek gorge.

3.0   Climb through a break in the cliffline, passing a smaller rockhouse to your right. Keep along the gorge rim.

3.4   Come to a signed four-way trail intersection. Here a short spur goes right to Lawsons Rock while another spur goes left to Poplar Spring campsite. Check out the fine view from the pale outcrop. In the distance, clifflines meld with forest in Suck Creek while the maw of the Suck Creek gorge opens to the abyss of the Tennessee River. Backtrack toward Tower Road.

6.8   Arrive back at Tower Road.

6 Natural Bridge via Snoopers Rock

This hike visits two scenic features with the opportunity for another highlight. Hike a short distance then open onto aptly named Snoopers Rock, with extensive views of the Tennessee River Gorge. From there, join the Cumberland Trail and ride the gorge rim, traversing indented hollows before reaching Natural Bridge, a stone span that you can walk over and under. Consider a side trip to Blowing Wind Falls on the Ritchie Hollow Trail.

Start: Snoopers Rock trailhead

Distance: 6.2 miles out and back

Hiking time: About 3 hours

Difficulty: Moderate; a few ups and downs

Trail surface: Natural

Best season: Sept–June

Other trail users: Backpackers

Canine compatibility: Leashed dogs allowed

Land status: State forest

Fees and permits: No fees or permits required

Schedule: Daily, dawn to dusk

Maps: USGS Wauhatchie; Prentice Cooper State Forest hiking trail map

A late morning fog hangs over the Tennessee River

Trail contacts: Prentice Cooper State Forest, PO Box 160, Hixson, TN 37343; (423) 658-5551; tennessee.gov/agriculture/forestry

Finding the trailhead: From the junction of US 27 and US 127 northwest of Chattanooga, take US 127 North for 1.6 miles to TN 27 West. Turn left on TN 27 West and follow it for 8 miles to Choctaw Trail and a sign for Prentice Cooper WMA. Turn left on Choctaw Trail and follow it for 0.2 mile to Game Reserve Road. Turn left on Game Reserve Road and enter Prentice Cooper State Forest, where it becomes Tower Road. Keep straight on gravel Tower Road for 4.6 miles to the Cumberland Trail parking area on your right. GPS: N35 6.097' / W85 25.757'

The Hike

Note: Before taking this hike, check the Prentice Cooper State Forest website for hunt dates. During these dates, only hunters are allowed on forestland. Also, know that despite the possibility of crowds at the trailhead, the vast majority do not step foot beyond Snoopers Rock. Fall through spring is the best period to enjoy this adventure. Autumn will be cooler and the skies clear to soak in the views. During winter you can better appreciate the geology of Natural Bridge. A vibrant spring day will bring good views and wildflowers in the hollows you cross.

This hike first visits one of greater Chattanooga's iconic lookouts—Snoopers Rock. The large, wide-open stone slab seems more a natural deck than outcrop. From this perch you can overlook the heart of the Grand Canyon of the Tennessee River as it cuts a 1,000-foot-deep swath through the Cumberland Plateau. This is but a short walk from the trailhead, even shorter if you use a side road to access Snoopers Rock. However you reach it, the panorama remains rewarding. From there you will likely enjoy solitude en route to Natural Bridge, a capacious stone arch that is fun to visit—not only does the Cumberland Trail take you atop the span but you can also walk under it for a complete examination.

The hike to Natural Bridge leaves the Snoopers Rock Trailhead, where you can find picnic tables and a restroom. The trail descends easterly to reach a small parking area close to Snoopers Rock. After crossing the lot you soon reach Snoopers Rock. The view equals the name—there is plenty to snoop upon. From the stone breadth you can admire the Grand Canyon of the Tennessee River as it curves to the right upstream and to the left downstream, all embroidered with rock outcrops. Raccoon Mountain rises as a wooded wall on the far side of the river. This is a popular area for photos and videos, so expect company.

Looking up at Natural Bridge reveal's its arch

Snoopers Rock is renown for its views into the Grand Canyon of the Tennessee River.

From there you will join the Cumberland Trail, rolling south along the gorge, working in and out of hollows. Partial views open among the trees before you turn into the hollow of strangely named Muddy Branch, for under normal flows the stream runs clear. Stay with the white blazes as the path joins and leaves an old roadbed on a sharp slope high above the river.

Up high, you turn into Ritchie Hollow, a mix of woods, small streams, and ever-present emergent rock in the form of cliffs, boulders, walls—and stones at your feet. This is where you can make the side trip to Blowing Wind Falls (see option below). You next work your way out of Ritchie Hollow and once again are on the brink of the gorge. Natural Bridge is near, but not yet evident. Ahead, a spur leads left to an outcrop with views partly obscured by tree cover. Most people don't realize it, but they can see the opening of Natural Bridge from this perch. After returning to the Cumberland Trail, the path goes directly atop Natural Bridge, and most people figure it out. Steep accesses to the base of Natural Bridge can be found on both ends of the stone span, stretching about 40 feet in length and standing about 25 feet above the ground, though the mountain slope makes the arch's exact height variable. After you walk atop and under it, you will

Natural Bridge via Snoopers Rock

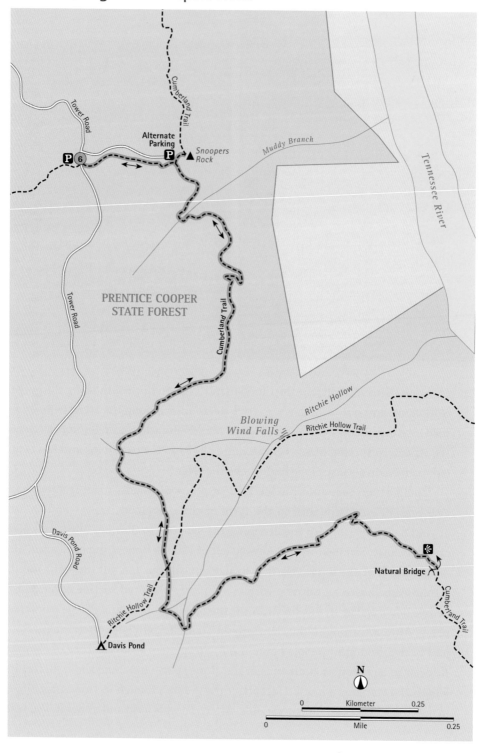

have a full understanding of this natural landform that is just one more reason to engage in a hiking adventure on the Cumberland Trail at Prentice Cooper State Forest.

Option: Consider adding a side trip to Blowing Wind Falls, especially during winter and spring. This 30-foot spiller makes its splash in Ritchie Hollow on the Ritchie Hollow Trail, opened in 2018. It starts at the bottom of the river gorge, climbs to meet the Cumberland Trail, then heads onward to Davis Pond. The side trip to Blowing Wind Falls is about 0.7 mile one-way with a decided downward trend, adding 1.4 miles to the hike to Natural Bridge.

Miles and Directions

0.0   Start at the trailhead kiosk at the south end of the Snoopers Rock parking area. Join a short spur then head left toward Snoopers Rock. Descend a wooded hollow along an intermittent stream.

0.3   Reach a parking area to your left as you meet the Cumberland Trail. Cross the parking lot and walk a short bit of trail that opens onto expansive, deck-like Snoopers Rock. Follow the gorge of the Tennessee River as it curves away in both directions while Raccoon Mountain stands tall across the water. Backtrack beyond the parking area to join the Cumberland Trail, southbound.

0.6   Cross normally clear Muddy Branch in its steep hollow. Curve back out toward the rim of the Tennessee River Gorge.

0.9   The Cumberland Trail makes a sharp switchback to the right and climbs. Level off then walk south, with rock outcrops about.

1.2   The trail turns into Ritchie Hollow, cut by two major branches.

1.6   Cross the first branch of Ritchie Hollow.

2.0   Meet the Ritchie Hollow Trail. Stay straight with the Cumberland Trail. (*Option:* Head left 0.7 mile to Blowing Wind Falls.) Ahead, cross a pair of small streams.

2.8   Make a switchback and climb.

3.1   Come to a spur leading left to a partly wooded view. Just ahead, the Cumberland Trail crosses the span of Natural Bridge. Cross the bridge then descend to view it from below. Backtrack to the trailhead.

6.2   Arrive back at the trailhead.

Looking out toward
Mullens Cove

7 Ransom Hollow and Mullens Cove Vistas

Hike to two overlooks on one hike, enjoying a cool hemlock-filled hollow in between. The Cumberland Trail is the conduit as you trek through the 25,000-acre Prentice Cooper State Forest. First you dip into a cool evergreen vale then work to an outcrop where you can look down the gorge of Mullens Creek to the Tennessee River. Backtrack a bit to pick up new trail to a remote piney overlook with a distant westerly panorama reaching clear to Alabama.

Start: Snoopers Rock trailhead

Distance: 4.8 miles out and back with spur

Hiking time: About 2.2 hours

Difficulty: Moderate

Trail surface: Natural

Best season: Year-round; mornings best in summer

Other trail users: Backpackers

Canine compatibility: Leashed dogs allowed

Land status: State forest

Fees and permits: No fees or permits required

Schedule: Daily, dawn to dusk

Maps: Prentice Cooper State Forest Hiking Trail Map; USGS Wauhatchie

Trail contacts: Prentice Cooper State Forest, PO Box 160, Hixson, TN 37343; (423) 658-5551; tennessee.gov/agriculture/forestry

Finding the trailhead: From the junction of US 27 and US 127 northwest of Chattanooga, take US 127 North for 1.6 miles to TN 27 West. Turn left on TN 27 West and follow it for 8 miles to Choctaw Trail and a sign for Prentice Cooper WMA. Turn left on Choctaw Trail and follow it for 0.2 mile to Game Reserve Road. Turn left on Game Reserve Road and enter Prentice Cooper State Forest, where it becomes Tower Road. Keep straight on gravel Tower Road for 4.6 miles to the Cumberland Trail parking area on your right. GPS: N35 6.097' / W85 25.757'

The Hike

Note: Before coming here, check the Prentice Cooper State Forest website for hunt dates; only hunters are allowed in the forest during those times.

This worthwhile hike to two lesser visited overlooks—Mullens Cove and Ransom Hollow—is often overshadowed by other, more popular destinations in Prentice Cooper State Forest. However, this can be a good thing if you are trying to avoid the crowds heading to nearby Snoopers Rock or just want to trod the trail less traveled. These two overlooks provide westerly vantages from the mountaintop upon which Prentice Cooper State Forest stands, a protected parcel of wildness bordered by the Tennessee River on three sides. It is a haven for flora and fauna of the Cumberland Plateau as well as home of the most southerly segment of the Cumberland Trail.

The large trailhead can be busy and the hike's beginning unclear. Nevertheless, once you are hiking on the west side of Tower Road on a singletrack connector trail, you will be leaving the crowds behind. You are now descending into an evergreen-rich valley with Hemlock Branch and several other tributaries converging to drop westerly toward Mullens Creek below. Step over stony tributaries of Hemlock Branch on your descent. The pathway is flanked by American holly trees. Hollies range widely in the eastern United States, from east Texas to Florida to Massachusetts—and right here on the Cumberland Plateau. This evergreen is easy to identify. It's leaves are spiny, thick, stiff, and leathery, with a dull green color on top and a yellowish green below. The bark is light gray or tan and often mottled. The bright red berries give holly the familiar look that makes it a popular decoration during Christmas. Hollies growing in the wild have a treelike form, as opposed to the cultivated bushes trimmed in ornamental or hedge fashion that you see in suburban settings.

The hemlocks in this hollow are being protected from the hemlock woolly adelgid that has been killing the eastern hemlock. The hemlocks here are being injected with an insecticide to keep the bug from killing the trees. Look for a painted dot at the base of these healthy evergreens, indicating they have been treated. For now at least, Hemlock Hollow will live up to its name.

The vale is also a designated backcountry campsite. Small camps are nestled along both sides of the stream before it dives off the rim of Mullens Creek gorge. You will have a good opportunity to inspect the sites for future overnight adventures. The tree cover changes to pines, oaks, and sourwood as you climb out of moist Hemlock Hollow.

Don't worry about missing Mullens Cove Overlook—the steep spur trail is signed. Here a short path leads down to a rock, creating an opening in the surrounding dense forest. From the stone promontory, the gorge of Mullens Creek clears a view down to the Tennessee River, with Raccoon Mountain rising in the distance. The vista is limited to a southerly look, since the valley of Mullens Creek opens in that direction. The outcrop has limited room and is not conducive to

The view down to the Tennessee River from Ransom Hollow Overlook

hanging out; if you want to eat lunch or just relax, head back to Hemlock Branch or, better yet, enjoy an extended break at Ransom Hollow Overlook.

After recrossing Hemlock Branch, continue southbound on the Cumberland Trail. The path here is signed but less used, so be watchful while climbing away from Hemlock Branch. The trail now wanders along the slope of the Mullens Creek gorge under tall oaks and lesser hickories while delivering a real sense of being "out there." Ahead, as you walk the woods lost in contemplation, the trail seemingly ends at a stone jumble. However, upon closer inspection, the Cumberland Trail slips between a pair of monstrous boulders then opens onto a small stream, easily crossed. As you continue, look below for a waterfall cascading from sight. The whole scene is just one more example of the sublime scenery found at Prentice Cooper State Forest.

Ahead, follow the spur to Ransom Hollow Overlook. This larger rock flat, bordered by pines, is a fitting reward, and one less frequently visited. To your left, Ransom Hollow drops deeply to Mullens Creek while the sprawling view is dead ahead. Here you can stare westerly into island-dotted Nickajack Lake, nestled in

Ransom Hollow and Mullens Cove Vistas

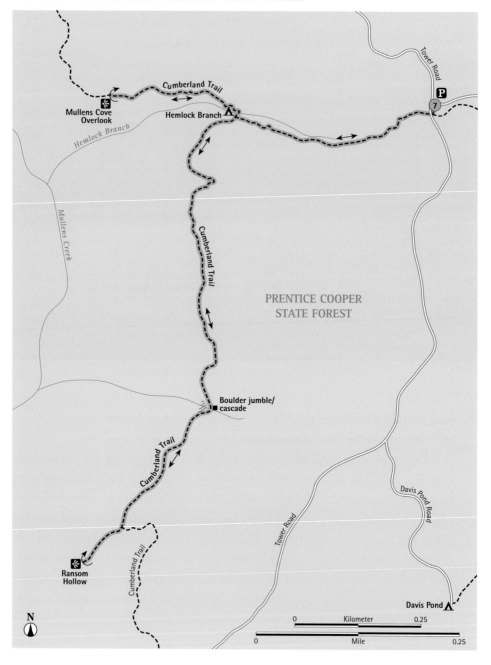

the western reaches of the Grand Canyon of the Tennessee River where it has curved around Prentice Cooper State Forest. To the west, the Tennessee River flows into Alabama, winding among the lands of that state. After soaking in the panoramas and relaxing to your heart's content, a 2.0-mile backtrack to the trailhead awaits.

Miles and Directions

0.0 Start from the kiosk on the south end of the Snoopers Rock trailhead and walk just a short distance on a connector trail then reach an intersection. Turn right toward Hemlock Branch campsite, crossing Tower Road. Begin dipping into the vale of Hemlock Branch, forming to the right of the trail.

0.6 Intersect the Cumberland Trail. You will be going in both directions. First, head right, descending to Hemlock Branch, dancing through the rocks to your right. Follow the Cumberland Trail down to Hemlock Branch, crossing the stream on boulders and cutting through the middle of the Hemlock Branch backcountry campsite. Climb back into hardwoods after bisecting the campsite.

0.7 Meet an old roadbed. Follow the track left and downhill before quickly leaving right, back on the climbing singletrack.

1.0 Reach the short signed spur dropping left to Mullens Cove Overlook. Here you can peer down the Mullens Creek gorge to the Tennessee River and beyond. Backtrack to the trail intersection near Hemlock Branch. Continue on the Cumberland Trail, heading south toward the Ransom Hollow Overlook on a decidedly fainter narrow trail.

2.3 The trail cuts between a pair of boulders then crosses a small stream above a stair-step cascade.

2.7 Reach a signed intersection. Head right toward Ransom Hollow Overlook, roughly paralleling an old roadbed.

2.8 Come to the Ransom Hollow Overlook, with a stellar view to the west of Nickajack Lake and points beyond. Backtrack toward the trailhead.

4.8 Arrive back at the trailhead.

8 Foster Falls Hike

Foster Falls is the worthy centerpiece of this hike that takes you not only to the 60-foot spiller but also along the view-rich rim of a gorge on the highly acclaimed Fiery Gizzard Trail. Ultimately, this hike leads down into the gorge of Fiery Gizzard Creek, where old-growth trees, climbing walls, boulders, and Little Gizzard Creek will be appreciated after its headlong tumble as Foster Falls. Backpack campsites add overnighting possibilities to the adventure.

Start: Foster Falls Trailhead

Distance: 4.7 miles out and back with loop

Hiking time: About 2.8 hours

Difficulty: Moderate

Trail surface: Natural

Best season: Fall–spring

Other trail users: Rock climbers, backpackers

Canine compatibility: Leashed dogs allowed

Land status: State park

Fees and permits: No fees or permits required

Schedule: Daily, dawn to 10 p.m.

Maps: USGS White City; South Cumberland State Park–Fiery Gizzard

Trail contacts: South Cumberland State Park, 11745 US 41, Monteagle, TN 37356; (931) 924-2980; tnstateparks.com

Finding the trailhead: From exit 155 on I-24, west of Chattanooga, take TN 28 North for 1.5 miles. Join US 41 North and follow it through Jasper for a total of 9.5 miles to Foster Falls Road; turn left into the park. The trailhead offers restrooms, water, and a covered picnic shelter. GPS: N35 10.9357' / W85 40.4402'

The Hike

Part of South Cumberland State Park—several disparate tracts of wildland on the Cumberland Plateau northwest of Chattanooga—the Foster Falls tract anchors one end of the Fiery Gizzard Trail, a rewarding path traversing the rim and gorge of Big Fiery Gizzard Creek. Sixty-foot Foster Falls is the main attraction as it plummets from a rock rim into a plunge pool of epic proportions. The rest of the hike is more than worth your time.

Foster Falls dives into
a stone cathedral.

A face-on view of Foster Falls
and its huge plunge pools

Originally preserved as part of a Tennessee Valley Authority (TVA) wild lands program, Foster Falls was conferred to the State of Tennessee, which now manages not only the trails of Foster Falls but also the day-use area with picnic tables and shelter, plus a nice little auto-accessible campground that makes a fine base camp for exploring this extraordinary locale.

So how did the place get the name Fiery Gizzard? An unusual moniker even for name-rich Tennessee, legend has it that none other than Daniel Boone christened the creek when he burned dinner here over a campfire and threw the remains over the rim of the gorge, a flaming piece of meat lighting up the night as it went over the cliff into the depths below.

This hike adventure is divided into two distinct parts—on top of the rim and below the rim. The rim hiking part is easy on the feet and the eyes; the second part, below the rim, traverses irregular rough terrain, presenting vertical variation as well. The hike starts in innocuous fashion at the nice trailhead with restrooms, picnic area, shelter, and water. A little boardwalk leads over an upland bog-like stream, and then you are at a power line cut. Foster Falls is already echoing in the depths below. The Fiery Gizzard Trail takes you to a swinging bridge over Little Gizzard Creek, a tributary of Big Fiery Gizzard Creek. Lush forest of hemlock, bigleaf magnolia, mountain laurel, and holly envelop the span and the stony waterway below.

Your anticipation grows after climbing away from Little Gizzard Creek among hardwoods. Ahead, a side trail leads to the Father Adamz campsite, a backcountry camp mainly used by rock climbers who ply the nationally known walls found here. The latter part of the hike takes you past some of these climbing spots—and then comes the overlook of Foster Falls. Here Little Gizzard Creek plunges from a stone lip headlong into a massive plunge pool bordered by perpendicular rock walls. If the stream is flowing well, the power of the stream dive is palpable. Use caution—the drop from the overlook to the stream below is a doozy.

After lingering at the falls overlook, continue on the Fiery Gizzard Trail as it weaves along the gorge rim amid pines, hardwoods, and occasional hemlocks. The second spur trail to the Father Adamz campsite quickly merges with the Fiery Gizzard Trail as you span occasional wetlands on boardwalks. Hiker-created spurs lead to lesser overlooks on the rim, where eager hikers seek distant views. The walking is easy and free.

Ahead, meet one of the two climber access trails leading down into the gulf below. Stay with the Fiery Gizzard Trail, passing the second climber access trail. You will use this later to get below the rim of the gorge, but for now continue the rim walk, passing small seasonal creeks quietly winding through the woods before plunging into the gulf below. Enjoy looks into the 700-foot-deep chasm as the trail turns into the side gorge of Laurel Branch.

After passing the Small Wilds backcountry campsite, you cross Laurel Branch and come to the hike's last overlook from an outcrop into the Laurel Branch gorge and beyond. From there it's a backtrack to Climbers Access 2, where you enter the geologically fascinating world below the gorge rim of rockhouses, sheer bluffs, and massive boulders on a rough, stony track. You will also see climbing areas with bolts inserted into the walls for those who challenge the vertical bulwarks of rock. Look for regal old-growth tulip trees as you dodge seeps dripping overhead.

Soon the sounds of Little Gizzard Creek drift through the density of trees, brush, and boulders. Reach the lower viewing area of Foster Falls, with its oversized plunge pool. Hemlocks rise in dark ranks here. Enjoy the locale then take the swinging bridge over Little Gizzard Creek to climb back out of the gorge. A final limited view of Foster Falls awaits on the rim before you backtrack a short distance to complete the hiking adventure.

Miles and Directions

0.0   Start from the parking area and walk toward the picnic shelter, passing a sign-in registration and kiosk. After crossing a boardwalk, join the Fiery Gizzard Trail, leaving right along a power line clearing. Foster Falls is audible. Cross Little Gizzard Creek above the falls.

Foster Falls Hike

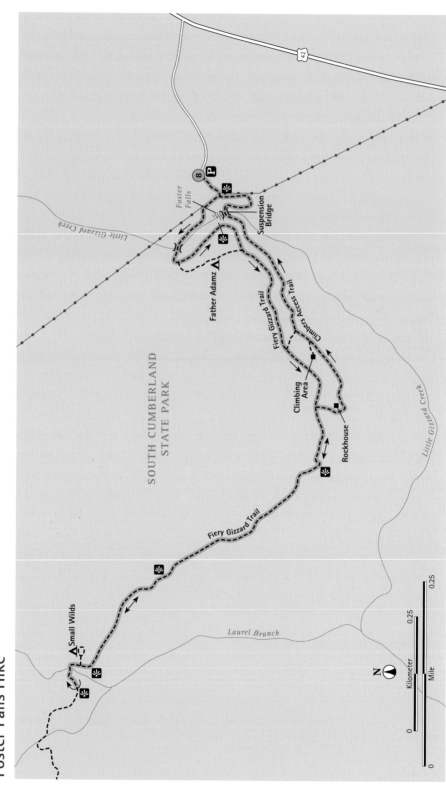

SOUTH CUMBERLAND
STATE PARK

Fiery Gizzard Trail

Fiery Gizzard Trail

Small Wilds

Laurel Branch

Rockhouse

Climbing
Area

Climbers Access Trail

Father Adamz

Suspension
Bridge

Foster
Falls

Little Gizzard Creek

Little Gizzard Creek

42

P

8

N

Kilometer
0   0.25

Mile
0   0.25

0.3 A spur trail leaves right to the Father Adamz campsite.

0.5 Reach the rocky first overlook of Foster Falls. The 60-foot spiller plunges from a vertical rock precipice then smashes into a colossal plunge pool.

0.6 Pass the second spur trail to the Father Adamz campsite.

0.9 Reach a trail junction. Climbers Access 1 splits left. Keep straight on the Fiery Gizzard Trail.

1.1 Reach Climbers Access 2. Turn left here and descend off the rim via steps, reaching a rockhouse. Cruise the base of the cliff.

1.3 Cross a hiker bridge over a small, dark, unnamed creek. Immediately turn left onto the rim to hear the unseen falls dive from the rim and also gaze south into Fiery Gizzard Gulf.

1.8 Cross another small creek via bridge and come to another overlook into Fiery Gizzard Gulf.

2.2 A spur trail leads left to an overlook. Just beyond the overlook spur, the first of two trails leads right to the Small Wilds backcountry campsite. Stay left and cross Laurel Branch.

2.3 Come to an overlook on your left after walking a bit on the Fiery Gizzard Trail beyond the Laurel Branch crossing. Here you can look back along the rim you traversed as well as down into Fiery Gizzard Gulf. Backtrack toward the trailhead.

3.5 Turn right at Climbers Access 2, quickly descending by stairs and steps into the gorge and passing a noteworthy rockhouse. Cruise the base of a cliffline.

3.8 Stone steps lead left to a designated climbing area.

3.9 Climbers Access 1 leads left, ascending to the gorge rim. Stay along the cliffline base, shaded by overhanging rockhouses.

4.2 Reach a suspension bridge. From here you can access the plunge pool of Foster Falls and enjoy a face-on perspective of this powerful rumbler. Cross the suspension bridge after viewing Foster Falls, ascending the gorge.

4.6 Come to a wooden platform offering a distant view of Foster Falls.

4.7 Arrive back at the trailhead.

9 Falls of Grundy Forest

You can bag five waterfalls on this hiking adventure, each distinct from the others. First, drop off the Cumberland Plateau, passing an ancient hemlock, and hike along Little Fiery Gizzard Creek. View wide Blue Hole Falls, with its legendary swimming hole. Next, join Big Fiery Gizzard Creek and visit curtain-like Sycamore Falls. Stretch your legs on the Fiery Gizzard Trail, climbing the rim of the gorge to view modest Yellow Pine Falls. Backtrack and make a loop past the slide of Hanes Hole Falls. Finally, visit slender and delicate School Branch Falls. Geological wonders enhance the aquatic highlights of this magnificent hike.

Start: Grundy Forest trailhead

Distance: 5.5-mile lollipop

Hiking time: About 3.3 hours

Difficulty: Moderate; rocky trails

Trail surface: Natural

Best season: Fall–spring

Other trail users: Backpackers

Canine compatibility: Leashed dogs allowed

Land status: State park

Fees and permits: No fees or permits required

Schedule: Daily, dawn to dusk

River level view of
Sycamore Falls

Maps: USGS Tracy City, Burrow Cove, Monteagle, White City; South Cumberland
State Park–Fiery Gizzard
Trail contacts: South Cumberland State Park, 11745 US 41, Monteagle, TN 37356;
(931) 924-2980; tnstateparks.com
Finding the trailhead: From Chattanooga, take I-24 West to exit 135 near Mon-
teagle. Join US 41 Alt South toward Tracy City for 0.5 mile to join US 41 South.
Stay with US 41 South toward Tracy City. Hit your odometer as you pass the
South Cumberland State Park Visitor Center on your left (better yet, stop and get
information). Drive for 2.2 miles beyond the visitor center to turn right on Third
Street. Continue for 0.4 mile then turn right on Marion Street. Continue for 0.1
mile; turn right on Fiery Gizzard Road to dead-end at the trailhead, passing the
overflow parking area. The trailhead offers restrooms, picnic tables, and a shelter.
GPS: N35 15.103' / W85 44.853'

The Hike

Back in the 1930s, citizens of Tracy City donated a 212-acre parcel known as
Grundy Forest just south of town to be preserved for its superlative natural features. Later, the Civilian Conservation Corps (CCC) came in and laid out trails.
Ultimately, the land was preserved as part of South Cumberland State Park. The
concentration of features in Grundy Forest and the adjacent gorge of Big Fiery
Gizzard Creek deserve preservation. For here you have waterfalls, old-growth
trees, rock shelters, cliff-rim views, and everywhere-you-look natural splendor
rivaling anywhere in the Southeast. Much of this hike lies within a designated
state natural area.

If you want to see the plethora of waterfalls in all their finery, I recommend
taking this hike from late fall through spring. Summer and early fall can reduce
the streams to less than their best. Spring hikers will benefit from wildflowers
in the moist vales. The hike wastes no time hitting the constant highlights as it
leaves the picnic area/trailhead then dips into the gorge of Little Fiery Gizzard
Creek, reaching the clear stream then cruising to marvelous Cave Spring Rockhouse, where a hemlock five centuries alive rises in its own grandeur. Ahead, more
hemlocks, rocks, and boulders of every size and description pepper the water
and land. Blue Hole Falls is your first cataract, named for the sizable azure pool
below the 10-foot falls. Generations of nearby Tracy City residents have cooled
off on hot summer days in this pool. After that, cross Little Fiery Gizzard Creek

then come to its confluence with Big Fiery Gizzard Creek. Together the streams merge and cut the mini slot canyon known as Black Canyon. Its slender depths hold more cataracts. Ahead stands another geological wonder—the columnar spires known as the Chimney Rocks. Then you reach Sycamore Falls. The stream-wide spiller drops 14 feet off a stony lip, making a sonorous splash. The best views are from the falls pool, though you can enjoy the falls from atop as well.

The hike continues south down the gorge of Big Fiery Gizzard Creek on a stony track above which rises forbidding terrain of rocky soil and forest. Climb from the gorge bottom past a ragged cliffline to reach the rim of the gulf. Here, walk uplands amid gently rolling terrain to meet the spur to 15-foot Yellow Pine Falls. This modest low-flow spiller pours in a uniform drop over

Backpacker traverses a rock garden deep in the Fiery Gizzard gorge

a mossy stone ledge. This part of the hike gives you added perspective on the Fiery Gizzard experience.

From Yellow Pine Falls a backtrack is in order, and you return to Grundy Forest to complete the loop portion of the hike. Hike upstream on Big Fiery Gizzard Creek to unusual Hanes Hole Falls. The cataract slides over a smooth stone deck before pirouetting into a reverberating pool. The trailside view is best, but head to the base of the pool for a supplementary vantage. After climbing from the stream, pass the site of the historic CCC camp where a taxpayer-funded group of young gents built the trail system we enjoy today. It is now a backcountry campsite. The now mostly-level path leads to School Branch and a final cataract, School Branch Falls. The hard-to-see faucet-type fall freefalls 20 feet over naked rock. It is not long before you close the loop, emerging at the trailhead parking area.

Falls of Grundy Forest

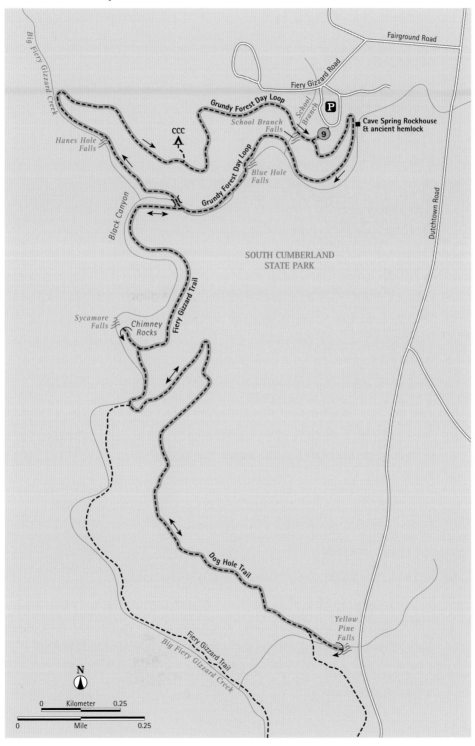

Fairground Road

Big Fiery Gizzard Creek

Fiery Gizzard Road

Grundy Forest Day Loop

School Branch

P

School Branch Falls

Cave Spring Rockhouse & ancient hemlock

9

CCC

Hanes Hole Falls

Grundy Forest Day Loop

Blue Hole Falls

Black Canyon

Dutchtown Road

SOUTH CUMBERLAND
STATE PARK

Fiery Gizzard Trail

Sycamore Falls

Chimney Rocks

Dog Hole Trail

Yellow Pine Falls

Fiery Gizzard Trail

Big Fiery Gizzard Creek

N

| 0 | Kilometer | 0.25 |
| 0 | Mile | 0.25 |

Miles and Directions

0.0 Start on the Grundy Forest Day Loop. Quickly split left, turning down to Little Fiery Gizzard Creek.

0.1 Come to Cave Spring Rockhouse, a huge stone shelter from which Cave Spring flows. Look for the 500-year-old hemlock that stands just outside the shelter.

0.4 School Branch comes in on your right.

0.5 Reach Blue Hole Falls.

0.6 Pass an unnamed slide cascade and plunge pool. Rock walls rise from the creek.

0.7 Reach a trail intersection. Head left on the Fiery Gizzard Trail, crossing a bridge over Little Fiery Gizzard Creek. Hike past the confluence of Big Fiery Gizzard and Little Fiery Gizzard Creeks. Below the confluence, the stream slams through a slender slit of sandstone dubbed the Black Canyon. Watch for the Chimney Rocks ahead.

1.2 Reach a trail junction. Take the spur trail leading right toward Sycamore Falls.

1.3 Reach Sycamore Falls, making its wide jump. Backtrack to the Fiery Gizzard Trail and continue on it southbound, following Big Fiery Gizzard Creek as it cuts a wild canyon.

1.6 Reach a trail intersection. Head left on the Dog Hole Trail, climbing past a cliffline.

1.8 Make the rim of the gorge and resume hiking south.

2.7 Take the spur left to Yellow Pine Falls, soon reaching the 15-foot spiller. Backtrack on the Dog Hole Trail to the Fiery Gizzard Trail then follow it north.

3.8 Pass the spur to Sycamore Falls. Keep north on the Fiery Gizzard Trail.

4.3 Rejoin the Grundy Forest Day Loop. Head left and ascend a steep hill, rising above Big Fiery Gizzard Creek, which you follow upstream.

4.5 Reach Hanes Hole Falls.

4.6 Turn away from Big Fiery Gizzard Creek, ascending in thick woods.

4.9 Reach the spur trail leading left to the historic CCC camp, now a hiker-accessible campsite.

5.4 Reach School Branch Falls at a bridge. Below, the delicate ribbon streams 20 feet off a cliff. It can be accessed by continuing past the falls then dropping right.

5.5 Arrive back at the trailhead.

10 Collins Gulf Hike

Tap into some of what Collins Gulf has to offer. A bucolic cruise along the rim of the Cumberland Plateau takes you past a primitive backcountry campsite to a view of Collins Gulf below. Then you drop off the rim into another world, where Rocky Mountain Creek cuts a canyon to behold. You will curve around a colossal rockhouse and see three consecutive waterfalls, including star-of-the-show Suter Falls as it spills off the rim of the rockhouse. The hike then leaves Rocky Mountain Creek for its mother stream—the Collins River. At the base of Collins Gulf you will find aptly named 20-foot-wide, 20-foot-high Horsepound Falls pounding over a ledge then strangely disappearing in a sinkhole.

Start: Collins Gulf trailhead

Distance: 5.4 miles out and back

Hiking time: About 2.9 hours

Difficulty: Moderately difficult due to elevation change and rocky trail

Trail surface: Natural

Best season: Fall–spring

Other trail users: Backpackers

Canine compatibility: Leashed dogs allowed

Land status: State park

Fees and permits: No fees or permits required

Schedule: Daily, dawn to dusk

Maps: USGS Collins; South Cumberland State Park—Savage Gulf

Trail contacts: South Cumberland State Park, 11745 US 41, Monteagle, TN 37356; (931) 924-2980; tnstateparks.com

Finding the trailhead: From the intersection of TN 28 and TN 283 in Whitwell, northwest of Chattanooga, head north on TN 28 just a short distance. Turn left onto TN 108 West and follow it for 18 miles; turn right onto 55th Avenue and follow it for 2.7 miles to the Collins Gulf trailhead on your left. GPS: N35 24.404' / W85 35.602'

The Hike

Collins Gulf is one of three canyons that together create the "crow's foot" of Savage Gulf State Natural Area, a place of waterfalls, overlooks, stream sinks, tall trees, wildflowers, and pioneer history. This state preserve is part of the greater

Author peers out from the
Collins Gulf Overlook

South Cumberland State Park. Savage Gulf State Natural Area contains a whopping 55 miles of hiking trails, with several backpack campsites too. Within easy
striking distance of Chattanooga, Savage Gulf is a must-visit destination for
Chattanooga-area adventurers.

Collins Gulf is a lesser trod segment of Savage Gulf, but after hiking here you
will wonder why it isn't more popular. I do. The hike follows the Collins Gulf Trail
the whole way. It leaves the trailhead kiosk and sign-in sheet to pick up an old
doubletrack road heading north. Descend in woods of pine, oak, and sourwood.
Ahead you will find a spring on trail left, marked by a sign. Pines and oaks rise
overhead as you reach a trail intersection. Here, follow a spur through the Collins
Gulf West campsite, a primitive locale with a fire ring and privy near the rim of
Collins Gulf. The spur ends at Collins Gulf Overlook, a stone promontory. Here
you can look left into the vale of Rocky Mountain Creek, with the balance of the
panorama opening down the carved canyon of Collins River. Rock outcrops contrast the densely wooded wilderness.

After backtracking to the Collins Gulf Trail, take stone steps down, briefly
joining an old jeep road before reaching the loop portion of the Collins Gulf Trail.
It is a full 13 miles to do the circuit; the path is rocky and slow but rewarding,
with three campsites along the way should you desire to overnight it. Our hike to
Horsepound Falls is but half the distance.

Head left on the Collins Gulf Trail, back on singletrack, working through extremely rocky terrain. The path takes you under the massive rockhouse beside Rocky Mountain Creek. The Cumberland Plateau features many rockhouses, but I believe this is one of the most spectacular of them all. In addition, look on Rocky Mountain Creek for three exciting back-to-back waterfalls. The lowermost one spills over a rock rim and out of sight. The next one cascades white for 20 feet atop an angled rock slab. Suter Falls tumbles in the distance. Walk deeper into the rockhouse, echoing the falling water. At the head of the rockhouse, Suter Falls dives 40 feet over a cliff. What a sight of raw beauty!

A swinging trail bridge transports you over Rocky Mountain Creek; then you work along a cliffline in rough terrain, where boulders and trees create an obstacle course. The Collins Gulf Trail breaks away from the cliffline then works deeper into the canyon of the Collins River. Numerous switchbacks ease the descent. The moist, north-facing vale is a haven for spring wildflowers, from trillium to phlox to foamflower and larkspur; overhead, yellow birch, rhododendron, and hemlock rise in thick ranks. You will also notice copious numbers of tulip trees, buckeyes, and sugar maples in this biologically rich preserve.

The singletrack path joins an old road grade, and the hiking eases. The Collins River flows within sight to your right. You are now in the depths of the Collins Gulf. Seemingly out of nowhere, the signed spur to Horsepound Falls splits right, leaving from the old roadbed. It isn't long before you are at the top of

Horsepound Falls is a great cataract with a great name.

Collins Gulf Hike

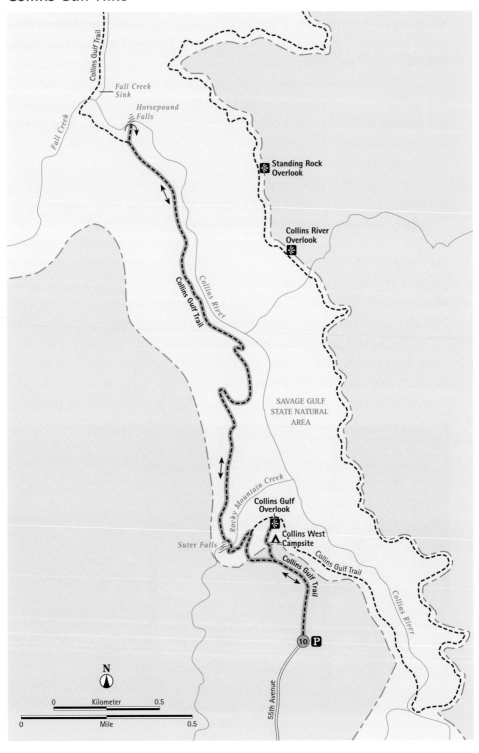

the cataract, pouring 20 feet over a uniform sandstone rim, frothing white then slowing in a large plunge pool bordered by gravel and rock. Depending on water levels, the Collins River can go underground here at Horsepound Falls. At higher flows it continues on then disappear in the Fall Creek Sink, a little ways downstream. At flood levels it keeps flowing aboveground nonstop. Horsepound Falls can be easily accessed along its top via an extended sandstone ledge and also at its base with a little rock scrambling. It's unlikely you will have much company at this remote waterfall, deep in the heart of Collins Gulf.

Miles and Directions

0.0 Start at the Collins Gulf trailhead kiosk and join the doubletrack Collins Gulf Trail. Descend on a gentle grade.

0.2 Reach a signed spring on your left, pumping clear water for the forthcoming Collins West campsite.

0.3 Come to a trail junction. Turn right here, passing through the Collins West campsite on the spur to Collins Gulf Overlook. Look over the deep canyon down the Collins River valley as well as Rocky Mountain Creek. Backtrack, leaving the campsite, then take stone steps into Collins Gulf on the Collins Gulf Trail.

0.6 The Collins Gulf Trail splits. Stay left here on a narrow trail heading under the huge Rocky Mountain Creek rockhouse. Below, a cataract drops from a rock rim. An upstream fall pours as an angled cascade. Farther upstream, Suter Falls makes a curtain-like drop 40 feet over a cliff at the head of the enormous curved rock house. Cross Rocky Mountain Creek on a swinging bridge then work past rockhouses and cliffs into the Collins River canyon.

1.1 Step over the streambed of a seasonal waterfall dropping from the cliffline above you. The hiking is slow and rocky. Ahead, the trail pulls away from the cliffline.

1.8 The trail joins an old roadbed after switchbacking down a singletrack path. The Collins River flows to your right. Step over seasonal drainages flowing from the hillside to your left.

2.6 Join the spur trail leading right down to Horsepound Falls.

2.7 Reach 20-foot Horsepound Falls. Backtrack toward the trailhead.

5.4 Arrive back at the trailhead.

11 Savage Day Loop

This hike takes you to not only two views of attractive Savage Falls but also a woodsy walk atop the Cumberland Plateau in one of Tennessee's premier preserves—Savage Gulf State Natural Area. Leave the Savage Gulf Ranger Station, cruising upland woods to cross a pair of swinging bridges and visit an old moonshine still site before reach the base of 30-foot Savage Falls as it dives over a stone shelf. Sheer stone bulwarks ring the cataract on three sides. Next the hike takes you to an elevated overlook of Savage Falls then to a distant panorama down Savage Gulf, an untamed valley. Enjoy additional forested trail before returning to the ranger station.

Start: Savage Ranger Station

Distance: 4.9-mile lollipop with spur

Hiking time: About 2.6 hours

Difficulty: Moderate

Trail surface: Natural

Best season: Year-round

Other trail users: Backpackers

Canine compatibility: Leashed dogs allowed

Land status: State park

Fees and permits: No fees or permits required

Schedule: Daily, dawn to dusk

Maps: USGS Collins; South Cumberland State Park—Savage Gulf

Trail contacts: South Cumberland State Park, 11745 US 41, Monteagle, TN 37356; (931) 924-2980; tnstateparks.com

Finding the trailhead: From the intersection of TN 8 and US 127 on the north side of Dunlap, north of Chattanooga, take TN 8 North/TN 11 North for 8.6 miles to TN 399 West. Follow TN 399 West 5.6 miles to the Savage Gulf Ranger Station on your right. GPS: N35 26.058' / W85 32.377'

The Hike

Savage Gulf State Natural Area is known as a rugged locale, where several canyons, locally known as gulfs, converge after cutting their way into the Cumberland Plateau. While the vast majority of the 55 miles of preserve trails are rough and tumble, this hike is decidedly more foot-friendly. Primarily using the Savage Day Loop, this adventure also includes a spur trail to the base of Savage Falls,

Left: Savage Falls plunges through a rock cleft into a fine swimming hole
Right: Peering into Savage Gulf from Rattlesnake Point

along Savage Creek. The trails on this hike are not only foot-friendly but also don't entail much elevation change, making it a great introductory hike at Savage Gulf State Natural Area, part of greater South Cumberland State Park. A pair of backcountry campsites are located along the way, providing overnighting opportunities. I have personally spent more than thirty nights backpacking at Savage Gulf and pronounce it one of the finest adventure destinations in the greater Chattanooga area. Hopefully this hike will inspire you to explore other pathways in this special preserve.

Savage Gulf is not only botanically significant but historic as well. In the mid-1800s, an old stage road passed through the area, connecting McMinnville and Chattanooga. Part of this road has been incorporated into the Savage Gulf trail system. At the bottom of the gorge stands the Decatur Savage Cabin, a frail remainder of the tough life settlers had in this land. His family name inspired the name of the state natural area, which came under state preservation in 1973.

Savage Gulf Ranger Station includes a picnic area and water spigot. A park ranger lives on-site. The Savage Day Loop leaves the wooden cabin ranger station and comes to a trailhead kiosk and trail registration. From here you enter upland hardwoods typical of the Cumberland Plateau—holly, hickory, oak, and sourwood. Just ahead a spur leads left to the Savage Station campsite, which must be reserved online. Meander north in gently rolling woods before descending to cool, dark, and damp woods of hemlock surrounding Boyd Branch, a tributary of Savage Creek. Carefully cross the swinging bridge over the gently gurgling stream. Treat these swinging bridges with care—they take abuse from everyday hikers plus thoughtless visitors who swing the bridges to excess, shortening their life span.

The Savage Day Loop now turns west to reach the actual loop of the hike. Head left on the loop and keep left again ahead, taking the South Rim Trail toward Savage Falls. Upon reaching Savage Creek you will come to a 100-foot suspension bridge that presents suitable opportunities to look up and down—and into—Savage Creek. Pass the first of two access trails to Savage Falls campsite. Keep downstream, tracing splashy Savage Creek under a mantle of black birch, rhododendron, and mountain laurel. Watch for the signed site of an old moonshine still next to Savage Creek. The stones of the fire pit mark the spot where mash was distilled into "white lightnin'."

You are nearing Savage Falls. Sounds of the cataract assail your ears, then you descend wooden stairs to the base of the spiller, where gray boulders stand in still repose under tall trees and mosses—a scene primeval. The big plunge pool stands between you and 30-foot Savage Falls, somersaulting from a cleft in a rising ledge. Sheer stone walls frame the pour-over. Savage Falls can range from trickle to torrent. A visit during winter through spring raises the odds of invigorating water flow.

Our hike backtracks on the South Rim Trail, continuing the loop part of the Savage Day Loop. Next you find the spur leading to the Savage Falls overlook. Hopefully the view will be cleared on your visit. From a small rock outcrop you can peer about 250 feet distant to see Savage Falls and its plunge pool forming a clearing in the thick forest of Savage Gulf. *Note:* Savage Falls cannot be accessed from this viewpoint.

The thrills aren't over yet as you climb along the rim of the gorge above Savage Creek to reach Rattlesnake Point Overlook. Here the depths of Savage Gulf open before you. A plaque honors Samuel and Ellen Werner, who in the 1920s acquired 3,800 acres here at Savage Gulf. The plaque's inscription states: "This magnificent creation of God will be forever protected for the inspiration and enjoyment of this and future generations." Amen to that.

Savage Day Loop

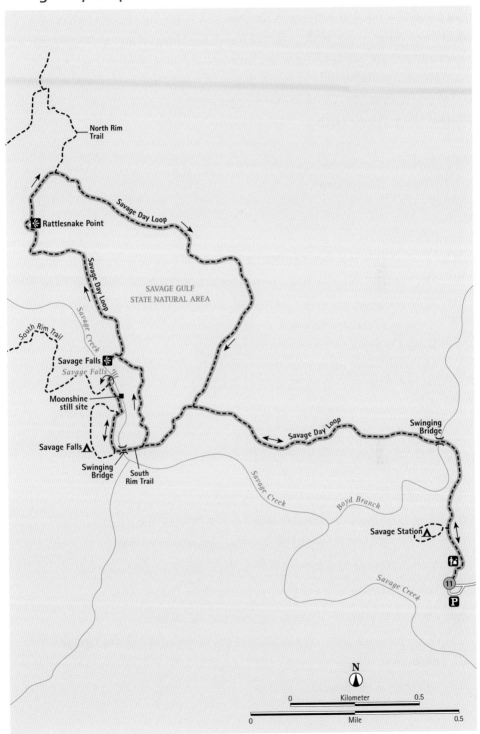

North Rim
Trail

Savage Day Loop

Rattlesnake Point

Savage Day Loop

SAVAGE GULF
STATE NATURAL AREA

South Rim Trail

Savage Creek

Savage Falls

Savage Falls

Moonshine
still site

Savage Falls

Savage Day Loop

Swinging
Bridge

Swinging
Bridge

South
Rim Trail

Savage Creek

Boyd Branch

Savage Station

Savage Creek

11

N

| 0 | Kilometer | 0.5 |

| 0 | Mile | 0.5 |

Beyond Rattlesnake Point Overlook, the hike passes the North Rim Trail then meanders through white oaks and pines. A moderate climb tops out on a hill before joining an old small-gauge rail line. It isn't long before the loop is completed and you are backtracking to the Savage Gulf Ranger Station, with a growing appreciation of the wild and scenic nature of Savage Gulf State Natural Area.

Miles and Directions

0.0 Start on the Savage Day Loop at the wooden cabin ranger station. Reach a trailhead kiosk and trail registration.

0.1 A spur trail leads left to the Savage Station campsite. Keep straight on the Savage Day Loop.

0.4 Cross a suspension bridge over Boyd Branch.

1.1 Stay straight at this first intersection with the loop portion of the Savage Day Loop.

1.3 Reach the second intersection with the loop portion of the Savage Day Loop. You will be back here later. For now, keep straight, joining the South Rim Trail. Cross Savage Creek on a 100-foot-long suspension bridge. Once across the bridge, pass a spur trail leading left to Savage Falls campsite. Pass the site of an old moonshine still, the round stones of the fire pit still visible.

1.6 Come to another trail junction just above Savage Falls. Here a stone outcrop looks down on the falls and plunge pool. Stay right with the falls access trail, descending on wooden steps to reach the base of Savage Falls. Backtrack to the second intersection with the Savage Day Loop.

1.9 Rejoin the Savage Day Loop. Head left, northbound, rising into evergreens.

2.1 Come to the spur trail leading left to Savage Falls Overlook. Find a small outcrop with a cleared view of Savage Falls. Backtrack then resume the loop.

2.5 Reach Rattlesnake Point Overlook with its plaque and view down Savage Gulf.

2.6 Stay right with the Savage Day Loop as the North Rim Trail leaves left.

3.3 Reach a high point then descend, soon joining an old rail line.

3.8 Complete the loop portion of hike and head left, backtracking toward the ranger station.

4.9 Arrive back at the trailhead.

12 Imodium Falls

Imodium Falls is just one highlight of many on this hike that uses the illustrious Cumberland Trail to explore the wilds of the Possum Creek gorge. The trek passes other waterfalls on Blanchard Creek before crossing the stony basins of Little Possum Creek and Possum Creek, with views of enormous clifflines and rockhouses. Grab a look into the Tennessee River Valley before hiking through a recovered mine area, reaching 25-foot Imodium Falls, effervescing into a pool equal in stature to the waterfall itself.

Start: Heiss Mountain trailhead

Distance: 9.8 miles out and back

Hiking time: 5–6 hours

Difficulty: Difficult due to rocky trail and distance

Trail surface: Natural

Best season: Year-round

Other trail users: None

These unnamed falls tumble within 100 yards of the trailhead

Canine compatibility: Leashed dogs allowed

Land status: State park

Fees and permits: No fees or permits required

Schedule: Daily, dawn to dusk

Maps: USGS Soddy; Cumberland Trail—Possum Creek Gorge Section

Trail contacts: Justin P. Wilson Cumberland Trail State Park, 220 Park Rd., Caryville, TN 37714; (423) 566-2229; tnstateparks.com

Finding the trailhead: From Chattanooga take US 27 North to Soddy-Daisy. From the intersection of TN 111 and US 27 just north of Soddy-Daisy, take TN 111 North for 4 miles to the Jones Gap Road exit. Turn right on Jones Gap Road and follow it just a short distance. Turn right on Heiss Mountain Road and continue for 0.5 mile to the trailhead on your left. GPS: N35 20.757' / W85 10.492'

The Hike

The Cumberland Trail is a hiking jewel of Tennessee, and greater Chattanooga is blessed with easy access to this exciting trail that courses along the Cumberland Plateau from Signal Mountain in the south, near the Georgia state line, to historic Cumberland Gap in the north, bordering Kentucky and Virginia. Still a work in progress, the Cumberland Trail is slated to stretch approximately 300 miles when complete. The Possum Creek Gorge section is finished, providing a rugged and challenging hike that rewards every rocky step you take. First the Cumberland Trail leaves Heiss Mountain Road and immediately comes alongside falling water after squeezing betwixt a pair of big boulder "gates," seemingly symbolizing your entrance into a geologically entrancing wonderland, where cliff-lines rise overhead, stone outcroppings rise as silent sentinels, boulder jumbles form slalom courses for the streams flowing off the Cumberland Escarpment from Walden Ridge; where overhangs form rockhouses and smaller stones slow your footfalls. Yet, while scanning the ground with every step, you cannot help but notice the amalgamation of forests and wildflowers, flowing water, and still stone that make this section of the Cumberland Trail one special hike, culminating in the splashing dive of Imodium Falls into a plunge basin of the first order.

Judging from the trailhead, a simple pull-off with a few spots on both sides of the road, you would never know what kind of hike you are in for. From here the Cumberland Trail leads you down into that stony world of rocky gorges. After passing a trailhead kiosk, you are instantly hit with your first highlight—the

Imodium Falls on a late summer morning

waterfalls of Blanchard Creek. The spill makes an 18-foot double dive over a slick ledge before merging into one flow. You are following the Cumberland Trail between the aforementioned boulder gates then crossing Blanchard Creek and turning down the stream, making its own course, straining to give its waters to Big Possum Creek. If the water is up you will hear additional waterfalls below, to be enjoyed by the determined off-trail waterfall enthusiast.

For the rest of us, the trailside scenery will more than do as the Cumberland Trail skirts Bare Point, diving into rhododendron and moss and rock, making its slow, rocky way down the defile of Big Possum Creek. This is a world primeval, yet where you briefly follow an old narrow-gauge railway line, long ago used to extract towering timber from the gorge of Big Possum Creek. The forest has since recovered magnificently. After that respite, the Cumberland Trail leads up along a towering tan cliffline. Walk the base of this geological wonder known as The Amphitheater, perhaps for its propensity to echo the falling waters of Big Possum Creek. The cliffline is pocked with overhangs where dripping water freezes in winter.

The Cumberland Trail leads up through pines to a knob known as Perkins Point. Evergreens thicken in this briefly level, foot-friendly trail segment, where pine needles carpet the trailbed. Beyond the pines, the woods open to a spur trail and outcrop where the Perkins Point vista reveals—through the opening of the Big Possum Creek gorge—the extent of the habitations, lands, and waters of the Tennessee River Valley, lying below the Cumberland Escarpment.

Beyond the view, a long series of switchbacks leads down the gorge of Little Possum Creek. The Cumberland Trail takes you up this closing defile, as rugged as its sister stream valley. A rocky and small campsite provides overnight refuge for those desiring a stay in this untamed land (I have stayed here a few times myself). Just as the Little Possum Creek gorge closes in, a hiker bridge leads across this stream and you ascend its stone-pocked wooded slopes, passing a columnar formation known as Stack Rock. The trail leads past this notable formation, first from its base and then to the top, which offers a partial view.

Ahead, the Cumberland Trail joins an old strip mine bench, where coal was mined in the 1940s. The layer of coal was extracted and the tailings pushed away from the mountain, forming a parallel rampart. Here you travel along the now wooded yet not quite natural slope of Bakewell Mountain. (After 1967, a law required mined slopes be returned to their natural contours.) The trek also crosses atop rock slabs flanked by colorful mosses and spindly pines as Little Possum Creek crashes below.

And then you come to Imodium Falls, aka Little Possum Creek Falls. Imodium Falls received its peculiar moniker from nervous, and crazy, whitewater kayakers who paddle Little Possum Creek and off the top of this waterfall. The overall locale impresses where the stream spills 25 feet off this rim, which overhangs a rockhouse bordered by verdant woodlands rising from the waters. Big boulders border the oversized plunge pool into which Imodium Falls spreads and slides then plummets. The cataract can be accessed from both the bottom and top, though exercise caution if observing from above.

Miles and Directions

0.0 Start from the Heiss Mountain Road trailhead, joining the Cumberland Trail. Pass a trailside kiosk and watch for an unnamed 18-foot waterfall to your left. Squeeze through a pair of boulders then cross Blanchard Creek on a footbridge. Turn down Blanchard Creek, bordered by rich forest.

Imodium Falls

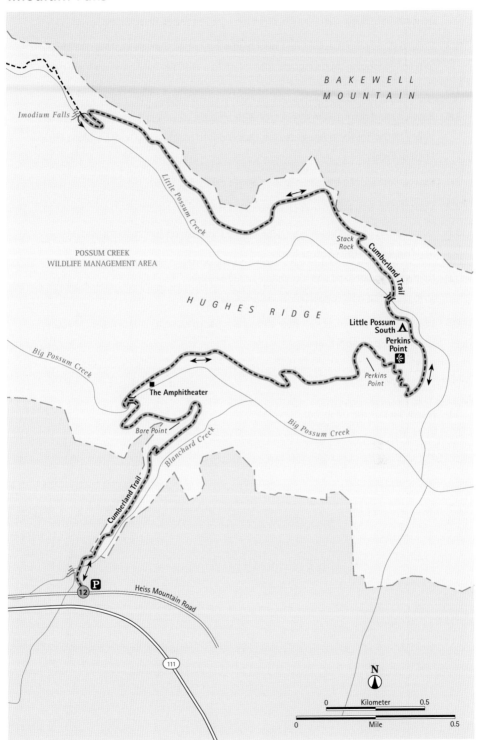

Imodium Falls

BAKEWELL MOUNTAIN

Little Possum Creek

POSSUM CREEK
WILDLIFE MANAGEMENT AREA

Stack Rock

Cumberland Trail

HUGHES RIDGE

Little Possum South

Perkins Point

Perkins Point

Big Possum Creek

The Amphitheater

Bare Point

Big Possum Creek

Blanchard Creek

Cumberland Trail

12 P Heiss Mountain Road

111

N

0   Kilometer   0.5

0   Mile   0.5

0.6 Come along a cliff line, shortly passing a rockhouse. The Cumberland Trail curves beneath Bare Point. Gain limited views into the Tennessee River Valley.

1.3 Cross bouldery Big Possum Creek on a high hiker bridge. Turn downstream to briefly join an old logging railroad grade then climb to a cliffline, back on singletrack trail.

1.5 Walk under a large rockhouse dubbed The Amphitheater. Circle Perkins Point.

2.6 Reach a short spur trail to a rock cliff with an open view across the Tennessee River Valley to the Southern Appalachians. Descend into rough, rocky territory along Little Possum Creek.

3.1 Pass a short spur to the Little Possum South campsite.

3.2 Cross a long trail bridge over Little Possum Creek.

3.5 Come to the base of Stack Rock, a pillar. The Cumberland Trail makes a switchback and reaches the top of Stack Rock.

3.9 Hike near private land and a primitive road then join a roadbed. Hike along a 1940s strip mine cut, now reforested. Some areas can be wet.

4.5 Leave the old strip mine cut. Hike a natural wooded slope, eventually switchbacking toward Little Possum Creek.

4.9 Reach Imodium Falls, also known as Little Possum Creek Falls. Backtrack toward the trailhead.

9.8 Arrive back at the trailhead.

13 North Chickamauga Creek Gorge State Natural Area

This popular hike takes you into the gorge of North Chickamauga Creek where it cuts a stony swath through Walden Ridge. Follow the Cumberland Trail through a designated Tennessee state natural area, passing numerous highlights, including a wild tumbling creek, clifflines, views, rockhouses, even a waterfall.

Start: Montlake Road trailhead

Distance: 4.8 miles out and back with small loop

Hiking time: About 3 hours

Difficulty: Moderately difficult due to rocky trail

Trail surface: Natural

Best season: Year-round; can be hot in summer

Other trail users: Swimmers

Canine compatibility: Leashed dogs allowed

Land status: State natural area

Fees and permits: No fees or permits required

Schedule: Daily, 8 a.m. to 7 p.m.; strictly enforced

Maps: USGS Daisy, Soddy, Fairmount, Henson Gap; Cumberland Trail—North Chickamauga Creek Section

The beauty of Strip Mine Falls far outstrips its unappealing name.

Trail contacts: Justin P. Wilson Cumberland Trail State Park, 220 Park Rd., Caryville, TN 37714; (423) 566–2229; tnstateparks.com

Finding the trailhead: From the intersection of TN 153 and US 27 just north of Chattanooga, take US 27 North for 2 miles to the Thrasher Pike exit. Take Thrasher Pike west 0.7 mile to a traffic light and the junction with Dayton Pike. Turn right on Dayton Pike and follow it 0.7 mile to cross North Chickamauga Creek then reach a traffic light and Montlake Drive. Turn left on Montlake Drive (the right turn will be Industrial Drive) and follow it for 1.1 miles to a large parking area on the left. The Cumberland Trail starts at the far end of the parking area. GPS: N35 14.258' / W85 14.067'

The Hike

Formerly a preserved pocket wilderness held by Bowater Corporation, a paper company, this 7,093-acre swath of wild land is now a Tennessee state natural area, conferred in 2007. A highlight reel of a segment of the Cumberland Trail has been routed through Chickamauga Gulch, an incredibly rough yet gorgeous vale created where North Chickamauga Creek cuts its way from Walden Ridge off the Cumberland Escarpment. In the gorge, North Chickamauga Creek slaloms amid huge boulders then slows in big pools, popular with swimmers in the summertime. During the warm season, the parking area can fill with the cars of scantily clad bathers seeking relief from torrid Chattanooga summers, while the Cumberland Trail remains lightly used. *Note:* The no-alcohol policy here is stringently enforced, although the rare boozing hiker is far outnumbered by illicitly drinking swimmers.

By all means, come here to enjoy this stellar hiking adventure, but try to come during off-times—early mornings during summer, weekdays during fall, and just about any time in winter. Spring can be busy on weekends as hikers seek the wildflowers rising prolifically in the gorge, including the federally threatened large-flowered skullcap. This hike on the Cumberland Trail leaves the parking area, passing picnic tables and designated accesses leading down to "gorge-ous" North Chickamauga Creek—a wild, rocky waterway, open to the sun above, bordered by sandbars and bus-sized boulders, around which whitewater swirls between pools. The trail at this point is tracing an old roadbed. Overhead, a roof of tree cover shades the trail as it pushes headlong into the heart of Chickamauga

Gulch. Just as you get your feet going, the Upper Hogskin Loop leaves right. This will be your return route.

For now, keep along North Chickamauga Creek as stony wooded slopes rise high. After a bit, the Cumberland Trail crosses Hogskin Branch (on the top-10 all-time Tennessee creek names list) then leaves the roadbed, zigzagging uphill while incredibly rocky and wide Hogskin Branch crashes downhill. The trail rises to an old mine access road, and the hiking gets much easier. Here you continue up the gorge, deeper into the canyon. You will not miss the massive rockhouse on trail right, almost a perfect shelter. No one uses it as a shelter today, but vandals have defaced the stone haven with spray paint. Nevertheless, you can still see its natural beauty, despite the disfiguring.

The Cumberland Trail gently rises, passing the concrete base of a former coal tipple. This area was both deep mined and strip mined. Now the trail turns into an unnamed stream, the stream of Strip Mine Falls. Here water froths white 24 feet over the gorge rim, gathers in a shallow rocky pool, then bounds through rocks in a continuous rapids for 130 more feet before slowing. In summer and autumn the falls can slow to a trickle, but following a rain, Strip Mine Falls is a thing of beauty. So is the massive adjacent rock shelter, very wide, so large that it must be seen to be believed. You will also find an open mineshaft. Do not go in to it! The mine shaft at these falls was likely the Montlake Mine, which was abandoned in 1926, though other parts of the lease were strip mined later, lending a name to the cataract.

The hike now takes you along the base of a rising cliffline. Look for panoramas down Chickamauga Gulch, courtesy of a fire that ravaged the gorge several years back. For now, the trees are low and brushy; eventually they will lessen the views. The minimal tree cover in this area also makes the path a hot proposition in summer. Nearer scenes are eye pleasing, especially the geology of the cliffline you are following, where boulders and rockhouses enhance the imposing cliff walls. The footing is rough in places as the trail undulates along the cliffline, dodging trees and rocks, running behind boulders in places. After passing under a low rockhouse, the trail leads up steep stairs—scaling the cliffline—to reach the rim of the gorge and Boston Branch Overlook. The view makes for a worthy destination—you can see up and down the gorge, as well as up Rogers Creek and Boston Branch. A house across the way detracts a bit from the natural attributes of the panorama. However, the overall experience is one of the finest hikes in the greater Chattanooga area. On your return, take the Upper Hogskin Loop, adding new mileage to the adventure.

North Chickamauga Creek Gorge State Natural Area

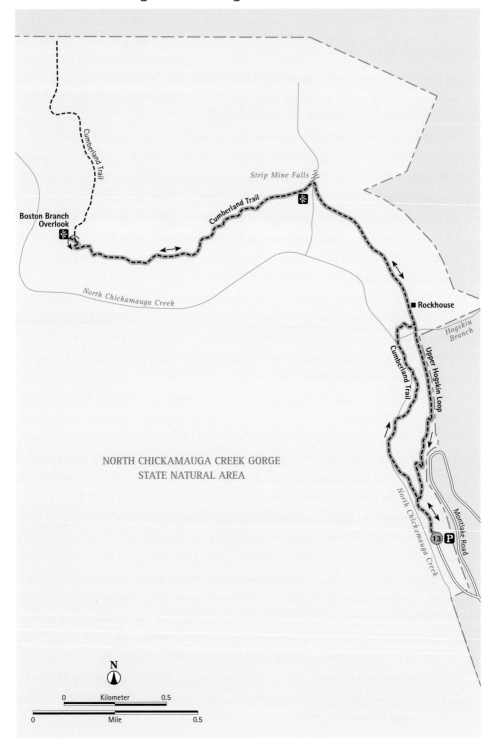

NORTH CHICKAMAUGA CREEK GORGE
STATE NATURAL AREA

Boston Branch
Overlook

Cumberland Trail

North Chickamauga Creek

Strip Mine Falls

Cumberland Trail

Rockhouse

Hogskin
Branch

Cumberland Trail

Upper Hogskin Loop

North Chickamauga Creek

Montlake Road

13 P

N

| 0 | Kilometer | 0.5 |
| 0 | Mile | 0.5 |

Miles and Directions

0.0   Start on the wide doubletrack Cumberland Trail at the north end of the large parking area. The white-blazed path passes picnic tables and near North Chickamauga Creek. Vertical gorge walls boldly rise across the creek.

0.1   The Upper Hogskin Loop leaves right. Stay straight with the Cumberland Trail. Head into the gorge, dotted with immense boulders used by visitors as sunning rocks overlooking large azure pools.

0.6   Reach an old auto ford crossing North Chickamauga Creek. Stay right as the now-singletrack Cumberland Trail wanders on the right-hand bank then turns away from the stream and climbs to cross Hogskin Branch, with its small cascades dashing betwixt big boulders.

0.8   Meet the other end of the Upper Hogskin Loop after climbing. Turn left here, continuing into the gorge.

0.9   Come to an overhanging rockhouse.

1.3   Reach Strip Mine Falls after passing the concrete abutments of an old coal tipple, used to load coal. Above, Strip Mine Falls spills over a rock rim then tumbles to and below the trail. An immense rockhouse stands to the left of the falls. Look for an open mine shaft to the left of the falls as well.

1.4   Pass a view to the left, open down Chickamauga Gulch, into the Tennessee River Valley, framed by the Southern Appalachians in the distance.

2.2   The now-westbound Cumberland Trail leads you under a low, protruding rockhouse on a south-facing segment of the gorge. Beyond, the Cumberland Trail joins steep wooden steps and surmounts the cliffline you have been following.

2.4   Come to and follow a spur leading left to Boston Branch Overlook. Here, from outcrops amid post-fire brushy trees, you can look up the gorge, across at a house, and into Boston Branch and Rogers Creek valleys. Backtrack toward the trailhead.

4.0   Meet the other end of the Upper Hogskin Loop. Keep straight on the old mine access road before descending right on a singletrack path in rocky woods.

4.7   Rejoin the Cumberland Trail after completing the Upper Hogskin Loop. Head left, toward the trailhead.

4.8   Arrive back at the trailhead.

14 Benton Falls

Start this waterfall hiking adventure at a popular Cherokee National Forest recreation area, including a lake, campground, picnic area, and trails aplenty. First circle pretty McCamy Lake, then descend the slopes of Chilhowee Mountain on a well-graded trail to reach 65-foot Benton Falls, spilling in a widening wonderment of white over layers of stone before slowing in a deep cool glen.

Start: Chilhowee Recreation Area Day Use Area

Distance: 4.0 miles out and back

Hiking time: About 2.1 hours

Difficulty: Moderate

Trail surface: Natural

Best season: Spring for boldest waterfall

Other trail users: Mountain bikers on some parts, swimmers near McCamy Lake

Canine compatibility: Leashed dogs allowed

Land status: National forest

Fees and permits: Parking fee

Schedule: Year-round, 24/7

Maps: USGS Oswald Dome; National Geographic #781: Cherokee National Forest Tellico and Ocoee Rivers

Trail contacts: Cherokee National Forest, Ocoee Ranger District, 3171 Hwy. 64, Benton, TN 37307; (423) 338-3300; fs.usda.gov/cherokee

Finding the trailhead: From exit 20 on I-75 near Cleveland, take the US 64 East Bypass for 6.4 miles. Turn right onto US 64 East and continue for 15 miles. Turn left on FR 77, just after the Ocoee District Ranger Station, and drive for 7.3 miles. Chilhowee Campground will be on your right. Turn right toward the campground and travel 0.4 mile, passing the spur to A and B loops. Come to a fee station and the day-use area, pay your parking fee, then take the next right to reach the trailhead. There is also parking near the fee station. GPS: N35 9.0139' / W84 36.4545'

The Hike

Benton Falls is the scenic centerpiece of Cherokee National Forest's Chilhowee Recreation Area. The easy but rewarding hike to the attractive spiller deserves its popularity.

Benton Falls can be a quite photogenic spiller

The immediate trailhead offers picnicking, restrooms, water, and even a nearby lake for swimming, so take advantage. On nice-weather weekends, the whole locale—along with the adjacent campground—can be hopping. You start the hike by circling 7-acre McCamy Lake on the McCamy Lake Trail, passing a swim beach then turning to the upper end of the clear impoundment, standing at around 1,900 feet in elevation. The impoundment is popular with swimmers, anglers, and folks fooling around in kayaks and canoes. You will reach the Benton Falls Trail after crossing the marshy upper reaches of McCamy Branch, the creek filling McCamy Lake. The majority of the hike traces the Benton Falls Trail, a wide natural-surface track built to handle the crowds. The path traverses the slope of Chilhowee Mountain, richly forested with dry situation species such as sourwood, black gum, pine, and dogwood.

After your mountainside meander, you come within earshot of Franklin Spring Branch, the stream of Benton Falls. Your pulse increases and you know the falls are near. Suddenly the route leaves the main trail and traces an attractive and robust stone path weaving toward the base of Benton Falls into a cool,

A PLETHORA OF BEAR SIGNS

You will see a host of bear warning signs at Chilhowee Recreation Area. Here's why.

In April 2006, 45-year-old Susan Cenkus and her two children, ages 2 and 6, visited Benton Falls. A black bear was spotted near the falls. Hikers attempted to scare the bruin away. Instead, the bear swooped in and grabbed 2-year-old Luke in its jaws. With a mother's frantic energy Susan hurled rocks and branches at the bear, which released its grip on Luke.

The bear then went after Susan, getting hold of her and dragging her from the trail into the forest. Other nearby hikers valiantly drove the bear away from Susan. Just when it seemed the ordeal was over, Susan realized that her daughter, Elora, was missing. The hikers desperately searched for the 6-year-old, who had run away during the initial encounter. A man spotted the bear hovering over the lifeless Elora.

The Tennessee Wildlife Resources Agency later trapped a bear, which was euthanized. However, the University of Tennessee veterinarian school could not conclusively determine that the trapped bear had been the culprit. Susan and her son survived the attack.

deeply wooded, rhododendron-ensconced glen. Here, reach the base of the 65-foot spiller, where waterfall mist settles over the creekside rock. Above, Benton Falls fans out over stratified layers of stone. For the most drama, come here from late fall through spring.

Along the way, if the trail is at all busy, you'll run into other people wondering if they are on the correct route to Benton Falls. The uncertainty comes as no surprise, despite the abundance of signage. It is the sheer number of trail intersections that must be navigated—nature trails around the trailhead; a host of mountain biking paths thereafter. Additionally, most of the hike to Benton Falls is completely away from water, adding further doubt.

Your first sight of Benton Falls will be from the top. It is tempting to look over the spiller. Be careful; many accidents have occurred at Benton Falls, most involving bad decision making. Many people are tempted to descend/climb this cataract and its layered rock strata. Don't—the rocks are slippery! The shallow waters at the base of the falls lend themselves to water play, but if you desire a swim, take a dip back at McCamy Lake, where you'll find a designated swim beach and deep water.

Miles and Directions

0.0 Numerous sidewalks in the Chilhowee day use area come together near McCamy Lake and a large restroom, including steps leading from the upper parking area to the lower parking area. Briefly join the Benton Falls Trail near the restroom building, then quickly turn right before coming to McCamy Lake and joining the McCamy Lake Trail. Begin walking with the swim beach and lake to your left. Pass the amphitheater and a connector to the campground.

0.3 Intersect another connector going to the campground. Head left here, immediately crossing the marshy headwaters of McCamy Branch. Continue circling the small mountaintop lake.

0.6 Reach the lake dam and a trail intersection after nearly encircling the impoundment. Join the blue-blazed Benton Falls Trail, a widish track, as the 0.4-mile Forest Walk Trail leaves right. It is a short nature trail for casual trail strollers. The Benton Falls Trail winds amid pines, sassafras, hickory, and black gum. (*Note:* The US Forest Service has used prescribed burning on this mountainside. Look for blackened trunks at the bases of trees and gnarled bushes such as mountain laurel.) Soon pass the intersection with the Elderberry Trail.

Benton Falls

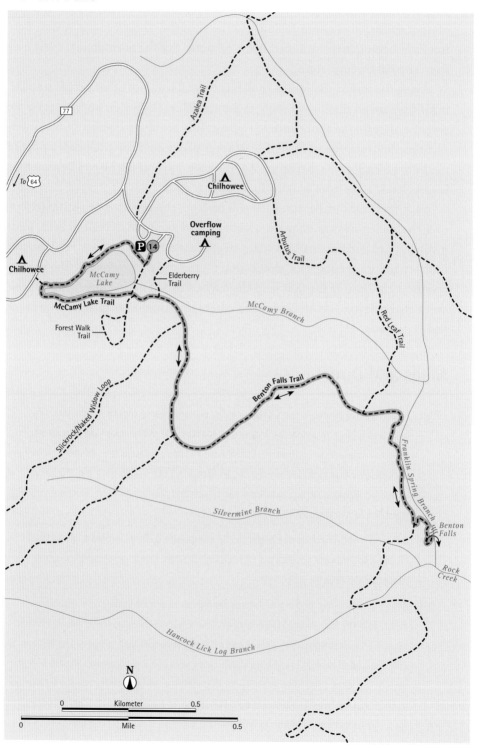

77

To **64**

Azalea Trail

▲ Chilhowee

Overflow camping
⛺

Arbutus Trail

P 14

McCamy Lake

▲ Chilhowee

Elderberry Trail

McCamy Lake Trail

McCamy Branch

Red Leaf Trail

Forest Walk Trail

Slickrock/Naked Widow Loop

Benton Falls Trail

Silvermine Branch

Franklin Spring Branch

Benton Falls

Rock Creek

Hancock Lick Log Branch

N

0   Kilometer   0.5
0   Mile   0.5

0.8 Reach the first intersection with the Slick Rock/Naked Widow Trail. It leaves right. Keep straight with the Benton Falls Trail on a gentle downtick. Cross occasional rock slabs under a partial tree canopy. In other places you will find clay and sand underfoot.

1.0 Intersect the Slick Rock/Naked Widow Loop a second time. Stay straight with the wide Benton Falls Trail, still among pines and oaks. The path is nearly level in places.

1.6 The Red Trail leaves left. Stay with the Benton Falls Trail, descending a bit.

1.7 Come close to Franklin Spring Branch, coursing through the valley below. The stream lies in deep, moist woods. Cross more natural stone slabs bordered by bushes of mountain laurel.

1.9 Head left on the spur trail to Benton Falls. Attractive wood and stone steps lead you down to a switchback. Steps continue all the way to the falls.

2.0 Reach the base of Benton Falls, a widening sheet of white and a showpiece of the national forest's Rock Creek Scenic Area. The base of the falls is shallow and rocky, not conducive to swimming. Backtrack to the trailhead.

4.0 Arrive back at the trailhead.

15 Rock Creek Gorge Scenic Area Hike

This Cherokee National Forest adventure leads hikers through striking forest into the gorge of Rock Creek. Here you will find not only everywhere-you-look beauty but also two eye-catching waterfalls—one with a deep swimming hole. The hike as a whole is not difficult, yet the rewards are great. Give it a try.

Start: Clemmer trailhead

Distance: 3.2 miles out and back

Hiking time: About 1.8 hours

Difficulty: Easy to moderate

Trail surface: Natural

Best season: Spring for boldest waterfalls, fall for colors

Other trail users: Mountain bikers on a small part

Canine compatibility: Leashed dogs allowed

Land status: National forest

Fees and permits: No fees or permits required

Schedule: Year-round, 24/7

Maps: USGS Caney Creek, Oswald Dome; National Geographic #781: Cherokee National Forest Tellico and Ocoee Rivers

Trail contacts: Cherokee National Forest, Ocoee Ranger District, 3171 Hwy. 64, Benton, TN 37307; (423) 338–3300; fs.usda.gov/cherokee

Finding the trailhead: From exit 20 on I-75 near Cleveland, take the US 64 East Bypass for 6.4 miles. Turn right onto US 64 East and continue for 17.3 miles. Turn left on TN 30; continue just a short distance, then turn left onto the first gravel road and to reach the Clemmer Trailhead. GPS: N35 6.9024' / W84 34.7402'

The Hike

Rock Creek Gorge Scenic Area is the setting for this hike that leads to two rousing waterfalls. Comprising 244 acres of the gorge, the scenic area was designated in 1965 and harbors not only the two waterfalls at trail's end but other cataracts beyond, only accessible by off-trail enthusiasts. Rugged rock cliffs and imposing bluffs border much of the gorge, augmenting the waters of Rock Creek and the forest beneath which it flows. Rock Creek is the agglomeration of numerous branches flowing from the east slope of Chilhowee Mountain. The stream cuts its famed gorge below Benton Falls, slicing deeper and deeper through the

Morning sun pierces the forest in Rock Creek Gorge Scenic Area

highlands before flattening out near the trailhead of this hike. A series of hiking and mountain biking trails lace the east slope of Chilhowee Mountain, and you will cross some of these paths en route to your ultimate destination, alternately known as Rock Creek Falls and Rainbow Falls, as well as Falls of the Scenic Spur. The greater cataract consists of two waterfalls, one after another, each expressing its own unique form.

The lower falls at Rock Creek Gorge Scenic Area stairsteps into a deep plunge pool

The upper cataract—20 feet high—makes a slender dive then skims below a boulder before sliding across a stone slab and making a second drop. The lower fall makes a stairstep tumble 14 feet into a deep plunge pool that hikers use to take a mountain dip. A striking rock cliff rises from the lower fall, enhancing the scenery. Despite the steep walls on either side of the falls, boulders and flat areas can be found for repose. This is a truly fine spot for a greater Chattanooga adventurer to spend a day.

The trailhead is located near Parksville Lake, commonly known as the Clemmer trailhead. You will first join the Clemmer Trail, rising into woods on a red clay pathway. You aren't even in the Rock Creek valley yet, but actually cut through a gap then drop into the Rock Creek watershed. At this point the vale stretches wide and is anything but a gorge. Yet the woods are scenic, and you can hear Rock Creek gurgling in the distance. This flat was likely a homesite a century or more back. Where corn once grew, now rise oaks, sweetgum, and pines.

After a bit you leave the flat and come to clear Rock Creek, gently gurgling out from its gorge after a raucous waterfall-rich ride. You are heading up the creek, into the stony mouth of the gorge and into the scenic area. The name Rock Creek seems perfectly natural. The forest changes to moisture-loving species commonly found in Appalachian Mountain valleys, such as black birch, beech, and rhododendron. Look over the waterway as it dances among big boulders and lesser rocks in rapids of white then slows in deep pools bordered by sandbars.

Rock Creek Gorge Scenic Area Hike

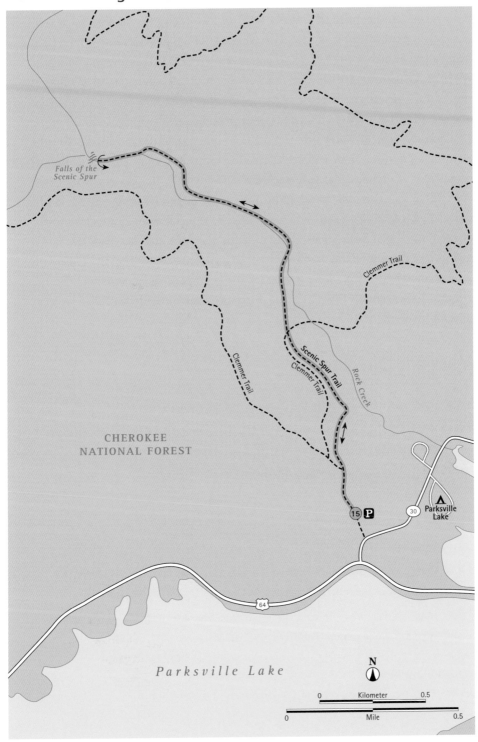

Falls of the
Scenic Spur

Clemmer Trail

Scenic Spur Trail

Clemmer Trail

Clemmer Trail

Rock Creek

CHEROKEE
NATIONAL FOREST

15 P

30 Parksville
Lake

64

Parksville Lake

N

| 0 | Kilometer | 0.5 |

| 0 | Mile | 0.5 |

Ahead, a sheer bluff forces you to cross the stream to the other side. When the stream roars at springtime flows, this may be a ford. At other times a dexterous rock hopper will make it across dry shod. After 0.5 mile working up the right bank, another high rock bluff forces you to make a second crossing, rejoining the left bank, still heading upstream. The Rock Creek gorge is living up to its name at this point. The walls are steep and stony. The rhododendron-lined stream drops one cascade after another, divided by plunge pools.

Soon the roar of water echoing off the stone ramparts above tells you the waterfalls are near. Then you are there. The lower waterfall with its deep pool comes into view first. Next you reach an imposing cliff. This is what Rock Creek Falls has to slice through, creating the upper falls. Be careful exploring the locale, especially after rains or during icy conditions. You can come quite close to the upper falls. Rock Creek slides along a nearly flat rock slab between the upper and lower falls, and in low water this can be a good place to relax. The lower falls is best approached from downstream, at the bottom of the plunge pool. Do not attempt to descend to the plunge pool from the top of the lower falls—you are inviting an accident.

Miles and Directions

0.0 Start from the trailhead on the Clemmer Trail, ascending a wide red-clay path.

0.1 Reach a trail junction. Join the Scenic Spur Trail, leaving right. Climb through a gap then dip into the Rock Creek valley, crossing a wide, wooded flat.

0.6 Intersect an arm of the Clemmer Trail. Keep straight on the Scenic Spur Trail, narrowing into a gorge.

0.9 Rock Creek comes into view. Enter the gorge of Rock Creek.

1.1 Cross Rock Creek at a bluff.

1.5 Cross back over to the left-hand bank. Bluffs rise above. Rock Creek is spilling in a series of pool and shoals. Rhododendron blocks clear views of the stream.

1.6 Reach the falls area. The main falls is upstream; the swimming hole falls is downstream. Exercise caution. Backtrack to the trailhead.

3.2 Arrive back at the trailhead.

16 Keown Falls Loop

This gorgeous circuit hike in Georgia's Chattahoochee National Forest takes you through a designated scenic area including two waterfalls plus multiple views and overlooks. The trail itself is a joy as it starts at an alluring picnic area then rises through attractive woods before topping out on Johns Mountain, a regal forested ridge. The loop takes you back down, winding through rocky portions of the deservingly designated scenic area.

Start: Keown Falls trailhead

Distance: 5.0-mile double loop

Hiking time: About 2.6 hours

Difficulty: Moderate; has a solid climb

Trail surface: Natural

Best season: Winter–spring for bolder waterfalls and clear skies

Other trail users: None

Canine compatibility: Leashed dogs allowed

Land status: National forest

Fees and permits: No fees or permits required

Schedule: Daily, dawn to dusk

Maps: USGS Sugar Valley; Chattahoochee National Forest

Trail contacts: Chattahoochee National Forest, Conasauga Ranger District, 3941 Hwy. 76, Chatsworth, GA 30705; (706) 695-6736; fs.usda.gov/conf

Finding the trailhead: From exit 336 on I-75 near Dalton, southeast of downtown Chattanooga, take US 41 North/US76 West for 2.6 miles to GA 201. Turn left on GA 201 South and follow it for 10 miles to the intersection with GA 136 (East Armuchee Road) at Villanow. Turn left on GA 136 and follow it 0.3 mile to Pocket Road. Turn right on Pocket Road and follow it 4.9 miles to the signed right turn for Keown Falls Recreation Area and FR 702. Turn right on FR 702 and follow it for 0.6 mile to dead-end at the trailhead. GPS: N34 36.806' / W85 5.308'

The Hike

This hike takes place in a lesser visited parcel of ridge-and-valley country in northwest Georgia. Located within the confines of the Chattahoochee National Forest's Keown Falls Scenic Area, the trek will deliver great rewards—if you hike it at the right time of year. Come here after the rains have been falling and the

The hiker behind Keown Falls gives it perspective

skies are at their clearest, meaning winter through spring. That way you can bag Keown Falls (pronounced COW-an) and South Keown Falls and gain rewarding panoramas from multiple overlooks. Hiking here on a hazy summer day will yield dribbling waterfalls and obscured views. Additionally, wildflowers brighten the woods in the season of rebirth.

The adventure begins by leaving the parking area on the Keown Falls Trail. Short gravel spur trails, lined with rocks, break off the main path and lead to picnic tables in a variety of sun and shade conditions. This is one attractive picnic area, and I heartily recommend adding a dining experience to your hike. The creek of Keown Falls—it has no name but is a tributary of Johns Creek—runs to your right. If the stream is running boldly, so will the falls. If it is trickling, focus on enjoying the views on the hike.

A sparse, fire-managed forest of hickory, pine, oak, sassafras, and sweetgum cloaks the rising hillside. Ahead, cross the stream of Keown Falls, then switchback up a slope. The sparse vegetation opens vistas to the south of Horn Mountain. Turn into the rugged stone cleft through which Keown Falls flows. Stone steps aid your passage in the shadow of a vertical stone wall. The trail splits, and you can view the slim 40-foot curtain-type falls. The undercut bluff forms a rockhouse behind Keown Falls.

After backtracking from the falls, top out on the stone steps, reaching a large wooden observation deck where you can view Keown Falls in the near and Horn Mountain stretching across the Johns Creek valley. Wow! Just beyond there you join the Johns Mountain Trail, continuing the counterclockwise circuit, with the rim of Johns Mountain ridge dropping to your right. A steady but gentle climb leads you to the Johns Mountains viewing deck, also accessible by FR 208. This observation deck replaced a fire tower first built in 1940 by the Civilian Conservation Corps and, later, another tower. See the patchwork of field and forest in the Armuchee Creek valley to the west, backed by Dicks Ridge and Taylors Ridge in the near, with Lookout Mountain in the distance.

From here the Johns Mountain Trail turns southbound, quickly passing a concrete block structure, left over from a transmitter tower operation. The trail narrows, winding amid lichen-patterned boulders shaded by hickories and oaks. The trail runs level on the ridge crest,

Keown Falls spills shower-like from its rock precipice

while the land slopes steeply below. Look for fallen wild grapes in September. The Johns Mountain Trail turns and begins dipping into the valley of the creek forming South Keown Falls. The fire-managed woods can be brushy here. Ahead, cross that small stream. You can hear South Keown Falls below and will have an opportunity to see it soon. You are walking above the cliffline forming Keown Falls and reach a trail intersection.

After soaking in your second view of Keown Falls, curve behind the spiller, flanked by ferns clinging onto the bluff. You will soon come to South Keown Falls, wider than Keown Falls but with less volume, making its 30-foot dive. From here the path wanders downhill in a slow, very rocky segment. A switchback moderates the descent until the land's slope softens before you reach the trailhead, agreeing that this area deserves its adventure-worthy scenic status.

Keown Falls Loop

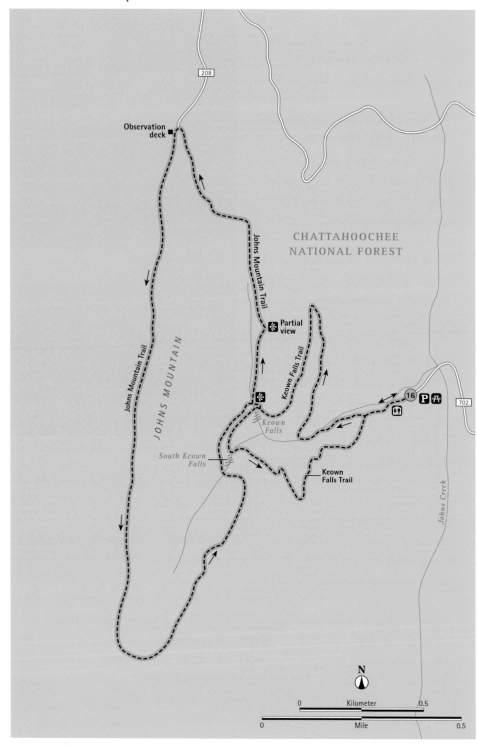

208

Observation deck

CHATTAHOOCHEE
NATIONAL FOREST

Johns Mountain Trail

Partial view

Johns Mountain Trail

Keown Falls Trail

JOHNS MOUNTAIN

Keown Falls

16 P

702

South Keown Falls

Keown Falls Trail

Johns Creek

N

0   Kilometer   0.5

0   Mile   0.5

Miles and Directions

0.0 Start from the trailhead on the Keown Falls Trail, passing the restroom to your left. Ascend on a rock-lined path.

0.1 Reach an intersection. Stay right on the Keown Falls Trail.

0.3 Step over the stream of Keown Falls. Angle away from the stream.

0.7 Make a switchback at a resting bench, now aiming for the hollow of Keown Falls. Ahead, partly open rocky slopes allow views to the east across the Johns Creek valley of Horn Mountain. Join stairs ascending the side of a stone bluff.

1.0 Reach a trail intersection amid stairs ascending the stone bluff. Go left for a minute to view Keown Falls, dropping 40 feet from an overhung bluff, then backtrack and ascend the stairs to reach a viewing platform. Here, look over the Johns Creek valley then reach the Johns Mountain Trail. Head right, northbound.

1.3 Pass a spur on the right to a partial easterly view.

1.9 Reach the Johns Mountain observation deck and a parking area reached via FR 208. Head south on the Johns Mountain Trail after gaining a panorama of the Armuchee Creek valley. Pass a small concrete building.

3.2 The Johns Mountain Trail curves east then north, leaving the crest of Johns Mountain.

3.9 Step over the small stream of South Keown Falls.

4.1 Complete the Johns Mountain Trail and turn right, passing the observation deck where you were before, and head back to Keown Falls. Continue behind Keown Falls on the Keown Falls Trail. Walk the base of the cliffline.

4.3 Reach the base of South Keown Falls. It spills curtain style 30 feet, splattering onto a rocky base below. Continue hiking through a rocky section of trail.

4.6 Make a big switchback left, still descending.

4.9 Complete the Keown Falls Trail. Backtrack to the trailhead.

5.0 Arrive back at the trailhead.

17 Chickamauga Battlefield Hike

This hike explores the south end of the battlefield, a semi-wild, accidental nature preserve. Here trek mostly hiker-only trails through a mix of environments, from tall pinewoods to fields to streamside bottoms to unique cedar glades—a globally rare ecosystem. Much of the route nears West Chickamauga Creek, where you can enjoy stream views. Since this area was a battlefield backwater, there are a few war monuments and interpretive information compared with other areas of this preserved place of conflict.

Start: Viniard-Alexander Road

Distance: 4.7-mile loop

Hiking time: About 2.2 hours

Difficulty: Moderate

Trail surface: Natural, a little gravel road

Best season: Fall–spring

Other trail users: Equestrians on short trail segment

Canine compatibility: Leashed dogs allowed

Land status: National military park

Fees and permits: No fees or permits required

Schedule: Daily, dawn to dusk

Maps: USGS Fort Oglethorpe, East Ridge; Chickamauga Battlefield trail map

Trail contacts: Chickamauga & Chattanooga National Military Park, 3370 Lafayette Rd., Fort Oglethorpe, GA 30742; (706) 866-9241; nps.gov/chch

Finding the trailhead: From exit 350 on I-75 in Georgia, southeast of downtown Chattanooga, take GA 2 West/Battlefield Parkway for 6.4 miles to Lafayette Road. Turn left on Lafayette Road and follow it for 1 mile to the visitor center on your right. (You may want to stop in and grab a trail map.) Continue past the visitor center for 2.5 miles. Turn left on Viniard-Alexander Road and follow it for 0.7 mile to a parking area on your right. GPS: N34 54.092' / W85 15.101'

The Hike

From both a natural and historical perspective, a hike at Chickamauga Battlefield is necessary to round out your greater Chattanooga hiking mosaic. Chattanooga was profoundly shaped by the Civil War, and Chickamauga Battlefield is an important part of that history. The site is part of the greater Chickamauga &

Parts of the battlefield are kept mown for historical accuracy

Chattanooga National Military Park, consisting of several preserves in the area protecting the past, where the Union and Confederacy fought for mastery of the railroads, roads, and rivers that were strategic for control of the South.

The Battle of Chickamauga was fought over three days in September 1863, a victory for the Rebels that only postponed the inevitable Yankee conquest. This site was the nation's first national military park, established in 1895, only thirty-two years after the actual battle was fought. One of the most studied battle sites of the Civil War, the officers who fought in this very conflict took part in placing monuments and developing interpretive information.

Thus we have a history-rich mix of woods, fields, and quiet roads scattered over 5,000 acres. However, there is more. Unbeknownst to the planners who established the boundaries of Chickamauga Battlefield, they also created a de facto nature preserve and within that preserve are biologically important cedar glades as well as other ecosystems. Unfortunately, the preserve is under onslaught by invasive nonnative vegetation such as Chinese privet. As with most urban or semi-urban preserves, controlled burns to curb such vegetation are not favored, since neighbors find burning highly objectionable. Therefore, places like Chickamauga Battlefield are forced to recruit volunteers to cut and pull exotic species, a slow and time-consuming process.

Cannons accompany historical information about one of the Civil War's most well documented battles

Nevertheless, it is better to have the battlefield in its imperfect state than to not have it at all. The preserve presents more than 50 miles of trails for hikers and equestrians to explore the park. The pathways are not named but go by color according to usage—whether horse and hiker or hiker only. This particular hike explores the southeast corner of the battlefield, a place that saw little action. To better understand the battle, enjoy a recommended bike ride (adventure 29: Chickamauga Battlefield Ride) or explore other trails in addition to this hike, which roughly parallels West Chickamauga Creek most of the way. If not for this creek, this part of the battlefield might not have been included at all. West Chickamauga Creek simply made for an expedient border.

The hike is fun, mostly level, and explores numerous ecosystems. I strongly recommend this hike from fall through spring. Do not hike here during summer—it is too hot, and the trails are often overgrown. Be watchful when the pathways come along fields, and take the opportunity to view West Chickamauga Creek as well as appreciate the cedar glades. Large portions of the trails traverse lands where limestone is at the surface, and in places it almost seems as if the trails were paved with the crumbly layer of rock.

Our hike leaves Viniard-Alexander Road, southbound on a gated gravel track bordered by forest of cedar, pine, and oak. You will shortly see the first of the few interpretive battle signs along the hike. The hike leaves the gravel road for hiker-only trails that make a near loop, coming directly beside West Chickamauga Creek as it bends sharply. For the next section you are roughly paralleling the creek among tall pines. Once along the creek bottoms, sycamores will rise above spring wildflowers and pawpaw bushes.

Then you make your way through a mix of fields and woods. The fields are kept mown in order to replicate the land as it was at the time of the battle. You will find the Hunt Cemetery back in these parts. The Hunts owned and farmed the land here during that turbulent period. From here the hike runs through low piney hills cut by intermittent limestone-bottomed drainages.

Look for a trail leading right just before reaching Viniard-Alexander Road. The spur takes you to a limestone bluff above West Chickamauga Creek. When the water is low, you can walk down to a waterside rock slab that is one of my favorite natural areas in the park. After crossing Viniard-Alexander Road, you enter an environment rich with cedar glades. Notice the exposed limestone locales, with stunted cedars and shrubby vegetation. It does not look like a place where a globally rare plant community would thrive, but it is the best place in Georgia to experience cedar glades, characterized by shallow limestone-based soils.

Beyond the glades, the loop returns to taller forests while using a horse trail. The final part of the hike turns south, back on hiker-only paths through a mix of woods, from pines to cedars to hardwoods. It is a scenic corner of the battlefield and a great way to appreciate the indirectly conserved ecosystem to complement the American history contained within.

Miles and Directions

0.0   Start south from Viniard-Alexander Road on an unsigned doubletrack gravel road flanked by forest.

0.2   Head right on a yellow-blazed trail amid hickory and oak.

0.3   Turn right again (westbound) on a little-used orange-blazed trail, also hiker only. This path descends to cross an intermittent stream.

0.5   Intersect a green-blazed trail in a seldom-hiked upon area. Head left (southbound) to quickly pass a yellow-blazed trail going right.

0.7   Come alongside West Chickamauga Creek, soon coming to a bend. Climb away from the stream over layers of rock.

Chickamauga Battlefield Hike

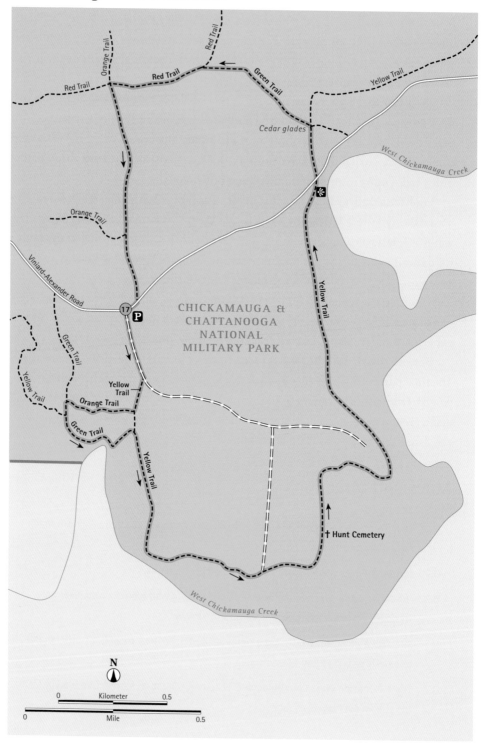

0.9 Return to the Yellow Trail. Here, some cannon emplacements indicate a troop's position atop this hill. Head right, back on a well-used pathway.

1.2 Come near West Chickamauga Creek again, now in sycamore-dominated bottomland. A spur trail heads to the water's edge

1.5 The Yellow Trail opens onto a field. Skirt the right side of the field, then trace a farm road past other fields to rejoin the signed Yellow Trail, keeping east through woods as the farm road turns north.

1.8 Open onto another field. Head left here to shortly reach the Hunt Cemetery. Wind through gentle hills in pines.

2.5 Reach a high point then keep almost due north, crossing then running beside a limestone-bottomed streambed bordered by beard cane.

3.2 Look right for a user-created trail leading to West Chickamauga Creek. After exploring the stream up close, cross Viniard-Alexander Road and enter Georgia's densest concentration of cedar glades.

3.4 Head left at an intersection with a fine cedar glade to your left, joining a green-blazed trail heading northwest. Hike through smaller cedar glades.

3.8 Intersect the Red Trail. Head left on a wider track used by equestrians. Watch for muddy spots.

4.1 Reach a four-way intersection. Head left, joining a yellow-blazed trail, making a level track among limestone outcrops and a few battlefield interpretive signs.

4.5 Pass a short orange-blazed trail leaving right. Keep straight.

4.7 Arrive back at Viniard-Alexander Road. The trailhead is just to your right (west) on the road.

18 Waterfalls of Daniel Creek via Sitton Gulch

Three tall noteworthy waterfalls are the rewards of this hike up an imposing canyon cutting through Lookout Mountain. Start at the base of Sitton Gulch on a first-rate trail, part of Georgia's Cloudland Canyon State Park, then make your way up a wildflower-rich chasm, thick with lofty trees and massive boulders, cut by a rugged stream. Ascend the closing canyon, passing an unnamed falls before crossing Daniel Creek to reach beautiful Hemlock Falls and Cherokee Falls.

Start: Sitton Gulch trailhead off Canyon Park Drive

Distance: 4.8 miles out and back

Hiking time: About 2.6 hours

Difficulty: Moderate; 700-foot elevation gain and hundreds of stairs

Trail surface: Gravel, stairs galore

Best season: Winter–spring for best waterfalls

Other trail users: None

Canine compatibility: Leashed dogs allowed

Land status: State park

Fees and permits: No fees or permits required

Schedule: Daily, dawn to dusk

Maps: USGS Durham; Cloudland Canyon State Park trail map

Trail contacts: Cloudland Canyon State Park, 122 Cloudland Canyon Park Rd., Rising Fawn, GA 30738; (706) 657-4050; gastateparks.org/CloudlandCanyon

Finding the trailhead: From exit 11 on I-59 southwest of Chattanooga, take GA 136 East for 1.5 miles to Canyon Park Road, running between a pair of stone gates. Turn left and follow Canyon Park Road past houses for 0.4 mile to Canyon Park Drive. Turn right on Canyon Park Drive, also lined with houses, and follow it for 0.1 mile; turn right into the park's Sitton Gulch access. GPS: N34 51.591' / W85 29.067'

The Hike

This hike leads you to three distinct waterfalls in the heights of Daniel Creek. The first fall, an unnamed cataract, makes a two-pronged drop over a pair of ledges, each bordered by rock walls and boulders, an overall rugged setting. A surprisingly complex series of stairs and bridges—and hundreds of steps—takes you through a sheer-walled gorge to the next two cataracts: Hemlock Falls and Cherokee Falls. Hemlock Falls drops a whopping 90 feet into its stone cathedral, fronted by a conspicuous boulder in its pool. You can view Hemlock Falls from an elevated deck. More steps lead upstream to 60-foot Cherokee Falls, boasting its own echo chamber of stone walls plus a huge plunge pool.

The hike up Sitton Gulch shows off its own splendor—wildflowers in spring, tree diversity, and geological wonderments from high stone walls to boulder fields and views up and down the canyon. Despite such primitive beauty, the trail itself is a breeze, a smooth

Hemlock Falls in Winter PHOTO BY PETER PILLIAMS

track of pea gravel that allows you to focus on the scenic surroundings rather than stumbling through rock gardens. The steps, walkways, and land bridges on the upper part of the hike are an engineering sight to behold, and also ease the burden of actually climbing through this craggy canyon.

The hike departs from the parking area at the bottom of Sitton Gulch. At this point, Sitton Gulch is at its widest. Flats stretch to your left, where Sitton Gulch Creek flows, well, part-time. The lower part of Sitton Gulch Creek runs underground during drier times of the year, leaving a bare rock streambed. If Sitton Gulch Creek is flowing here, the waterfalls will be bold. Hickories, maples, oaks, along with beech and even pines exhibit the vegetational variety found in the forest. Ferns sprinkle themselves at foot level. In spring wildflowers carpet the forest floor. As a testament to that, the Wildflower Trail soon leaves right. You shortly saddle alongside the west wall of Sitton Gulch, passing a spur loop leading to barred Case Cave. This cavern is closed to the public unless led by state park–sponsored guides.

An unnamed waterfall spills down
Sitton Gulch

Ahead, the gorge closes in, and Sitton Gulch Creek flows perennially. Boulders and rocks of all sizes litter the streambed and adjacent banks. Imagine the forces of water required to move these stones around—floods of frightening proportions. At times the trail is close to the water; at other places the path climbs above boulder jumbles. Be glad this smooth trail was built to explore this incredibly rugged gorge. Don't forget to look up the canyon walls at the horizontal layers of rock alternating with vegetation, delivering first-rate scenery. Also, look down on big pools of the stream below.

The canyon narrows and tightens once you turn up Daniel Creek. Vertical cliffs and boulder gardens stand in still defiance. At this point you may hear people yelling from the canyon rim above, trying to make their voice echo. Of course you will be hearing falling water as it tumbles down the vale.

After a couple of miles you reach the first bona fide waterfall—unnamed as it is. The two-tiered spiller drops a total of 35 feet, first cutting through a rock cleft in a swan dive, flowing a bit, then making a second, shorter drop. After that natural wonder, you will come to man-made wonders—the stream bridge, land bridges, and steel steps that combine to make the next section of hiking much less difficult than scrambling up the canyon. Nevertheless, it still amounts to hundreds of steps to ascend and descend—I counted more than 400 between this point and Cherokee Falls. Be sure to look around at the canyon while climbing the steps. The view will show the near impossibility of getting around here without the staircases.

Upon reaching the observation deck at Hemlock Falls, the 90-foot cataract will deservedly catch your eye, free-falling into an echoing gorge. But also appreciate the pair of huge old-growth tulip trees standing firm and proud directly beside the observation deck. These giants have been occupying their spot for centuries.

Waterfalls of Daniel Creek via Sitton Gulch

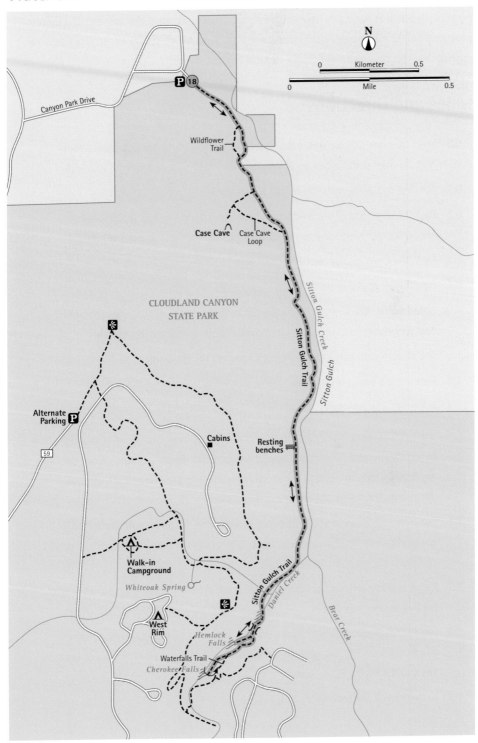

Next comes Cherokee Falls. The whole setting is superlative here—the pounding 60-foot cataract, the walls of the canyon around the waterfall, the big plunge pool, the boulders and evergreens at the foot of the pool. It is a place to appreciate the raw natural beauty of this locale.

Miles and Directions

0.0 Start from the parking area, passing around a pole gate to head up a wide, foot-friendly track under a canopy of deep woods. Sitton Gulch Creek is to your left.

0.2 The first end of the Wildflower Trail leaves right.

0.3 Pass the other end of the Wildflower Trail. Stay straight on the Sitton Gulch Trail. The walking remains easy as you bank up against the west side of the gulch.

0.5 Meet the lower end of the Case Cave Loop.

0.6 Pass the other end of the Case Cave Loop.

0.9 Sitton Gulch closes in, and Sitton Gulch Creek flows year-round among gigantic boulders, rising rock walls, and all-around inhospitable yet lovely terrain.

1.0 The smooth path cuts directly through a ragged boulder garden.

1.3 Pass a stone bench resting area.

1.7 The trail turns into the chasm of Daniel Creek, a much narrower, steeper gorge.

1.9 Bisect the rocky wash created by Whiteoak Spring.

2.0 Reach the unnamed two-tiered lowermost waterfall. Begin ascending steps, crossing Daniel Creek on a bridge, where you officially join the Waterfalls Trail. Look down from the bridge at the unnamed falls below.

2.1 Come to an intersection. Take the spur to a viewing platform of Hemlock Falls. Backtrack, then begin an eye-popping agglomeration of stairs and landings, coming along some sheer stone bluffs.

2.3 Reach another intersection, and catch your breath after all the stairs. Join the spur leading to Cherokee Falls.

2.4 Reach Cherokee Falls after hiking along the base of a bluff and reaching repose-worthy rocks at the foot of the pool below the 60-foot curtain-style spiller. Backtrack to the trailhead.

4.8 Arrive back at the trailhead.

19 West Rim Trail

This hiking adventure at Georgia's Cloudland Canyon State Park traces the highly acclaimed West Rim Trail, where designated overlooks, running streams, rock, and forest deliver continual beauty. A side trip into the upper Daniel Creek gorge to 60-foot Cherokee Falls enhances the experience. Be prepared to take your time, soaking in the scenery of this craggy vale atop Lookout Mountain.

Start: Scenic overlook next to picnic shelter

Distance: 5.2-mile lollipop

Hiking time: About 3 hours

Difficulty: Moderate

Trail surface: Natural; stairways and stone steps

Best season: Year-round

Other trail users: None

Canine compatibility: Leashed dogs allowed

Land status: State park

Fees and permits: No fees or permits required

Schedule: Daily, dawn to dusk

Maps: USGS Durham; Cloudland Canyon State Park trail map

Trail contacts: Cloudland Canyon State Park, 122 Cloudland Canyon Park Rd., Rising Fawn, GA 30738; (706) 657-4050; gastateparks.org/CloudlandCanyon

Finding the trailhead: From exit 11 on I-59 southwest of Chattanooga, take GA 136 East for 6.4 miles. Turn left into the state park. Follow the main park road to near its end at 1.5 miles, near the picnic shelter at the scenic overlooks. GPS: N34 50.0794' / W85 28.8324'

The Hike

Sometimes marketing and hype outstrip the actual qualities of the place being touted. However, when State of Georgia officials changed the name of Sitton Gulch to Cloudland Canyon before turning it into a state park, they were not using hyperbole. The chasm where Daniel and Bear Creeks slice through Lookout Mountain and together form Sitton Gulch, cutting a 1,000-foot rock-rimmed valley, is truly worthy of a name like Cloudland Canyon. The 3,538-acre state park is home to the highly acclaimed West Rim Trail, the nucleus of this hike. The park presents more than 60 miles of hiking trails, plus biking trails, equestrian

Looking across Daniel Creek valley and down Sitton Gulch

trails, wild cave tours, rock climbing, and every manner of overnight accommo-
dations, from backcountry camping to campgrounds to cabins, even round yurts
(you'll see one on this hike).

The West Rim Trail lives up to its hype as well. Expect a lot on this foot-
powered adventure—it will deliver. As its name implies, the track travels along
the rim of the canyon, passing several stony overlooks delivering views in multiple directions. Your first view is almost immediate after you pick up a paved path
leading from near the trailhead picnic shelter to canyon's edge. Here the gorge of
Sitton Gulch opens, revealing layers of sandstone in the near and the Tennessee
River Valley in the distance. Listen for Daniel Creek echoing in the canyon below
as you walk the well-trammeled track flanked by mountain laurel, rhododendron,
oaks, and pines.

Take your only detour from the West Rim Loop early in the hike. The side-
track is worth it as you trace the Waterfalls Trail down into the gorge via costly
and intricate stairways that lead into the canyon and beneath massive rockhouses. Make your way to 60-foot Cherokee Falls, spilling and echoing off the
canyon walls in a rocky glen enhanced by preserved hemlocks. Repose-worthy
rocks overlook the cataract as well as its huge plunge pool. While down here, you
can also head to Hemlock Falls, but prepare to navigate a whole slew of stairs.

After resuming the West Rim Loop, turn up now-quiet evergreen-bordered
Daniel Creek, crossing it to reach the far rim of Daniel Creek via switchbacks.

Note the trailside cave. Just ahead, you will hike near one of the yurts available for rental in the park. A yurt is a cross between a tent and a cabin. Check it out. Cruise the stony canyon rim bordered by pines and oaks on a sometimes sandy track. Wide rock slabs and deeply cut boulders lure hikers, and you soon reach a view. Here, scan directly across the gorge of Daniel Creek to the overlooks at the hike's origin.

From the overlook, the West Rim Loop turns into the hollow of Whiteoak Spring and reaches an intersection. Here you begin a counterclockwise loop. A pair of spur trails lead left to the Walk-in Campground, and you soon cross an intermittent streambed. The hike makes its

Cherokee Falls framed in blooming rhododendron

way to the west rim of Lookout Mountain. Lookout Creek valley and Trenton, Georgia, are visible through the pines below.

Ahead, you reach the best overlook of them all. Steps lead to a northerly tip of rock dividing Lookout Creek from Sitton Gulch. A fence-bordered developed overlook opens before you. Here Sitton Gulch opens to the Tennessee River Valley and beyond to the distant horizon. Soak it all in. This is what a hiking adventure is all about.

From here, the West Rim Trail heads south, now along the west rim of Sitton Gulch. More views lie ahead as you head up the closing gorge of Sitton Gulch. The streams are echoing again in the depths below. The layered stone and vegetation rock walls grow nearer. Enjoy the panoramas from the developed, fenced overlooks. Eventually you turn back into the gorge of Daniel Creek, completing the loop portion of the hike. From there, it is a simple backtrack to the trailhead.

West Rim Trail

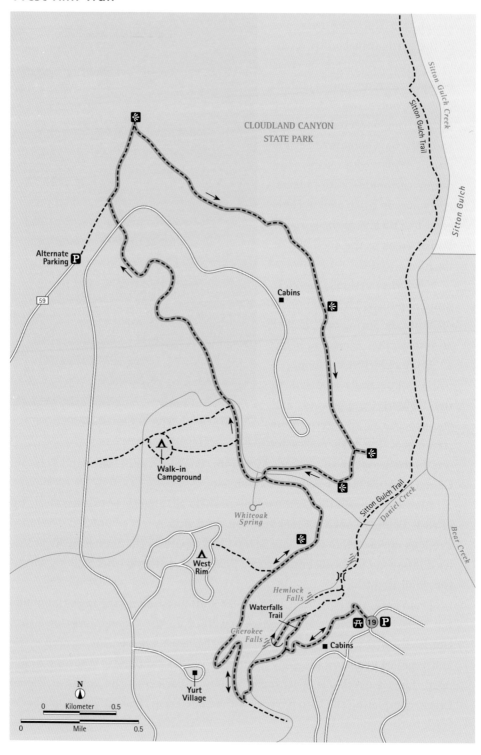

CLOUDLAND CANYON
STATE PARK

Sitton Gulch Creek

Sitton Gulch Trail

Sitton Gulch

Alternate
Parking

59

Cabins

Cabins

Walk-in
Campground

Whiteoak
Spring

Sitton Gulch Trail

Daniel Creek

Bear Creek

West
Rim

Hemlock
Falls

Waterfalls
Trail

Cherokee
Falls

19

Cabins

Yurt
Village

N

0   Kilometer   0.5

0   Mile   0.5

Miles and Directions

0.0 Start on an asphalt track heading past a picnic shelter and leading to the rim of the gorge. Enjoy views of Sitton Gulch below. Head left on the West Rim Trail, with the fence-bordered gorge to your right. Hike by park rental cabins.

0.3 Intersect the Waterfalls Trail. Take the Waterfalls Trail right, descending on a sheer gorge wall, aided by steps and stairs and walkways. Pass under an enormous rockhouse.

0.4 Come to an intersection. Here the Waterfalls Trail splits. Head left toward Cherokee Falls. (The right-hand trail leads to Hemlock Falls and Sitton Gulch.) The path dead-ends at a semicircular stone amphitheater where Cherokee Falls free-falls in a curtain of white. Backtrack to the West Rim Loop.

0.8 Cross Daniel Creek then ascend by switchbacks.

1.0 Gain the far rim of Daniel Creek, then walk near a yurt of the yurt village.

1.3 A spur trail heads left to the West Rim Campground.

1.4 Open onto the first major view, where you can look across Daniel Creek valley and down Sitton Gulch.

1.6 Reach the loop portion of the hike. Stay left on the West Rim Loop, heading up a small stream valley.

1.9 Step over an intermittent streambed after passing a pair of spur trails leading left to the Walk-in Campground. Ascend toward the west rim of Lookout Mountain.

2.4 Cross the park's cabin access road.

2.5 Come to an intersection. A spur leads left to CR 59. Stay right, hiking along the rim of Lookout Mountain.

2.7 Reach the most northerly overlook, with superlative views of the Tennessee River Valley below. Turn south, passing several spur trails to park cabins.

3.3 Come to a spur and view into upper Sitton Gulch.

3.7 Reach another view into the mouth of Daniel Creek, where it merges with Bear Creek to form Sitton Gulch. Turn into Daniel Creek gorge.

3.8 Come to another developed overlook in Daniel Creek.

4.0 Complete the loop portion of the hike. Backtrack toward the trailhead.

5.2 Arrive back at the trailhead.

20 Falls Loop at Desoto State Park

Waterfalls are the primary feature of this circuit hike at this Alabama state park atop Lookout Mountain. You will also enjoy CCC history, unusual rock formations, and overall beauty. The hike combines several trails to create this rewarding loop that starts on the Quarry Trail then passes clifflines, a quarry, and a backcountry campsite and shelter. Beyond, join the Family Bike Loop as it snakes toward Laurel Creek, where you will find three cataracts, fascinating stone formations, and mountain laurel and rhododendron aplenty.

Start: Old country store at Desoto State Park

Distance: 5.6-mile loop

Hiking time: About 3 hours

Difficulty: Moderate

Trail surface: Natural

Best season: Winter–spring for bolder waterfalls

Other trail users: Mountain bikers in some sections

Canine compatibility: Leashed dogs allowed

Land status: State park

Fees and permits: No fees or permits required

Schedule: Daily, dawn to dusk

Maps: USGS Valley Head, Dugout, Fort Payne, Jamestown; Desoto State Park

Trail contacts: DeSoto State Park, 13883 CR 89, Fort Payne, AL 35967; (256) 845-0051; alapark.com/DeSotoResort

Finding the trailhead: From exit 231 on I-59, southwest of Chattanooga, take AL 117 south for 5.7 miles, passing through Hammondville and Valley Head to reach the town of Mentone. Turn right on CR 89 and follow it for 5.8 miles; turn left at an intersection, still on CR 89. Travel for 0.5 mile then turn right again at another intersection, still on CR 89. Continue for 0.4 mile and turn right into the country store at DeSoto State Park; park here. *Note:* The route is signed the entire way for Desoto State Park. GPS: N34 30.085' / W85 37.130'

The Hike

DeSoto State Park is perched atop Lookout Mountain where the Little River cuts its astonishing canyon through the mountain—a fine natural location for this state park, which opened in 1939. Consider incorporating other amenities of

Lost Falls makes its double dive

Walking by Needle Eye Rock

the park into your hiking adventure. This northeast Alabama preserve offers it all—hiking, mountain biking, picnicking, backpacking, camping, cabins, a lodge, a restaurant, even a country store. The ol' country store happens to be where you begin this rewarding hiking adventure.

At the right time of year, this trek can be a real winner. Go in spring for the boldest waterfalls as well as colorful displays of wild azaleas, mountain laurel, and rhododendron in addition to other spring wildflowers. If you are wondering about the best bloom time, simply call the park office and ask about the current state of bloom.

The adventure starts on the Quarry Trail. As you are looking out the Country Store's front porch, walk left toward CR 618. The white-blazed Quarry Trail starts on the far side of CR 618. (As a whole the trails here at DeSoto State Park are well marked and maintained.) Enter woods of holly, oak, and pine on a singletrack path. Watch your feet, as the trailbed can be rocky and rooty. Meander along a hillside, gently ascending to enter a boulder garden flanked by a low, long bluff to your left. Continue west through this picturesque land of forest and rock. Ahead, come to the quarry excavated by Civilian Conservation Corps. Stone from this quarry was used by the CCC to construct roads and buildings at the state park. Look for cut blocks lying inside the quarry.

At the far side of the quarry you will find a spur leading to one of the park's two backcountry campsites. Each camp has a fire ring and a small shelter, open on the sides with a shed roof overhead. After exploring the campsite, continue the Quarry Trail, winding through woods. Avoid following the grassy road leading away from the quarry area. Shortleaf pines shade the trail. The hike then joins the Family Bike Loop as it makes a winding journey through mixed woods broken by small clearings. The path is more level than not, making for easy travel whether you are on foot or a bicycle. The multiple twists and turns add mileage to the hike and go literally in every direction. Sometimes you can even see the path you were on earlier.

After crossing CR 618 you join the Orange Trail. An inscribed stone from the CCC days shows the mileages ahead. This trail is going on a century old. The Orange Trail works downhill through stunted pines, thick mosses, and sparkleberry and atop open rock slabs, aiming for Laurel Creek. In spring you will step over flowing tributaries. And if these feeder branches of Laurel Creek are flowing, the chances are good the falls of Laurel Creek will be bold.

And then you find Lost Falls. Here a side loop curves by the cataract, spilling 15 feet in two stages over a semicircular stone ledge. Open rock slabs above the falls lure you toward them, but exercise caution—the rock can be slippery. Stone steps have been built to better access the base of the falls. The path then turns down Laurel Creek amid rich vegetation of deer moss, shortleaf pine, holly, and oaks, pulling away from the stream at points to meet the spur to Laurel Falls. Here the stream pours 6 feet from a horizontal ledge, splashes into a jumble of rocks, then slows in a pool.

Beyond Laurel Falls, the trail junctions come fast and furious. Make your way to Azalea Cascades, with its observation deck above the creek. This spiller makes an 8-foot angled drop into a pool amid huge boulders. The loop hike traces a boardwalk before splitting left to course among the big boulders, including Needle Eye Rock. Next thing you know, the Country Store is there and you will have completed your hiking adventure.

Miles and Directions

0.0 Start on the Quarry Trail, on the north side of the CR 618, north of the Country Store. Ascend among pine, oak, and holly trees.

Falls Loop at Desoto State Park

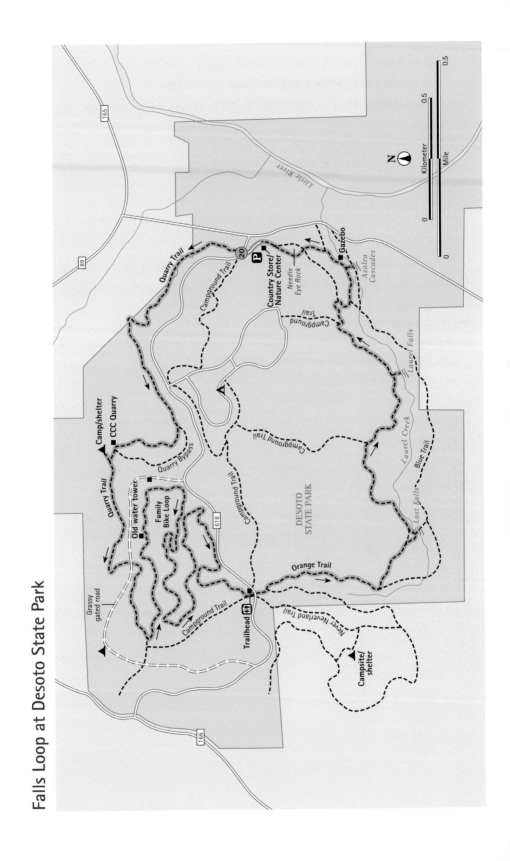

165

89

Quarry Trail

Camp/shelter
CCC Quarry

Quarry Bypass

Quarry Trail

Old water tower

Family
Bike Loop

Grassy
gated road

618

Campground Trail

166

Trailhead

Campground Trail

Orange Trail

Never Neverland Trail

Campsite/
shelter

DESOTO
STATE PARK

Lost Falls

Blue Trail

Laurel Creek

Laurel Falls

Campground Trail

Campground Trail

20

P

Country Store/
Nature Center

Needle
Eye Rock

Gazebo

Azalea
Cascades

Little River

N

Kilometer

Mile

0

0

0.5

0.5

0.5

0.4 Enter a boulder garden. Winding trails take you amid the burly gray stones. Watch as the trails split and come together around the boulders.

0.8 The trail officially splits as the Quarry Bypass heads left. This spur is primarily for mountain bikers to avoid excessively rocky areas ahead.

1.0 Reach the quarry excavated to provide stone for work on the state park. An interpretive sign goes more in-depth. After soaking in the interpretive info, continue the Quarry Trail.

1.1 Come to another intersection. Here a spur trail leads right to a backcountry campsite. Check it out then resume the Quarry Trail.

1.5 Cross a grassy road. Keep straight (southbound) on the Quarry Trail.

1.7 Come to a signed intersection. Head acutely left on the Family Bike Loop. Begin a winding, twisting, turning track.

2.0 Pass what is left of an old water tower in a small clearing.

3.7 Reach CR 618 and the Lost Falls trailhead with restroom. Keep straight here, crossing CR 618 and joining the hiker-only Orange Trail. Note the rock inscribed with trail mileages. The Never Neverland Trail on the right makes a separate mountain bike loop. The Campground Trail leaves left to the park campground.

3.8 Step over a seasonal tributary flowing among rocks.

4.0 Come to a trail junction in an open rock flat. The Blue Trail leaves right to cross Laurel Creek. Stay left with the Orange Trail, still aiming for Laurel Creek.

4.2 Follow the spur loop right to reach Lost Falls, which dives in two tiers from a wide rock lip. Turn downstream along mountain laurel.

4.6 Pass a spur trail leading left to the campground.

4.9 Head right at the spur to Laurel Falls. Check out this second spiller.

5.1 Pass another spur leading left toward the campground. Enter a maze of trails. Stay closest to Laurel Creek.

5.3 Reach a boardwalk and take a short right to reach Azalea Cascade and the observation deck above Laurel Creek. Continue down the boardwalk, passing a gazebo.

5.4 Head left from the boardwalk for the Country Store. Ahead, walk among a garden of massive boulders, including Needle Eye Rock.

5.6 Arrive back at the Country Store, completing the hike.

MOUNTAIN BIKING, GREENWAY AND ROAD RIDING

Bicyclers of all stripes have a treasure trove of pedaling opportunities in and around Chattanooga. The mountain biking community here is strong, dedicated, and involved, creating and maintaining trails for them—and us—to use. You will find every level of mountain biking difficulty among the many fat-tire trail systems in the area—and in this guide—though most of the treks here are in the beginner to intermediate range. Other bicycling opportunities exist beyond the natural-surface trails. Two-wheelers can also ply hard-surface greenways such as the nationally acclaimed Riverwalk and South Chickamauga Creek Greenway. A historic and serene road ride at Chickamauga Battlefield is also detailed. Whether you are looking for a technical singletrack challenge, a flat family pedal, or an in-city ride, there's a bicycling adventure here for you.

The concrete track makes for a smooth and scenic ride

21 Raccoon Mountain

Regarded as the most challenging mountain biking locale in greater Chattanooga, Raccoon Mountain lives up to its billing in both scenery and trail difficulty. However, a tiered system of pathways of differing difficulties laces this Tennessee Valley Authority property, opening it to bicyclers of all abilities. This recommended ride skirts the rim of the mountain most of the way, looping back toward the trailhead. You will have to work among big boulders along with easing through fast segments.

Start: East Overlook trailhead

Distance: 7.3-mile lollipop

Riding time: 1.3–2.7 hours

Difficulty: Moderate; some tough rocky segments

Terrain and surface type: Natural surface; some smooth areas, some bouldery segments; bridges

Highlights: Exceptional mountaintop beauty, first-rate trails

Hazards: A few walkers, boulders; some unmarked trail intersections and shortcuts

Other considerations: Gates closed between 7:30 p.m. and 5:30 a.m. Central Time

Maps: Raccoon Mountain mountain bike trail map

Trail contacts: Tennessee Valley Authority, 400 West Summit Hill Dr., Knoxville TN 37902; (865) 632-2101; tva.gov

Finding the trailhead: From exit 175 on I-24, west of downtown Chattanooga, take Browns Ferry Road north for 0.9 mile. Turn left onto Elder Mountain Road and follow it for 1.7 miles; veer left onto the TVA access road with a sign stating: "TVA Raccoon Mountain Visitor Center." Continue for 1.2 miles then turn left toward East Overlook. After just a short distance, arrive at the East Overlook and a short loop road. The access trail starts on the south side of the loop. GPS: N35 2.477' / W85 23.124'

The Ride

Raccoon Mountain is a Tennessee Valley Authority facility atop a peak that's home to a water storage facility. Water is stored here to generate electricity during periods of high demand. When demand gets high enough, TVA releases water from the lake up on Raccoon Mountain into tunnels in the mountain. The water turns generators located in the tunnels to provide electricity. During times of low power demand, water is pumped back up the mountain to fill the lake

Soak in this overlook at the trailhead

for the next high-demand period. The facility took eight years to complete and was finished in 1978. The 528-acre lake atop the mountain holds about 107 billion gallons of water. In the early 2000s, Southern Off-Road Bicycle Association (SORBA) Chattanooga worked with TVA to build a mountain bike trail system on TVA lands around the reservoir. The result is a nationally recognized, stellar mountain bike network that would be the pride of any region in the country, though we are blessed to have such a treasure right here in greater Chattanooga.

The trails at TVA's Raccoon Mountain are generally regarded as the most difficult, challenging mountain bike tracks in all of greater Chattanooga. Even the beginner trails here are harder than beginner trails elsewhere! Raccoon Mountain presents a comprehensive interconnected 30-mile network of paths that will sate even the most talented and experienced fat-tire enthusiast. These trails include mountain rim–running tracks, mostly level, sometimes smooth, but also with bouldery terrain. Other paths increase in difficulty, with grueling ascents and blistering descents, tough turns, rock gardens, and technical track. The legendary Chunky Freeride Area features big bouldery drops for experts only, and even they had better be clad in elbow and knee pads along with their helmet and any other armor they can strap on!

Raccoon Mountain is the place to rise to the next level, no matter what level you are currently on, and that includes beginners—aspiring mountain bikers ready to take that next step, to rise to the challenge. This ride, our challenge,

Rolling down the trail

starts at East Overlook, a southeast-facing clearing atop Raccoon Mountain that presents a stellar view of Chattanooga, the Tennessee River, and Lookout Mountain, with the Appalachians forming a green mantle in the distance. The ride joins the beginner-level Electric Avenue 1 (as noted, the trail ratings at Raccoon Mountain reflect the tougher nature of the trail network). It leads along the south brow of Raccoon Mountain in thick woods where you can gain the sense of a deep drop-off nearby yet are not pedaling over open rock edges. Instead you are winding in and out of small drainages on pure singletrack, with bridges over wet-weather streams. You can get up speed along this segment, as it is less rocky than other areas of Raccoon Mountain.

The ride then joins Electric Avenue 2, continuing the beginner theme as you wander through pinelands and eventually out to the rim of the gorge overlooking the Tennessee River. This is a fun segment among pines, with plenty of little bridges. Then you join the intermediate-level Laurel Point Trail. The mountain drop-off here is palpable, and the pedaling challenge rises as the Laurel Point Trail becomes decidedly more bouldery, with humpy rocks around and over which you must navigate, though elevation changes are relatively negligible. The trail curves past a picnic area. Next you work around the upper ends of hollows and rocky ridges. The last bouldery-to-the-extreme 100 yards of the Laurel Point Trail will let you know if you are ready to tackle the expert trails here.

Notes: The widely dispersed trail system keeps bicyclers from getting too packed together, even on busy days. Trails here are bidirectional. Water and picnic facilities can be found at the Laurel Point parking area. Almost all trail intersections are signed, though there are a few potentially confusing spots. An alternative bicycle experience can be had by circling the asphalt road around the Raccoon Mountain storage reservoir, a roughly 6-mile road ride.

Raccoon Mountain

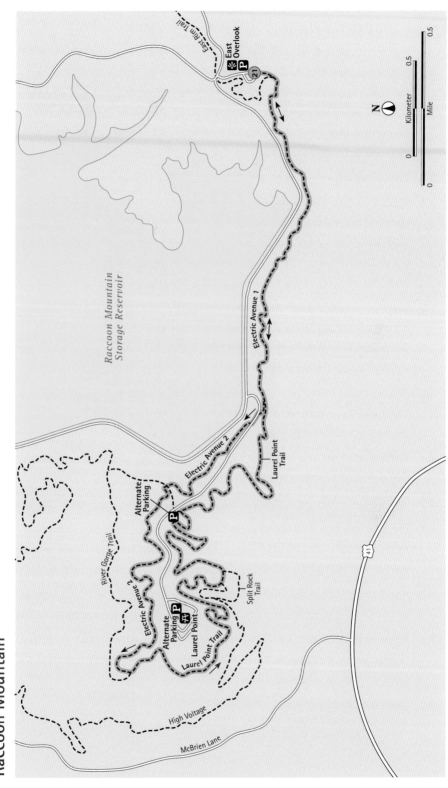

Raccoon Mountain Storage Reservoir

East Rim Trail

East Overlook

21

River Gorge Trail

Alternate Parking

Electric Avenue 2

Laurel Point Trail

Electric Avenue 1

Laurel Point Trail

Alternate Parking

Laurel Point

Split Rock Trail

Laurel Point Trail

High Voltage

McBrien Lane

41

N

Kilometer

Mile

0   0.5

0   0.5

Miles and Directions

0.0 Start south from the East Overlook parking area on a singletrack access path near the overlook; quickly join Electric Avenue 1. Keep straight here, pedaling westerly along the rim of Raccoon Mountain in oaks, pines, and cedars. Contour around hollows and hills with a steep drop-off to your left. A few brief punchy climbs and rocks add to the test. Cross drainages.

0.9 Open under a power line among thick grasses. Quickly reenter woods.

1.4 Reach a trail intersection. Here your return route, Laurel Point Trail, leaves left; we stay right, quickly joining a gravel road then the paved access road toward Laurel Point. Road ride a very short distance then split right into a strip of woods on the signed Electric Avenue 2. Ride northwesterly on singletrack in the strip of woods. Watch for interpretive signage detailing TVA's history in the region.

1.9 Reach an unnamed mountain bike access trail after crossing a closed TVA access road. The mountain bike access trail goes left to parking and right to the River Gorge Trail. Keep straight on Electric Avenue 2, entering a large stand of pines; turns are plentiful but the pedaling is easy as you frequently cross ephemeral wetlands.

3.0 Reach a signed trail intersection on the edge of the river gorge. Here the River Gorge Trail leaves right while you head left, joining the Laurel Point Trail and descending a rooty, rocky track.

3.3 Multiple spur trails lead left to the Laurel Point picnic area and fields. Bang your way over sloped boulders and gravelly sections.

3.9 Stay right as a spur goes left to the TVA access road.

4.1 The Split Rock Trail, with access to High Voltage Trail, splits right. Stay with Laurel Point Trail, rolling past the other end of the 0.5-mile Split Rock Trail. Ride over rock slabs as well as climbing and descending other embedded boulders in woods.

5.0 A spur goes left to an alternate parking area within sight of the trail. Stay with Laurel Point Trail, contouring on slopes amid rocks. Return to the brow of the mountain.

5.9 Return to the intersection with Electric Avenue 1 after passing through an extreme boulder garden. Backtrack to the trailhead. (*Option:* Use the asphalt road along the reservoir if you are beat up.)

7.3 Arrive back at the trailhead.

22 Stringer's Ridge

Stringer's Ridge presents mountain bikers with a quick-hitting 10-mile trail system near downtown Chattanooga. With a purposefully built trail system, Stringer's Ridge attracts mountain bikers from all over the area. Make a fast and flowy loop covering from one end of the park to the other. Come to Stringers Ridge when you just have to scratch that mountain biking itch.

Start: Spears Avenue trailhead

Distance: 3.4-mile loop

Riding time: 0.5–1 hour

Difficulty: Moderate

Terrain and surface type: Ridgeline hills on fast, smooth, fast-drying track

Highlights: Urban easy access park with well-marked, well-maintained trails

Hazards: Hikers and trail runners aplenty

Other considerations: More than 1,200 feet of climbing and descending on recommended ride. Trails are directional, based on day of the week.

Maps: Stringer's Ridge trails

Trail contacts: Stringer's Ridge Park, 1250 Market St., Chattanooga, TN 37402; (423) 643-6311; chattanooga.gov

Finding the trailhead: From exit 178 on I-24 in downtown Chattanooga, join US 27 North and follow it over the Tennessee River Bridge. Take the Manufacturers Road exit just after crossing the river; follow Manufacturers Road for 0.4 mile then turn left onto Cherokee Boulevard. Continue for 0.1 mile then turn right onto Spears Avenue. Follow Spears Avenue for 1 mile to dead-end at the Spears Avenue trailhead. GPS: N35 4.708' / W85 18.539'

The Ride

If you want to see—or be seen with—Chattanooga's hotshot mountain bikers, the best of the best, the cream of the crop, the demigods of the fat tire, then come to Stringer's Ridge. It seems the main trailhead parking lot off Spears Avenue is where these super athletes can be seen, where hard-core aficionados of the sport meet up and say, "Let's ride." Then they do.

It's not that the trails of Stringer's Ridge are the best of the best, but simply that Stringer's Ridge is conveniently located and is great for quick training rides, an after-work fix, or a speedy morning adventure. That is why you will find the

Catching air on the fast trails of Stringer's Ridge

royalty of the trail riders congregating at Stringer's Ridge (along with the rest of us). It is also where helmeted adventurers will be clacking around in their clip-on shoes, admiring and comparing bikes, racks, and of course places to ride.

It was almost not to be. As we all know, the ridges and mountains in and around Chattanooga are lined with houses sporting stellar views. Don't we all wish we had one of those? Naturally, Stringer's Ridge, across the Tennessee River from downtown but also overlooking the city, seemed a good location for condominiums. The four wooded knobs, running side by side, seemed destined for high-rises. Once the back of beyond, Chattanooga had slowly grown out this way, and in 2007 a six-story condominium development was announced on land where Union general John T. Wilder had been stationed and begun shelling Chattanooga and the Confederates in order to take the city back in 1863. However, it was not only the military history but also the aesthetic value of nature for nature's sake that led to the public outcry against this ridgetop housing plan. The Trust for Public Land came in and began a capital campaign to buy the 37-acre tract. The owner, Jimmy Hudson, was so moved by the desire of the populace to see Stringer's Ridge become a park that he agreed to donate an additional 55 acres to create 92-acre Stringer's Ridge Park.

Managed by the City of Chattanooga, Stringer's Ridge Park is now a mountain biker heaven as well an in-town nature preserve for plants and animals. The ball really got going when an avid cyclist by the name of Jim Johnson donated $50,000 of his own money toward construction of a permanent, sustainable trail system. And that is what we have today—a 10-mile network of almost all singletrack paths that range in difficulty. The trails are directional according to a daily schedule. The trails are open to runners and hikers, so be on the lookout on those blind turns. The park does have hiker-only trails, and that is usually where you'll find them. However, a common complaint is hikers getting lost or tired and going the wrong way on the multiuse trails, potentially causing accidents. Factor that into your speed—due to the flowy nature of the trails, you can really get going here on Stringer's Ridge.

Short climbs are followed by rolling descents, and despite the flowy nature of the trails, you can still get in 1,200 feet of ups and downs on this ride. Rocks and roots are minimal here. Speed has its price though; the wooded scenery and large hardwoods cannot be admired to the degree they deserve when you're rolling fast downtrail, watching the path ahead for obstacles and other trail users. You will see a few unofficial trails, often linking to adjacent neighborhoods.

On a side note, the hiker-only trails are pretty fun too. The Cherokee Trail follows an old roadbed, passing a developed overlook as well as circling around the highest knob of Stringer's Ridge. A picnic area is located on the south side of the park. The Spears Avenue trailhead, where this ride starts, has a restroom.

Just remember to be your best while riding Stringer's Ridge. You never know what kind of hotshots you will run into on the trail and in the parking lot.

Miles and Directions

0.0   Start from the Spears Avenue trailhead and join the singletrack connector rising away from the parking area. Soon come to an intersection. Head right, joining singletrack Hill City Trail. Remember: The trails are directional based on day of the week.

0.3   Join the Double J Trail, a rolling track on a very steep slope of the mountain. Have fun on the banked turns. You can really pick up speed in spots.

Stringer's Ridge

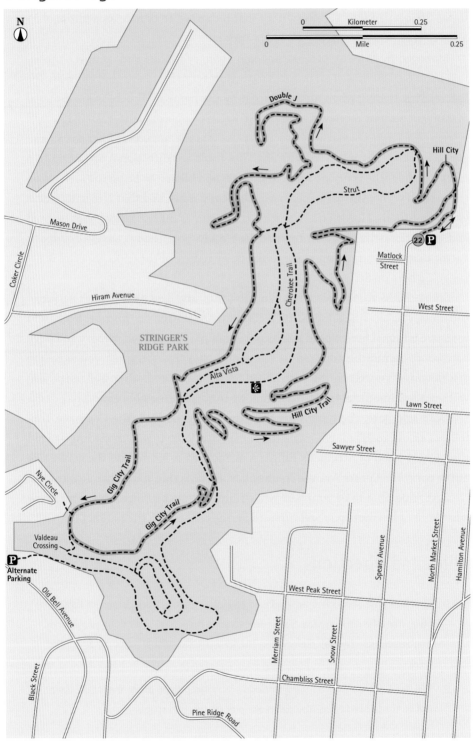

0.7 Pass a massive oak that was likely here during the Civil War when Stringer's Ridge was occupied by the Yankees.

1.0 Pedal through an area of big oaks then circle around the foundation of an old building.

1.0 A connector to Cherokee Trail and Strut leaves left. Stay straight with Double J. Enjoy a level section of trail on a steep slope.

1.4 Come to a major intersection. Here, head right with the Gig City Trail, climbing on a singletrack path overlaying a roadbed. Cherokee Trail comes into this gap as well.

1.7 Come near some houses off Nye Circle and an official neighborhood park access with no parking.

1.8 Stay with the Gig City Trail as hiker-only Valdeau Crossing Trail leaves right. Curve back north, passing a stone house foundation. The ridge slope remains steep.

2.0 Cross Cherokee Trail after descending several tight switchbacks and join the Hill City Trail. Begin some fast downhill and uphill on smooth track. This is where the pros get their tires in the air. Continue unimpeded, putting on your mojo. There are no trail intersections for the next 1.3 miles.

3.3 Complete the loop portion of the ride. Backtrack toward the trailhead.

3.4 Arrive back at the trailhead.

23 Riverwalk Ride

This popular greenway travels the banks of the Tennessee River from Chickamauga Dam into downtown Chattanooga and beyond, and is the centerpiece of a growing greenway system about which the city can brag. Our ride starts at Chickamauga Dam then traces the Riverwalk past several mini-parks and trail accesses while affording views of the Tennessee River and the mountains beyond. Nearing downtown, you detour to climb to the no-cars-allowed Walnut Street Bridge. Here, cross the river and soak in fantastic views then descend to Coolidge Park, a fine place to turn around.

Start: Chickamauga Dam access

Distance: 16.4 miles out and back

Riding time: 2–4 hours

Difficulty: Moderate to difficult due to distance

Terrain and surface type: Concrete trail, a few road crossings; all hard-surface pathways

Highlights: Riverside biking, numerous accesses and amenities, views from Walnut Street Bridge, Coolidge Park

Hazards: Pedestrians, a few road crossings

Other considerations: Can easily shorten bike ride if desired

Maps: Tennessee Riverpark

Trail contacts: Tennessee Riverpark, 4301 Amnicola Hwy., Chattanooga, TN 37402; (423) 842-0177; chattanooga.gov

Finding the trailhead: From exit 4 on I-75, northeast of downtown Chattanooga, take TN 153 north for 5.3 miles to TN 319, the Amnicola Highway. Exit north on TN 319 and follow it 6 miles to the right turn signed for "Riverpark—Chickamauga Dam Segment." Follow the entrance road for 0.3 mile then veer left onto another road signed "Tennessee Riverpark Chickamauga Dam Segment." Follow this road to park at the dam tailwater area. GPS: N35 6.130' / W85 13.874'

The Ride

Chattanooga's Riverwalk has been a boon for bicyclers, walkers, skaters, art lovers, river lovers, and general outdoor enthusiasts. Today, throngs of folks ply the greenway as it runs along the Tennessee River. Riverwalk is the backbone of the expanding greenway system in the greater Chattanooga area. In the early 1980s the idea of building urban greenways swept across the nation, and Chattanooga

The trail leads along the Tennessee River, complemented by mountain vistas

caught the fever. Riverwalk was the result, and now you can enjoy this linear track along the river, enhanced with mini-parks and accesses, adding to the total trail mileage.

One thing that did not catch on was the name "Tennessee Riverpark," the official moniker for this trail. Just about everyone refers to it as the Riverwalk. Therefore don't be surprised if you get uncomprehending stares should you say, "Let's ride bikes at Tennessee Riverpark!"

The Riverwalk also provides a connection to the historic Walnut Street Bridge, part of this fun bike ride. Built in the late 1800s, the truss bridge slowly fell into disrepair, and was closed to auto traffic in 1978. Slated for demolition, the span was saved after some smart people came up with the idea to make it a pedestrian bridge and part of a linear park. In 1993 the bridge was reborn for downtown walkers, hikers, and bicyclers. It has been wildly popular ever since, carrying folks across the river and helping to revitalize downtown. We can use it as part of our bike ride and a link to Coolidge Park, our scenic turnaround point.

This is one of the best greenway bike rides in the entire South, and I personally guarantee you will be pleased with the adventure. The ride stays on dedicated bike/pedestrian trails almost the entire way (save for a couple of blocks in the Bluff View Art District). In addition, the ride across the Walnut Street bridge presents enriching views of the river and downtown and is exciting for people watching too. The end of the line, Coolidge Park, allows you to hang out in some green space beside the river before backtracking to Chickamauga Dam. On your return trip, inspect the trailside art and abundant historical information. By this time you will have noted that even the greenway mileage markers are within pieces of art. Self-service bike rentals can be found all along the route.

Crossing the historic Walnut Street Bridge

Start your adventure just below Chickamauga Dam, where you join the River-walk as it winds among park facilities. This was the first segment of the greenway to be built, and it remains very popular to this day. After passing under a railroad bridge, you will reach a boat ramp used on a paddle adventure in this guidebook (Adventure 31: Tennessee River at Chattanooga). Park relaxers and nearby students of Chattanooga State Community College flood the locale.

The Riverwalk soon settles down to what you imagine a greenway to be. Benches and shelters overlook river views. The Riverwalk continues to meet hub parks and other accesses such as Fishing Park, where multiple fishing piers extend into the river. Fishing Park features a network of short interconnected paths, picnic areas, bike rentals, and a snack bar.

The Riverwalk winds westerly to another mini-park known as Riverpoint. Here a spur trail leads out to the confluence of South Chickamauga Creek and the Tennessee River. The South Chickamauga Creek Greenway links to the Riverwalk here. The trail then stays back from the river, reaching the next access at Amnicola Marsh, a wildlife wetland. The greenway continues in an industrial area, crossing occasional roads linking the businesses to TN 58 before returning to the Tennessee at a bend with good views, passing the Curtain Pole Road and Rowing Center accesses along the way.

You are nearing downtown and before long are winding your way among residences and businesses to emerge at the Bluff View Art District, where both views and artworks are to be seen. A short pedestrian bridge at the Hunter Museum of Art links the Riverwalk to the Walnut Street bridge. This historic span will not

Riverwalk Ride

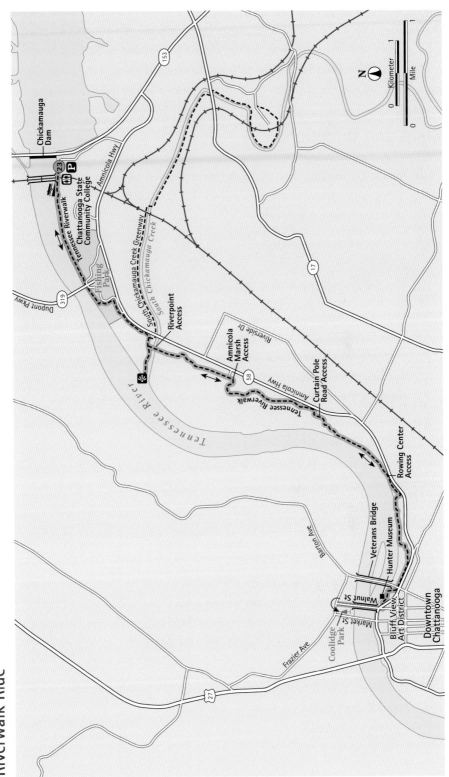

Chickamauga Dam

Chickamauga Dam

153

Amnicola Hwy

Tennessee Riverwalk

Chattanooga State
Community College

23 P

Dupont Pkwy

319

Fishing Park

South Chickamauga Creek Greenway

South Chickamauga Creek

Riverpoint
Access

17

Amnicola
Marsh
Access

Riverside Dr

58

Amnicola Hwy

Curtain Pole
Road Access

Tennessee Riverwalk

Tennessee River

Rowing Center
Access

Baton Ave

Veterans Bridge

Hunter Museum

Walnut St

Market St

Bluff View
Art District

Coolidge
Park

Frazier Ave

27

Downtown
Chattanooga

N

0   1   Kilometer
0   1   Mile

disappoint. Enjoy the panoramas, the people, and the downtown Chattanooga vibe as you pedal across the bridge, dipping to Frazier Avenue. From here it is just a short distance toward the river to reach Coolidge Park and its sister, Renaissance Park, where you can relax by the water before returning the way you came.

Miles and Directions

0.0 Start at Chickamauga Dam, tracing the Tennessee River on a concrete trail past a gazebo, picnic tables, benches, and more. This is a busy area, with park enthusiasts of all stripes congregating here.

0.8 The Riverwalk bridges a stream then opens onto an expansive green space. Watch for trailside art.

1.4 Pass through Fishing Park. Resume the greenway while pulling away from the river.

1.7 Come within sight of TN 58, Amnicola Highway.

2.2 Come to the Riverpoint access, with parking, picnic area, nature trails, and a link to the South Chickamauga Creek Greenway, an expanding bike trail. Take the spur out to a view at the confluence of South Chickamauga Creek and the Tennessee River, backtrack, then continue the Riverwalk, crossing South Chickamauga Creek.

3.8 Bike through the Amnicola Marsh access, with parking, restrooms, spur trails, and a wetland. You will pass another pond ahead.

5.1 Bike through the Curtain Pole Road access and a bike rental station. Soon come near the river again, with sweeping views of Lookout Mountain, Signal Mountain, and Erlanger Hospital.

6.0 Cut through the Rowing Center access amid good river views.

6.8 The Riverwalk winds among buildings and crosses a few roads.

7.5 Emerge at the Bluff View Art District. Follow the painted road markers for 2 blocks to the Hunter Museum of Art. Join the pedestrian bridge leading from the front of the museum to the south end of the Walnut Street bridge. Cross the river on the Walnut Street bridge, enjoying the vistas and the people.

8.2 Reach the north end of the Walnut Street bridge. From here you can make your way to the north bank of the river and enjoy Coolidge Park or next-door Renaissance Park. Backtrack toward Chickamauga Dam when done.

16.4 Arrive back at the trailhead.

24 South Chickamauga Creek Greenway

This fun greenway ride incorporates a completed portion of this expanding trail coursing along a major stream of the greater Chattanooga area. Start at Camp Jordan Park then cross West Chickamauga Creek to join an elevated berm paralleling South Chickamauga Creek. Pedal above the stream and adjacent wetlands to end near Shallowford Road. Backtrack to Camp Jordan Park, finishing a loop at the park.

Start: Camp Jordan Park

Distance: 9.4-mile lollipop

Riding time: 1.5–2.5 hours

Difficulty: Moderate

Terrain and surface type: Asphalt almost the whole way

Highlights: Amenities at Camp Jordan; elevated views and wildlife viewings along South Chickamauga Creek

Hazards: Sun along open berm part of greenway

Other considerations: Good for walking, too

Maps: South Chickamauga Creek Greenway

Trail contacts: Camp Jordan Park, 323 Camp Jordan Pkwy., East Ridge, TN 37412; (423) 805-3111; eastridgeparksandrec.com

Finding the trailhead: From exit 1 on I-75, southeast of downtown Chattanooga near the Georgia state line, take US 41 South and follow it for 0.1 mile. Turn left on Camp Jordan Parkway and follow it for 0.7 mile; cross West Chickamauga Creek then enter Camp Jordan Park. Immediately turn left into a large parking area. The greenway is near the auto bridge at the park entrance. GPS: N34 59.884' / W85 12.008'

The Ride

South Chickamauga Creek Greenway makes for a fun and fast ride in different environments. It rolls around Camp Jordan Park before heading along the elevated Brainerd Levee, built in the 1970s to prevent flooding of the nearby East Ridge neighborhoods. Later, someone saw the levee as a potential trail. Additionally, the lands around the levee provided a wildlife wetland—excellent bird habitat for blue herons, egrets, bitterns, and more.

This is an example of how we see public green spaces in a different light these days. The average city park of the 1950s—with a metal swing set, a seesaw, a few

Author stops to peer into West Chickamauga Creek

picnic tables with peeling paint, and a dusty baseball diamond—are now passé. City dwellers of the twenty-first century are demanding more than just a little park for their neighborhoods. In addition to traditional ball-field parks, they want greenways where they can bicycle, hike, even in-line skate through a strip of nature connecting their neighborhoods.

The past two decades have seen phenomenal growth in greenways for Chattanooga, with the Riverwalk its centerpiece. Exactly what is a greenway? A greenway is a linear park—a corridor of protected land overlain with a path that travels along or through specific natural features.

These paths can be asphalt, gravel, or mulch. Greenways often follow creeks or lakes. Greenways can utilize former railroad rights-of-way, utility rights-of-way, or already established parklands, linking two parks together. New land is sometimes purchased; other times easements are granted across private land. South Chickamauga Greenway is an asphalt path following South Chickamauga Creek and uses the existing Brainerd flood levee right-of-way as a trail conduit.

Greenways are most often linear, but can be a loop confined to one city park, such as part of this ride at Camp Jordan Park. Greenways are primarily used for recreational travel, but they can also be used by commuters and other citizens simply trying to get from point A to point B.

Greenways have broad appeal. You will see mothers pushing their newborns in strollers, runners huffing and puffing, couples strolling hand in hand, dogs walking their masters, or birders with binoculars pushed against their eyeballs. Bicyclists use greenways for exercise and travel. Greenways provide an attractive outdoor venue for exercise that could help reduce America's sky-high obesity rate.

Riding the Brainerd Levee

Greenways are more than family recreation venues. Urban wildlife inhabits these oases of nature amid the city. The corridor along South Chickamauga Creek is rich in birdlife. Critters use greenways to travel from one larger green space to another, wildlife corridors if you will. Animal health is improved because gene pools are not isolated, and greenways allow overall larger territories for wildlife to exist. Shaded streams make for richer aquatic habitat, further improving stream quality.

Greenways have practical benefits too. Wooded streamsheds cut down on urban flooding, reducing erosion for property owners. Wooded streams also absorb and filter pollutants from urban runoff. Greenway forests help keep cities cooler, reducing the urban heat island effect, and cut down on summertime electric bills. Trees also filter air, improving air quality in the Tennessee River Valley.

Greenways also improve property values of adjacent lands. Most residents realize greenways are more likely to carry alert citizens on the lookout for criminals than criminals themselves.

What does the future hold? Greenways are being integrated into overall urban planning. When finished, the South Chickamauga Creek Greenway will stretch from the Tennessee River—where it currently connects to the famed Riverwalk—15 miles to Camp Jordan Park, where this ride begins.

Integrating greenways into developments addresses many questions. For example, a greenway can cut down on stormwater runoff, reducing flooding, which addresses public safety. A greenway helps protect the natural resource of an area. Developing a greenway enhances overall aesthetics, improving the "quality of place." The whole process is known as "integration"—government-speak

South Chickamauga Creek Greenway

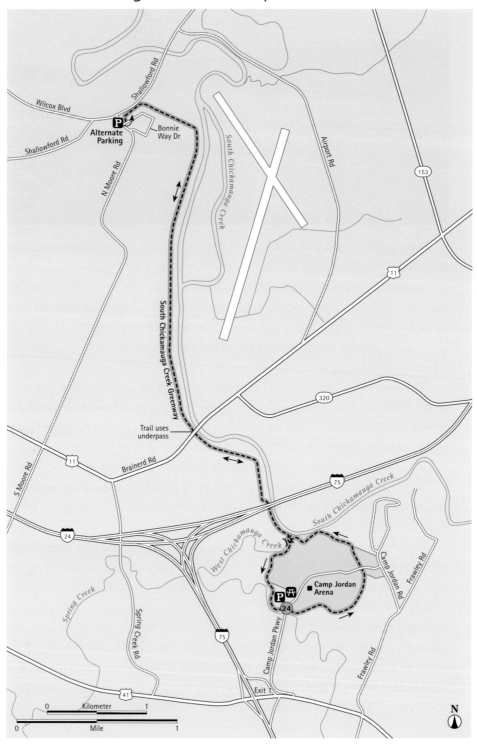

for putting it all together. Greater Chattanooga is growing fast. Let us continue to add greenways as we develop new areas of the region.

A few additional things to know about this ride: There is a shaded picnic pavilion with water near the Camp Jordan Trailhead. Contemplation benches are situated at intervals along the route. Be sure to stop and soak in the watery views from the top of the West Chickamauga Creek bridge as well as the confluence of West Chickamauga and South Chickamauga Creeks. Stay tuned as this greenway is completed all the way to the Tennessee River.

Miles and Directions

0.0   Pick up the South Chickamauga Creek Greenway near the road bridge entrance to Camp Jordan Park. Head east, counterclockwise, on the loop portion of the ride on level trail. West Chickamauga Creek is off to your right. Circle past Camp Jordan Arena and park amenities, even a zip line.

0.9   Cross Camp Jordan Parkway a second time. Continue in open terrain.

1.4   Reach the greenway bridge over West Chickamauga Creek, just upstream of its confluence with South Chickamauga Creek. Cross the bridge then drop to the confluence of the two streams.

1.7   Pass under I-24 then climb a bit, joining the Brainerd Levee, now the conduit for the South Chickamauga Creek Greenway. Head north, bordered by wetlands on both sides of the levee, with South Chickamauga Creek to the right.

2.5   Come to Brainerd Road. Here you can use the stoplight and crosswalk or use the stairs to a concrete trail going under Brainerd Road. Obviously, using the stairs necessitates carrying your bike. Continue on the levee, running parallel to South Chickamauga Creek. Look for birdlife in the marshes.

4.5   Curve west, now aiming toward Shallowford Road.

5.1   Reach the trail's current end at Bonnie Way Drive and Moore Road near Shallowford Road. Backtrack toward Camp Jordan Park.

8.8   Return to the bridge over West Chickamauga Creek near the stream's confluence with South Chickamauga Creek. Pedal across the span then bear right to ride the yet-to-be-bicycled portion of the loop at Camp Jordan Park. Pass the popular disc golf course at Camp Jordan.

9.4   Arrive back at the trailhead.

25 Enterprise South Nature Park Ride

Make a double loop on this fun ride at Enterprise South Nature Park using purpose-built dedicated mountain bike trails in attractive woods that were once munitions plant property. Get warmed up on the Black Forest Trail, winding over hills and hollows before tackling the more difficult TNT Trail. Excellent signage, trails, and trail conditions keep this park's mountain bike trails hopping.

Start: Poe Run trailhead

Distance: 7.1-mile double loop

Riding time: 1.5–2.5 hours

Difficulty: Moderate

Terrain and surface type: First-rate natural surface singletrack paths throughout rolling forested terrain

Highlights: Excellent, flowy trail network; historic munitions storage sheds

Hazards: None

Other considerations: Park offers road ride possibilities

Maps: Enterprise South Nature Park

Trail contacts: Enterprise South Nature Park, 190 Still Hollow Loop, Chattanooga, TN 37416; (423) 893-3500; parks.hamiltontn.gov

Finding the trailhead: From exit 9 on I-75, northeast of downtown Chattanooga, take Volkswagen Drive west, over the interstate, and follow it for 1.1 miles to a roundabout and a right turn into Enterprise South Nature Park. Drive just a short distance to reach a four-way stop. Keep straight on Poe Run Road and follow it 0.6 mile to the large Poe Run trailhead on your right. GPS: N35 5.087' / W85 6.963'

The Ride

Enterprise South Nature Park is a newer style park built with a plethora of trails for different users. For mountain bikers, it includes approximately 16 miles of dedicated mountain bike trails designed and built by SORBA Chattanooga. Generally considered fast, flowy, and not too difficult, these paths are great for beginner mountain bikers, intermediates, and those who like to add a little speed to their ride. Two additional factors make going fast here desirable: 1. The trails are one direction, switching every other day (and well signed about what day and what direction, so you can't mess up unless you try). 2. Pedestrians have a set of hiker-only trails they

Pedaling through an old dynamite storage facility along the trail

can enjoy, so you are unlikely to encounter someone on foot. An additional set of gated and open roads are designated for bicyclers and pedestrians.

Enterprise South Nature Park, 2,800 acres in size, has become very popular with not only mountain bikers but also hikers, joggers, and road cyclers, as well as all-around nature lovers, since its opening in December 2010. What became the park was formerly a munitions plant that specialized in making—and storing—dynamite.

The plant was opened during World War II, a time of high demand for dynamite. Owned by the military but run by a civilian contractor, at its height the plant employed around 3,500 people! After the war the plant survived until 1977, when it was closed but still guarded by the US Army. Over time, the Army began looking to dispose of its unused assets, and in the late 1990s they pitched idea of selling the property to the City of Chattanooga. The city ended up buying the property as a potential industrial park. Eventually, Volkswagen located on the majority of the parcel, with another parcel developed as Enterprise South Nature Park.

The rolling wooded park is a fine haven to preserve local flora and fauna. However, you will notice while biking here that remnants of the munitions plant still dot the park, mainly in the form of dynamite storage bunkers. These bunkers resemble small rounded hills with a concrete front and reinforced steel door. Each bunker is numbered and remains numbered to this day. On your ride you will have the opportunity to pedal your bike right through one of these bunkers (nearly all are closed). Roads and gates once used to access these bunkers serve as roads and gated paved trails within the preserve. These munitions bunkers and the history of the property may seem strange to you at first, but after a time or two, you will appreciate the integration of parklands and trails onto what was once a dynamite factory and storage place.

This ride utilizes the beginner-level Black Forest Trail and the intermediate TNT Trail. The two other major mountain bike trails here are the intermediate Log Rhythm Trail and the expert Atlas Trail. Log Rhythm features alternate parallel tracks with log jumps and elevated boardwalks. Atlas Trail also offers jumps and rock options that you can bypass, as well as some technical ups and downs.

In case you want to road ride, more than 9 miles of paved paths are available to pedalers. Hikers have an additional 9 miles of hiker-only natural-surface trails to ply. Enterprise South Nature Park also boasts a visitor center, three historical bunker displays, a scenic drive, restrooms, and a picnic area.

Our mountain bike ride starts at the Poe Run trailhead, joining the Black Forest Trail, so named for a dense stand of pines near the trailhead that casts thick shade upon the area. The trailhead has a large parking area, restrooms, changing area, and a bicycle repair area. Remember, trails are directional by set days. The Black Forest Trail quickly rises from the parking area and begins winding through the woods, working uphill at a modest tick, leveraging the hillside with turns and switchbacks, and keeping ascents doable by beginner mountain bikers. The trail is pure singletrack, mostly flowy and smooth.

It isn't long before you see your first dynamite storage bunker, bunker #100. Go ahead and jump off the bike on your first visit and check it out. From there the trail rolls, never too much up or down, keeping the gradients manageable. Roll through piney woods in places. Enjoy some banked turns. Log berms keep the trail from getting wider. The Black Forest Trail remains biker friendly.

Then you join the intermediate TNT Trail, but its increased difficulty lies in the more challenging elevation changes rather than trail conditions. It is a bit rougher with rock obstacles, but I wouldn't call it a rocky trail by any means. You will roll through hollows, enjoy some humps, and cross intermittent drainages

Enterprise South Nature Park Ride

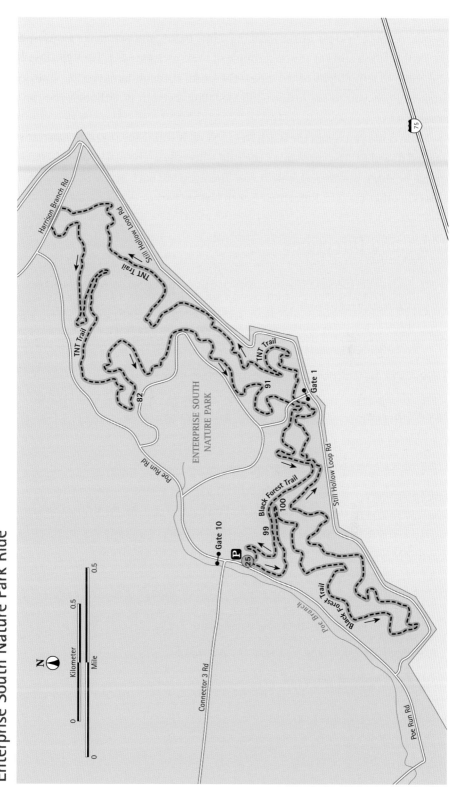

on quartz-lined bridges. After reaching a low point, you will make an extended but doable climb and encounter a couple of brief rock gardens. Then you descend and come to a highlight of the ride—the pedal through bunker #91. This open bunker allows you to see inside while pedaling through it, although you can go around.

From there you rejoin the Black Forest Trail. It will seem a breeze, especially as you roll downhill. The very end of the ride—literally in the black forest—makes a couple of sharp but manageable turns. Then you are back at the trailhead, ready to tackle other trails at Enterprise South Nature Park.

Miles and Directions

0.0 Start at the Poe Run trailhead and join the Black Forest Trail, ascending from the trailhead into dense woods.

0.3 Make a sharp right, passing near bunker #100. This is your first chance to see one of these former dynamite storage areas.

1.5 Come near Still Hollow Road, but stay with the Black Forest Trail.

2.3 Emerge at the paved road near gate #1. To your right, it is a short distance to an alternate parking area on Still Hollow Road. Keep straight here, joining the intermediate TNT Trail.

2.6 Reach a high point then go mostly downhill for the next period.

3.9 Reach gated and paved Harrison Branch Road after a prolonged descent. Log Rhythm Trail starts on the other side of the road. To continue the TNT Trail, head left on Harrison Branch Road, follow it just a short distance, and turn left at the sign for TNT Trail. Resume the singletrack path, now on an extended climb.

5.1 Pass bunker #82.

5.4 Top out on a knob near a small rock garden.

6.0 Pedal to and through—or around—bunker #91.

6.3 Rejoin the Black Forest Trail. Keep mostly downhill.

7.1 Arrive back at the trailhead.

26 Red Loop at White Oak Mountain

The White Oak Mountain Trail system provides mountain bikers with a fine network of settled and signed paths coursing through hilly woods. Considered flowy and fast down low and rockier and more technical up top, the singletrack trails challenge with elevation too as they work the east slope of White Oak Mountain. This adventure traces the Red Loop from trailhead to mountaintop and back down. Expect both a fast ride and a rocky one on this intermediate trek with connections to technical expert trails if you choose to make the ride more difficult. Easier routes are also available.

Start: Trailhead #1 near University and Morningside Drives

Distance: 4.4-mile loop

Riding time: 1–1.5 hours

Difficulty: Moderate

Terrain and surface type: Natural surface mountainside trails, almost all pure singletrack

Highlights: Fast, well-marked and well-maintained trails

Hazards: Hikers on the trail, blind curves

Other considerations: Over 1,100 feet of climbing and descending on Red Loop; numerous but well-marked trail intersections

Maps: White Oak Mountain trails, Southern Adventist University

Trail contacts: Southern Adventist University Outdoor Education Center, 4689 University Dr., Collegedale, TN 37315; (423) 236-2416; southern.edu

Finding the trailhead: From exit 9 on I-75, northeast of downtown Chattanooga, take Apison Pike East for 3.9 miles. Turn right onto University Drive and stay with it for 0.9 mile. Turn right onto Morningside Drive; the main parking area with nine spaces is on the left, just after you make the right turn onto Morningside Drive (even though the official trailhead address is 4713 Colcord Drive). GPS: N35 2.573' / W85 3.266'

The Ride

White Oak Mountain is located on the campus of Southern Adventist University, a Christian college in Collegedale, Tennessee, situated northeast of downtown Chattanooga. The official mission statement of the university is to "nurture Christlikeness, traditional Seventh-day Adventist values, academic excellence, and a lifelong pursuit of truth, wholeness, and service."

Singletrack trails here make the mountain biking fun

Good physical health is part of wholeness, and to that end the college has developed two trail systems open to the public—White Oak Mountain and Bauxite Ridge—totaling 30 miles of exploring pleasure for greater Chattanooga area mountain bikers.

This ride tackles the White Oak Mountain trail system. The network of mountain tracks has fully evolved, and it is good to see the White Oak Mountain trails in such fine shape. The trails are maintained by Landscape Services at Southern Adventist University, and they do a stellar job. The trail complex is broken down into major loops of varying difficulties, with the Green Loop the easiest and the Yellow Loop by far the most difficult, rocky, and technical, banging along at the top of White Oak Mountain. The Red Loop is rated more difficult. Trails can be ridden in both directions. Be sure to call out on blind curves.

In the old days, mountain bike trails were often very problematic to follow when trying to create an exploratory loop ride. You would almost have to be with someone who had been there before, or get lost a few times on your own. And then you factor in user-created trails, with thoughtless mountain bikers shortcutting trails or creating their own jumps and hazards, shortcuts, and side paths, adding to the confusion. What you end up with is an erosive mess of a trail network that can be neither followed nor sustained.

Not so here at White Oak Mountain. The individual loop routes the university has created have been signed so well that you can follow them straight out of the gate on your first run. Additionally, trail maps are available at major intersections, just in case you get turned around or want to alter your route without being caught in a maze. When you first contemplate the trail map here, you will expect a maze, but on the ground the trails are very easy to follow, even while you're tooling along (or going really fast). User-created trails, extracurricular paths, and hazards are quashed at White Oak Mountain. Furthermore, the trail layout is integrated into the contours of the mountain, giving the pathways a natural feel.

The network does have additional perks. Trailhead #1, where this ride begins, has shaded picnic tables with attached restroom building, a water station, as well as a bike repair area and large trailhead kiosk with map. However, there is one drawback—parking is limited at the trailhead, and the spaces can be taken quickly. Consult the signboard and map for alternate parking areas. Some alternate parking areas are available after 5 p.m., on weekends, and during other situations. However, despite having around 30 miles of trails, the trailhead turnover is fairly rapid, for White Oak Mountain also sees its share of trail runners and dog walkers. Be watchful of hikers; since, despite having specified hiker-only paths, the two-legged set can be found on the mountain biking trails (all trails are open to them).

At Six Shooter trail junction

Red Loop at White Oak Mountain

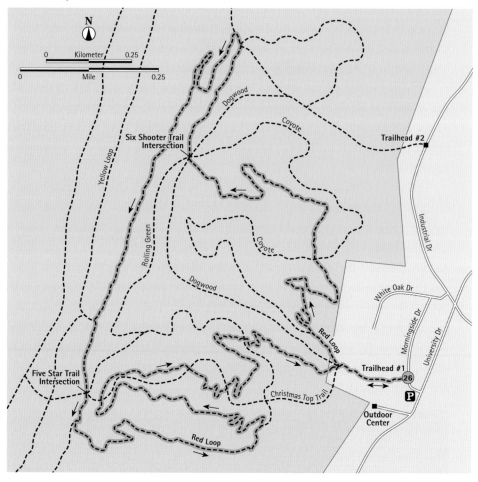

The Red Loop, using almost all pure singletrack, leaves Trailhead #1 and heads west up along a stream. It then begins its winding ways, contouring up the mountain, using switchbacks to gain elevation. The trail reaches a gap and multi-trail intersection known as Six Shooter. Here you climb a bit more and then roll south, zigzagging among roots and rocks. Ahead, you will get a chance to intersect the Yellow Loop—the expert circuit atop the ridge. Continuing on, the Red Loop descends and becomes easier and faster at lower elevations, eventually taking you back to Trailhead #1. If you haven't had enough, tackle another loop here at White Oak Mountain, or check out the Bauxite Trail system, also here at Southern Adventist University.

Miles and Directions

0.0 Start from Trailhead #1 on the wide gravel Dogwood Trail, passing through a pair of boulder gates. A small creek flows to your left. Southern Adventist University's Outdoor Recreation Program building is on the far side of the creek.

0.1 Reach a trail junction. Head right, joining the Red Loop, a signed circuit mountain biking route. Ascend on singletrack, rising using switchbacks. Stay with the red diamond blazes, marked on plastic Carsonite posts. There are signs at every major trail junction, and all trails are blazed. Work up a ridgeline as the route becomes rockier and more piney. You can see old trails that were eliminated before the trail network was stabilized.

1.1 Come to the Six Shooter trail intersection. Six different paths converge here in a gap. Stay with the Red Loop as it climbs a bit then turns south along White Oak Mountain. Here you will be challenged by rocky, rooty sections, with gravelly path in places.

2.1 The Yellow Loop leaves right. This is the most difficult loop of the White Oak Mountain trail system—a technical stone-pounding route among the rocks of White Oak Mountain. The Red Loop keeps straight.

2.3 Come to the Five Star trail intersection in a gap. Trails split five different ways here. The Red Loop turns east down the mountain. Make a fun controlled downhill with banked turns and fairly smooth track.

2.8 Turn back up the mountain, shooting through an area of tight, spindly trees. Watch your handlebars!

3.3 Come near the Five Star trail intersection then turn back down the mountain.

3.6 Top out on a knob and get ready for some action-packed downhill with banked turns and jumping humps. Watch for potentially loose-gravel sections.

4.3 Complete the loop portion of the ride. Backtrack toward Trailhead #1.

4.4 Arrive back at the trailhead.

27 Chilhowee Mountain Bike Ride

This is a true "mountain" bike ride as you take on a big loop on pathways from beginner to expert in the Chilhowee trail system of the Cherokee National Forest near Parksville Lake. Make an extended climb from the Clemmer trailhead, then cruise over small highland creeks by bridge and by tire. Make a stop by Benton Falls before looping around the upper Rock Creek watershed. Enjoy mountain views then tackle a tough stony segment before returning to the trailhead after an opportunity to visit Rock Creek Falls.

Start: Clemmer trailhead

Distance: 11.1-mile loop

Riding time: About 3.5 hours

Difficulty: Difficult due to climbs and some ultra-rocky segments

Terrain and surface type: Mountainous terrain with singletrack overlain on old roadbeds; pure singletrack; rocky sections in places; water features

Highlights: Mountain views, waterfalls, streams; vertical challenge

Hazards: Incredibly rocky descent segment on Clear Creek Trail

Other considerations: Almost 2,900 feet of ascent and descent throughout the ride; some streams have bridges, others do not.

Maps: Chilhowee Trail System, Ocoee Ranger District; National Geographic #781: Cherokee National Forest Tellico and Ocoee Rivers

Trail contacts: Cherokee National Forest, Ocoee Ranger District, 3171 Hwy. 64, Benton, TN 37307; (423) 338-3300; fs.usda.gov/cherokee

Finding the trailhead: From exit 20 on I-75 near Cleveland, take the US 64 East Bypass for 6.4 miles. Turn right onto US 64 East and continue for 17.3 miles. Turn left on TN 30; follow TN 30 for just a short distance then turn left onto the first gravel road to reach the Clemmer trailhead. GPS: N35 6.9024' / W84 34.7402'

The Ride

You will know the true meaning of mountain biking after your pedaling experience on the scenic trails of Chilhowee Mountain, ensconced in the Appalachians of the Cherokee National Forest east of Cleveland, Tennessee. Chilhowee Mountain has long been a recreation destination in the greater Chattanooga outdoor sphere, and it was only natural that mountain biking would follow suit after its rise in

Appalachian mountain vegetation borders the trails here

popularity, perhaps outstripping hiking in some areas. Managers of the Cherokee National Forest recognized that mountain bikers could also enjoy the wildlands of Chilhowee Mountain and developed or reworked trails with the two-wheel set in mind. Although all trails here are shared with hikers, this route (except for short portions near Benton Falls and Rock Creek Falls) is mostly used by mountain bikers. In fact, mountain bikers use most of the trails in the entire Chilhowee Recreation Area, save for the trails in the immediate vicinity of Chilhowee Campground. The trails here can be ridden in both directions.

This ride starts miles away from the mountaintop campground, at the Clemmer trailhead, located at the base of Chilhowee Mountain. Of course starting at the bottom means a big climb, but I prefer starting with a climb while fresh then enjoying downhill at the end. Before you imagine straight up then straight down, here is a rough breakdown of the mileage: The first 2.5 miles are mostly uphill, followed by 5 miles of mostly level or rolling terrain, followed by a 0.5-mile climb, then 3 miles of mostly downhill.

The trail terrain and biking difficulty range all over the place. With much of the trail network on singletrack overlain on old roadbeds, the initial climb on the Clemmer Trail is eased since you are not dancing through rock gardens, yet it is a climb of 900 plus feet. After leveling off, the ride wanders in and out of thickly wooded and lush upland streamsheds. Some of the streams have bridges; others force a rolling splash.

You will run into hikers for 0.5 mile near Benton Falls. Park your bike and make the short walk to the falls—it is worth seeing this 65-foot spiller, tumbling over layered rocks in widening pyramid fashion into a cool, rocky glen. After splitting from the waterfall hikers, you will circle around the top of the Rock Creek watershed on a series of fun paths near the campground, shared with a few pedestrians. Then you turn away from the camp and run along the rim of the gorge of Rock Creek, with Benton Falls and other cascades echoing up to the Clear Creek Trail. This section offers plenty of solitude as well as partial mountain vistas. You then open onto an old burn on Chestnut Mountain, with rocks, brush, and views; the segment is more difficult than what you have been riding. Then comes the legendary stony section of the Clear Creek Trail, a steep singletrack on a sharp slope pocked with boulder gardens that are a true test of your expertise. (Don't feel bad—most mountain bikers walk this segment.)

After leaving Clear Creek Trail in the lowlands, you cross Rock Creek without benefit of bridge, almost a sure ford. This can be avoided by taking Clear Creek Trail to TN 30 and making a mile or so road ride back to the Clemmer trailhead. However, if you do that you'll forfeit a chance to visit Rock Creek Falls, also known as Rainbow Falls and Falls of the Scenic Spur. This does require parking your bike then walking for the final 0.7 mile of the hiker-only track. Rock Creek Falls is a two-stage show stopper with a swimming hole par excellence at the bottom. The final part of the ride leads you a short distance back to the trailhead. Allow for plenty of time to enjoy the waterfalls and tackle the ups, downs, and bouncy sections of this exciting mountain bike adventure.

Miles and Directions

0.0   Start from the trailhead on the Clemmer Trail, ascending a wide red-clay path.

0.1   Reach a trail junction. Stay left, still on the Clemmer Trail, as the Scenic Spur Trail, your return route, leaves right. Keep ascending on a singletrack path overlaying an old roadbed shaded by pines and oaks. Ahead, the Clemmer Spur leaves right. Keep with the Clemmer Trail. Rock Creek flows down below.

1.1   Grab a partial view into the Rock Creek gorge in an area of rock and pine. Ahead, curve along a rock bluff. Cross occasional seeps amid rhododendron.

2.2   Pedal through Laurel Branch. Your steady ascent is almost over. Quickly roll through a second stream with slick stone. Continue in gorgeous forest on level track.

Chilhowee Mountain Bike Ride

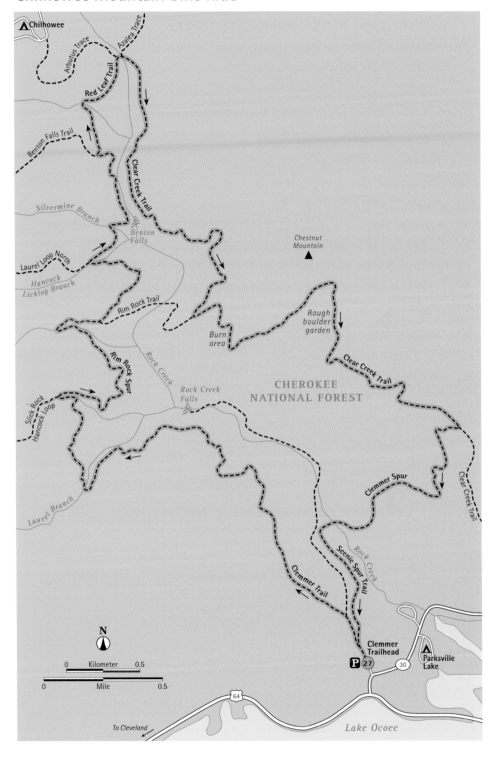

Chilhowee

Arbutus Trace

Azalea Trace

Red Leaf Trail

Benton Falls Trail

Clear Creek Trail

Silvermine Branch

Benton Falls

Laurel Loop North

Hancock Licklog Branch

Rim Rock Trail

Chestnut Mountain

Rough boulder garden

Burn area

Rim Rock Spur

Rock Creek

Rock Creek Falls

CHEROKEE NATIONAL FOREST

Clear Creek Trail

Slick Rock Hancock Loop

Clear Creek Trail

Laurel Branch

Clemmer Spur

Rock Creek

Scenic Spur Trail

Clemmer Trail

N

Clemmer Trailhead

P 27

30

Parksville Lake

0   Kilometer   0.5

0   Mile   0.5

64

To Cleveland

Lake Ocoee

2.8 Come to a trail intersection and stream bridge. Stay right here, still on the Clemmer Trail, crossing a stream as the Slick Rock Hancock Loop goes left.

2.9 Split right on the Rim Rock Spur as the Clemmer Trail stays left. Drop onto narrow singletrack, bouncing amid evergreen brush along the edge of the valley before climbing.

3.5 Rejoin the Clemmer Trail. Turn into the vale of Slickrock Branch. Splash across the stream and head east, curving around a ridge. Wander among pines on a level cruise.

4.4 Intersect the Laurel Loop North near Hancock Licklog Branch. Stay right here toward Benton Falls. Cross open rock slabs.

4.7 Reach the hiker-only 0.1 mile spur to Benton Falls after crossing Silvermine Branch. Do not pass up viewing the 65-foot cataract; then continue, now on the Benton Falls Trail. The next 0.5 mile can be crowded with hikers trekking atop rock slabs.

5.1 Leave the crowds by turning right onto the Red Leaf Trail. Soon bridge McCamy Branch.

5.6 Come to an intersection near Franklin Spring Branch. Here the Arbutus Trail leaves left for Chilhowee Campground. Stay straight, bridge Franklin Spring Branch, and then reach another intersection. Turn right here on the Clear Creek Trail as the Azalea Trail leaves left, also for Chilhowee Campground. Ride the rim of the gorge.

7.3 Intersect the Rim Rock Trail on a ridge. Stay left with the Clear Creek Trail, heading for a brushy burn area with loose, rocky trail tread in places.

8.0 Reach the high point of your climb over Chestnut Mountain. Prepare for some truly gnarly, rocky, steep singletrack downhill that will test your skills to the max.

9.4 Reach a trail junction. Turn right on the Clemmer Spur, heading toward Rock Creek, riding some easy trail. (Stay straight to avoid fording Rock Creek.)

10.4 Come to an almost-sure ford of Rock Creek. Cruise bottomland, and soon join the Scenic Spur Trail left toward Clemmer trailhead. Watch for hikers heading to Rock Creek Falls.

11.0 Make one last climb through a gap just before rejoining Clemmer Trail. Backtrack toward the trailhead.

11.0 Arrive back at the trailhead after your challenging adventurous ride along Chilhowee Mountain.

28 Tanasi Trails

Set in the Ocoee River gorge at the Ocoee Whitewater Center, site of the 1996 Summer Olympics, the Tanasi Trail system presents more than 20 miles of mountain biking tracks with a mix of singletrack and old forest roads as well as riverside riding. Start this 8.6-mile loop by cruising along the nationally renowned Ocoee River past whitewater to then climb 600 feet. From there rock and roll through the woods of the river gorge, returning to earth near the Ocoee Whitewater Center. Build in extra time before or after your ride to explore the whitewater center and the river, perhaps even overnighting at nearby Thunder Rock Campground.

Start: Ocoee Whitewater Center parking area

Distance: 8.6-mile loop

Riding time: About 2 hours

Difficulty: Moderate to difficult; 600-foot climb

Terrain and surface type: Sloped river valley. Part of the trail goes over pea gravel and forest road, but it is mostly natural-surface track.

Highlights: Ocoee River, land bridge above river, occasional views, Ocoee Whitewater Center

Hazards: None

Other considerations: Parking fee; 2,500 feet of ascent and descent throughout the ride. Watch for hikers on the Rhododendron Trail.

This land bridge allows you passage alongside a sheer rock wall

Maps: Tanasi Trail System, Ocoee Ranger District; National Geographic #781: Cherokee National Forest Tellico and Ocoee Rivers

Trail contacts: Cherokee National Forest, Ocoee Ranger District, 3171 Hwy. 64, Benton TN 37307; (423) 338-3300; fs.usda.gov/cherokee

Finding the trailhead: From the junction of US 64 and US 64 Bypass, just east of Cleveland, take US 64 East for 28 miles, 1.3 miles past Ocoee Dam #3 and Thunder Rock Campground. Reach the Ocoee Whitewater Center on your right. Enter the whitewater center then park in the large lot downstream of the main building near the bridge over the Ocoee River. There is a parking fee. GPS: N35 4.1505' / W84 27.9753'

The Ride

When the 1996 Summer Olympics came to Atlanta, Georgia, the whitewater events were held on the famed Ocoee River in southeast Tennessee. Decades earlier, the waters of the Ocoee River had been diverted from the streambed into a wooden flume to generate power. When the flume began to leak, the water was again let loose into the Ocoee so that the wooden flume could be repaired.

When that happened, whitewater enthusiasts saw the Ocoee as a first-rate destination for daring rafters, kayakers, and a few intrepid canoeists. A

Looking across the river at the Ocoee Whitewater Center

This bridge spans the fabled Ocoee River, whitewater paddling site of the 1996 Olympics

whitewater mecca was born. The new recreational opportunity has been an economic boon to the area ever since, with paddlers coming from all over the world to test the waters. Therefore, it was only natural that the Olympic whitewater events would be held here. The USDA Forest Service began developing the Ocoee River corridor—including the whitewater center near the trailhead for this ride as well as a slew of trails for hikers and mountain bikers—to enhance the area.

Thus the Tanasi Trail system came to be. The well-marked and maintained trails can be ridden in both directions. After decades, the Ocoee River corridor continues to thrive recreationally, with visitors tackling the river and biking the trails, as well as hiking, camping, and fishing. Today, a bevy of outfitters will guide you down the crashing whitewater on a hair-raising raft ride—a classic outing for adventure enthusiasts in the greater Chattanooga region.

Our mountain bike ride starts with the Rhododendron Trail, a super scenic pea gravel path slicing through evergreens. The air here is cool year-round as you look on the river through the woods. A part of the ride uses a land bridge to work around a bluff, providing clear views and an additional highlight. A lot of money went into this trail. Reach Ocoee Dam #3 powerhouse and then climb FR 45 after passing near Thunder Rock Campground. The wide forest road does make the ascent easier until you jump on the West Fork Trail. Wind along the north slope of Chestnut Ridge among drainages flowing into the Ocoee River divided by piney ridges.

The final part of the ride joins the Bear Paw Loop, where you roll along slopes descending toward the Ocoee River. Finally, follow a slim stream valley, returning to the Ocoee River. Once near the water, make sure to pedal out on the bridge connecting to the Ocoee Whitewater Center to gaze up and down the river. You can also bike directly along the waterway in places as you return to the trailhead. Note the shady picnic area on the south side of the river near the parking area. It makes an additional place to enjoy the outdoor opportunities available in the Ocoee River corridor.

Miles and Directions

0.0 Start from the Ocoee Whitewater Center parking area. Head south across the bridge over the Ocoee River—the bridge near the parking area restrooms, not the bridge behind the whitewater center. Cross the correct bridge and turn right, joining the Rhododendron Trail. Join a pea gravel path heading west, downstream along the Ocoee River. Cross side streams entering the river. Watch for hikers on this path.

0.3 Cross a land bridge working around a sheer bluff. Soak in views of the Ocoee River and lands to the north.

0.8 The trail splits, with a spur going right, closer to the water, before reconnecting with the main branch of the Rhododendron Trail.

Tanasi Trails

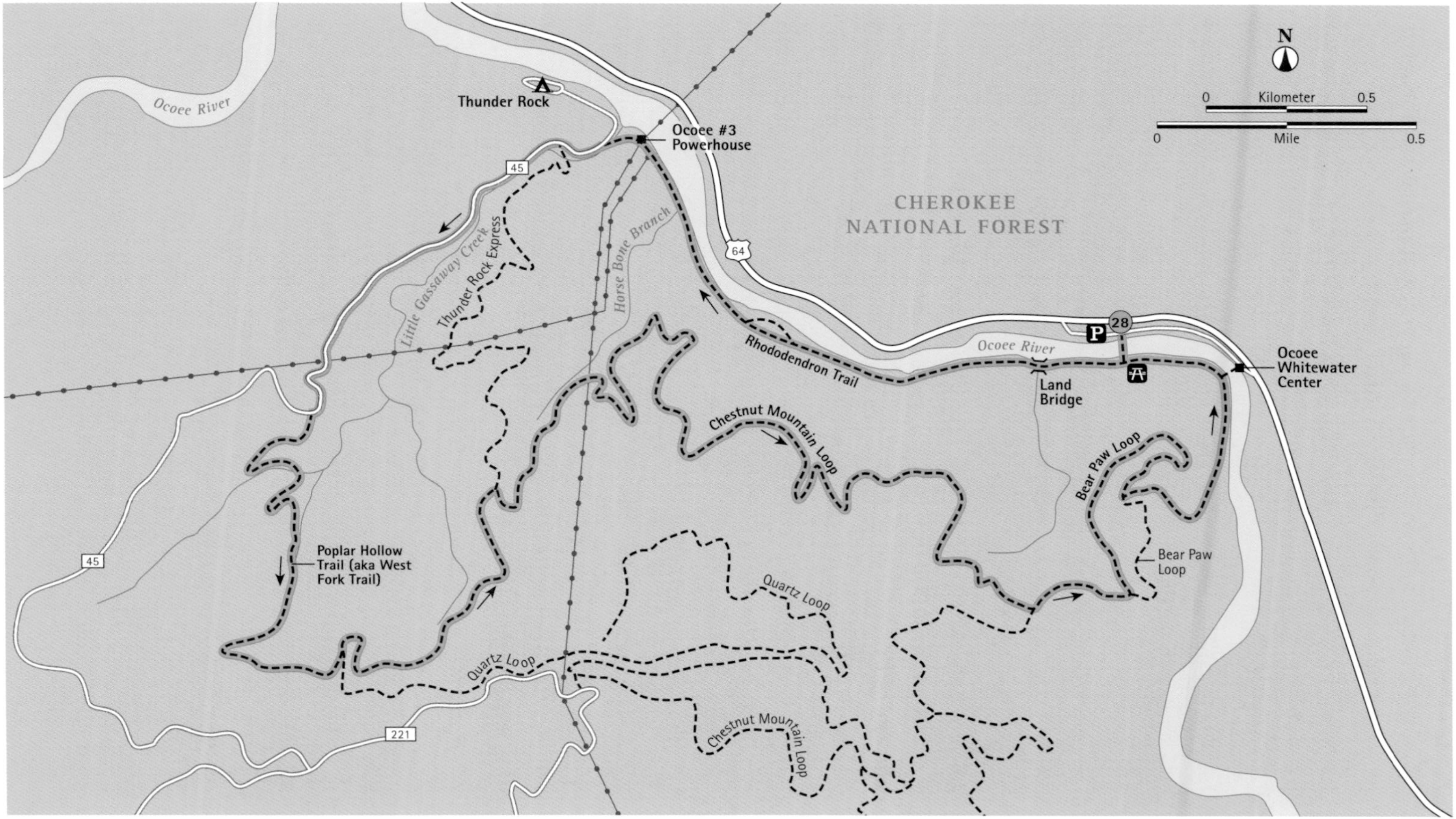

Ocoee River
Thunder Rock
Ocoee #3
Powerhouse
45
Little Gassaway Creek
Thunder Rock Express
Horse Bone Branch
64
CHEROKEE
NATIONAL FOREST
N
0
Kilometer
0.5
0
Mile
0.5
P
28
Ocoee River
Rhododendron Trail
Land
Bridge
Ocoee
Whitewater
Center
Chestnut Mountain Loop
Bear Paw Loop
Bear Paw
Loop
Poplar Hollow
Trail (aka West
Fork Trail)
45
Quartz Loop
Quartz Loop
221
Chestnut Mountain Loop

1.2 Bridge Horse Bone Branch then emerge at an electric grid. Cruise along the electric grid fence.

1.3 Reach the Ocoee Dam #3 powerhouse. Head left, joining FR 45 as a spur road goes to Thunder Rock Campground. Ascend the gravel road up a richly forested hollow created by Little Gassaway Creek.

1.5 The Thunder Rock Express Trail enters on your left. It is a very popular downhill fast track for mountain bikers. Keep climbing on FR 45.

2.3 Leave FR 45 after a sharp left bend in the road, followed by a right bend. Split left, joining the Poplar Hollow Trail (shown on some maps as the West Fork Trail). Cut across Little Gassaway Creek and a few tributaries, then climb. Look for a huge trail-side tulip tree ahead.

3.6 Reach an intersection atop a hill. Head left with the Chestnut Mountain Loop. Descend, losing hard-won elevation. Enjoy fun riding.

4.3 Stay with the Chestnut Mountain Loop as the Thunder Rock Express leaves left. The trail becomes more rocky and rooty.

5.1 Make the first of two cleared power line crossings. You are close to but way above the Ocoee River. The trail becomes pure singletrack, very narrow in places. This segment is exciting and pretty, especially when you ride the nose of a ridge between two hollows at 6.0 miles.

6.9 Come to an intersection. Stay left, heading east on a spur of the Chestnut Mountain Loop as the main Chestnut Mountain Loop leaves right. Keep a general downgrade.

7.1 Meet the Bear Paw Loop. Head left, riding rooty, piney, yet pretty trail. Watch for quartz outcrops. Turn downhill again.

7.8 Reach the other end of the Bear Paw Loop in a hollow. Turn left down the hollow. Shortly come near the Ocoee. Watch for pedestrians.

8.3 Come to the big bridge crossing the Ocoee to reach the whitewater center. Keep straight on a trail connector, shortly coming to a picnic area.

8.6. Return to the trailhead after crossing the bridge to the whitewater center parking area. Note the concrete submergible tracks directly along the river. Consider adding whitewater rafting to your bike ride.

29 Chickamauga Battlefield Ride

This road ride takes place at Chickamauga & Chattanooga National Military Park, where the route you take is quiet, scenic, and historic. Pedal tree-, monument-, and field-lined roads through the preserved battlefield. The paved pathway traverses mostly gentle terrain with few hills, and not nearly the traffic of regular roads outside the battlefield. Learn about the battle before, during, and after your ride.

Start: Chickamauga Battlefield visitor center

Distance: 8.8-mile loop

Riding time: 1.5–2.5 hours

Difficulty: Moderate

Terrain and surface type: Paved roads throughout

Highlights: Historic battlefield with monuments, interpretive information, historic structures

Hazards: Slow-moving cars on the roads

Other considerations: Most battlefield roads are very quiet; bicyclers are expected.

Maps: Chickamauga Battlefield trail map

Trail contacts: Chickamauga & Chattanooga National Military Park, 3370 Lafayette Rd., Fort Oglethorpe, GA 30742; (706) 866-9241; nps.gov/chch

Finding the trailhead: From exit 350 on I-75 in Georgia, southeast of downtown Chattanooga, take GA 2 West/Battlefield Parkway for 6.4 miles to Fort Oglethorpe, Georgia, and Lafayette Road. Turn left on Lafayette Road and follow it for 1 mile to the visitor center on your right. The large visitor parking area is just south of the visitor center. The ride starts here. (If you pass the Florida Monument on your left, you have gone just a little too far.) GPS: N34 56.406' / W85 15.566'

The Ride

This ride explores 5,300-acre Chickamauga Battlefield, part of Chickamauga & Chattanooga National Military Park, a series of locations preserving Civil War sites in the greater Chattanooga area. During the Civil War, Chattanooga was prized by both the Confederates and the Union. Chattanooga was a confluence of river, road, and railroad transportation, and the South needed to protect the town's transportation lines, while the Union saw the town as key to its plan to split the South in half. Attempting to stop the Union, the Confederates met them at what became Chickamauga Battlefield, located just south of Fort Oglethorpe,

The smooth quiet roads at Chickamauga Battlefield make for excellent bicycling.

Georgia. The September 1863 battle was the last major Confederate victory of the Civil War. Later that autumn, Chattanooga fell to the North, ultimately allowing Sherman's merciless scorched-earth march to the sea.

While pedaling a clockwise circuit through the battlefield, you will see monuments commemorating troops and individual battle participants from both sides. Roadside plaques explain the battle moves during the clash. However, for the best understanding of the battle, explore the visitor center at the trailhead. The visitor center offers a host of exhibits, a video describing the battlefield, a detailed battlefield map, historical artifacts from that time, and military items, including a special collection of shoulder arms.

Chickamauga & Chattanooga National Military Park was the first of its kind, dedicated by the US Congress in 1890; it encompasses more than 9,000 acres at a half dozen sites in and around Chattanooga. Here at Chickamauga Battlefield, the setting has a bucolic air, serenity unexpected at a former place of conflict. Today we have not only a historic, somber, yet scenic location but also a rewarding place to ride your bicycle, touring in appreciation of the human and natural history found in this preserve. The entire route is along two-lane paved roads open to motor vehicles.

After spending some time at the visitor center, grab a battlefield map and hit the road. You will first join Lafayette Road (old US 27), the busiest road in the park. It runs north–south, bisecting Chickamauga Battlefield. However, drivers here have a low speed limit, unlike on neighboring roads. You will be on Lafayette Road but briefly, joining Alexanders Bridge Road. Cruising southeast on Alexanders Bridge Road, make sure to stop at one of the most moving spots on the battlefield—the gravesite of Private John Ingraham. A young local who joined the Confederates, he was killed the first day of fighting. After the clash, his friends searched the battlefield, buried him on the spot, and marked it, where he remains to this day. Imagine searching a battlefield full of dead to find your friend and bury him. Sights such as this underscore the solemnity of the park.

From there you continue southeast, descending more than not to come near Chickamauga Creek before turning away on Viniard-Alexander Road. This locale is one of the most biologically important of the battlefield, richly forested and dotted with cedar glades—rare plant communities found only in a few places in the Southeast. You will also pass a few short spurs leading to overlooks of Chickamauga Creek. The ride briefly rejoins Lafayette Road then heads into relatively hilly terrain on Glenn-Viniard Road, where it rolls by the impressive Wilder Monument. You will continue winding through rolling terrain, climbing to a high point on Dyer Road then cruising amid fields. This section of the ride seems like a rural outing.

After turning on Glenn-Kelly Road, you have an opportunity to make a side trip to the Snodgrass Cabin, where Union soldiers were treated during and after the battle. This area exudes a relaxed pastoral air that contrasts greatly with our hurried life of today. Ahead you will return to the visitor center.

A few other things to consider: Battlefield trails are not open to bicyclers. All trails in the park are open to hikers, some to equestrians. However, designated

Some of the hundreds of memorials that stand in Chickamauga Battlefield

Chickamauga Battlefield Ride

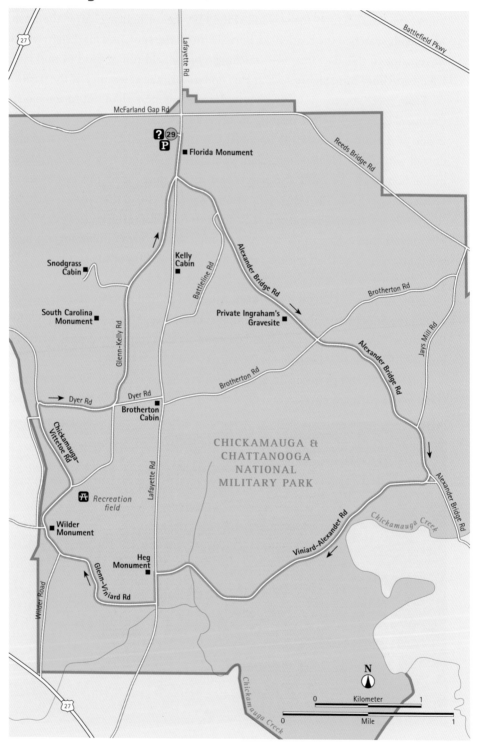

US 27

Battlefield Pkwy

Lafayette Rd

McFarland Gap Rd

29
P

■ Florida Monument

Reeds Bridge Rd

Snodgrass
Cabin ■

Kelly
Cabin ■

Battleline Rd

Alexander Bridge Rd

Brotherton Rd

South Carolina
Monument ■

■ Private Ingraham's
Gravesite

Glenn-Kelly Rd

Alexander Bridge Rd

Jays Mill Rd

Brotherton Rd

Dyer Rd   Dyer Rd

■ Brotherton
Cabin

Chickamauga–
Vittetoe Rd

CHICKAMAUGA &
CHATTANOOGA
NATIONAL
MILITARY PARK

Alexander Bridge Rd

Lafayette Rd

🏕 *Recreation
field*

Chickamauga Creek

Wilder
Monument ■

Heg
Monument ■

Viniard–Alexander Rd

Glenn-Viniard Rd

Wilder Road

N

US 27

Chickamauga Creek

0   Kilometer   1

0   Mile   1

gravel roads—of which there are many in the park—are open to bicycles. The Chickamauga Battlefield trail map details all the park's trails and roads.

Miles and Directions

0.0   As you look out the front door of the visitor center head left (east). Immediately reach old US 27, Lafayette Road. Turn right (southbound), crossing a creek and passing the conspicuous Florida Monument, the first of hundreds of monuments and statues commemorating regiments and individual battle participants. A mix of field and forest borders the road.

0.3   Bear left from Lafayette Road onto quiet Alexanders Bridge Road. Gently roll through woods.

0.6   Stay straight with Alexanders Bridge Road as Battleline Road leaves right.

1.3   Reach the grave of Private John Ingraham, to the right of the road. Stop here to learn about this young man killed in the conflict.

1.6   Cross Brotherton Road, passing a picnic area on your left at the intersection. Keep straight on Alexanders Bridge Road.

2.4   Stay with Alexanders Bridge Road as Jays Mill Road enters on the left.

2.7   Head right onto Viniard-Alexander Road as Alexanders Bridge Road keeps straight to cross Chickamauga Creek and leave the park. Consider a side trip down Alexanders Bridge Road to overlook the creek from the road bridge. Ahead, pedal through cedar glades and come near Chickamauga Creek.

4.7   Head left on Lafayette Road amid fields and monuments aplenty. Quickly turn right onto Glenn-Viniard Road.

5.8   Pedal near the tall Wilder Monument.

6.2   Turn left on Chickamauga-Vittetoe Road. You are near a picnic area and recreation field. Ahead, pass an equestrian loading area.

6.7   Turn right on Dyer Road. Climb, then roll through fields.

7.2   Turn left on Glenn-Kelly Road. Bike a quiet lane bordered by split-rail fence. You can see the hilltop South Carolina Monument above fields to your left.

7.9   A spur road leads left to the Snodgrass Cabin.

8.6   Turn left on Lafayette Road.

8.8   Arrive back at the visitor center.

30 Five Points Trails at Cloudland Canyon

On the site of former mine property, the Five Points trail system at Cloudland Canyon State Park provides two-wheel action atop Lookout Mountain. Make a loop ride using some of the 30 miles of trails open to mountain bikers, some of which scale and roll atop piles of mine tailings.

Start: Five Points trailhead

Distance: 5.3-mile loop

Riding time: About 1 hour

Difficulty: Moderate

Terrain and surface type: Natural surface, mostly smooth but irregular in mine areas and tailings

Highlights: Fast, well-marked trails for all levels

Hazards: None

Other considerations: Parking fee

Maps: USGS Durham; Cloudland Canyon State Park trail map

Trail contacts: Cloudland Canyon State Park, 122 Cloudland Canyon Park Rd., Rising Fawn, GA 30738; (706) 657-4050; gastateparks.org

Finding the trailhead: From exit 11 on I-59, southwest of Chattanooga, take GA 136 East for 7.3 miles. Turn left on GA 189 and follow it north for 2.6 miles. Turn right on Ascalon Road and follow it for 1.4 miles to a left turn onto GA 157 North. Continue for 0.7 mile and turn left into the Five Point trailhead. *Note:* The Five Points trailhead is well east of the main state park property. GPS: N34 51.056' / W85 25.489'

The Ride

Talk about turning a lemon into lemonade! What once were the wooded, overgrown relics of a mine from a century back is now an exciting trail network for mountain bikers. The trails are atop Lookout Mountain, all within the protected confines of Cloudland Canyon State Park.

The original portion of Cloudland Canyon State Park was established in 1938, and the addition of the trails of Five Points adds significantly to the park's former trail mileage. An agglomeration of pathways—some hiker-only, some equestrian trails, but mostly mountain biking tracks—the Five Points trails open up the scenic destination to fat-tire fans. Purposefully laid out for mountain bikers

Cloudland Canyon State Park features mountain biking trails for all levels.

of all levels, the Five Points trails present a recommended destination for beginner mountain bikers but also offers challenging expert paths. The now-wooded mine area delivers some unusual terrain amid a nicely recovered forest that is enjoyable for riding and pleasing on the eyes as well.

Centered on Round Mountain, a peak of greater Lookout Mountain, the locale was mined for coal from 1850 to 1922. Given time, what was known as the Durham Mine became reforested. The land was acquired thanks to the efforts of SORBA Chattanooga and the Lula Land Trust. The trails were laid out by mountain bikers and the area opened to riders in 2011. Twenty of the 30 miles are singletrack mountain bike trails. The Cloudland Connector Trail, a multipurpose path, links the Five Points trails to the heart of Cloudland Canyon State Park.

Interestingly, many of the expert trails are laid out on old mine tailings, including a part of our recommended ride. Since the mine tailings are not natural, they present surprises as you pedal over them amid trees and roots, twists and turns. It's really fun! However, most of our ride is a beginner route, where budding mountain bikers can learn the ropes and get the feel of their bikes—not too many hills but enough to build endurance. The tracks are smooth, allowing you to handle—and love—speed!

Our ride starts at the main Five Points trailhead, with parking available for about ten cars. If the lot is full, you can park at the larger trailhead off Ascalon Road. From the trailhead, our mountain bike adventure joins Peace Can Trail, designated as a beginner-level mountain bike trail. (Note to all expert mountain bikers: Remember, we were all novices once.) It soon passes the intersection with the Tailings Trail, an expert-level path that traverses mine tailings on irregular terrain. The terrain on Peace Can remains mostly level, lightly undulating with minor bank turns, running smooth. Trees grow close to the path as it runs along the slope of the ridge.

After figuring out which way to go at a well-signed junction, you will pick up the Cloudland Canyon Connector Trail. This path has been hardened and makes for a fast track. However, watch out for hikers and equestrians, as this is a multi-use track, a little wider than the rest of the pure mountain bike tracks. The path is flowy under rich woods, exhibiting enough up and down to keep it stimulating.

Then you reach another trail junction in a gap on Round Mountain. Our ride keeps straight on the wider Cloudland Canyon Connector Trail, but keep this spot in mind for future rides. No fewer than eleven trails can be accessed from here, giving you a multiplicity of pedaling possibilities, from beginner to expert. Mountain bikers doing multiple "laps" in the trail system will come to this intersection time and again over a day's outing.

Our adventure stays on the connector to eventually join the Shale Flats Trail, a speedy singletrack with few obstacles, a trail where newbies can learn to pedal fast and experts can fly. Remember, the trails here are bidirectional, so keep your eyes on both the terrain below and the trail ahead.

Join the North Hogsback Trail. Here's your chance to shine and have a ball, going up and over pile after pile of partly wooded mine tailings. Drop-offs fall away on both sides. The ride is fun, but if you believe North Hogsback too tough, just backtrack on the connector and join the Bankhead Trail. After descending from the wild tailings ride, you wind among small ponds. Ahead, the Bankhead Trail leaves left. Just a short piece to the trailhead, and you will have another biking adventure notched up—and a whole new trail network to explore.

Miles and Directions

0.0   Start from the Five Points trailhead and head north on the Peace Can Trail. Rise a bit on a singletrack path beneath pines and oaks. After 176 feet, come to a trail

Five Points Trails at Cloudland Canyon

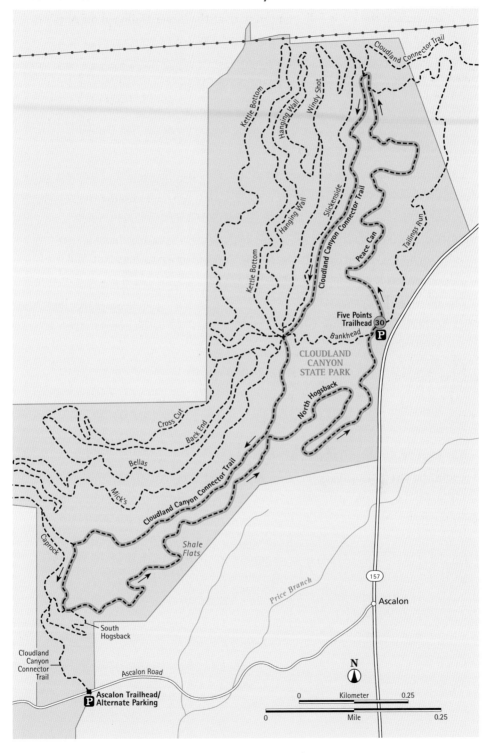

Cloudland Connector Trail

Kettle Bottom

Hanging Wall

Windy Shot

Hanging Wall

Slickenside

Kettle Bottom

Cloudland Canyon Connector Trail

Peace Can

Tailings Run

Five Points
Trailhead
30
P

Bankhead

CLOUDLAND
CANYON
STATE PARK

North Hogsback

Cross Cut

Back End

Bellas

Mick's

Caprock

Cloudland Canyon Connector Trail

Shale
Flats

Price Branch

157

Ascalon

South
Hogsback

Cloudland
Canyon
Connector
Trail

Ascalon Road

Ascalon Trailhead/
P Alternate Parking

N

	Kilometer	
0		0.25

	Mile	
0		0.25

intersection. Stay left with the Peace Can Trail as the expert-level Tailings Run Trail leaves right.

1.2 Come to a major intersection after passing the other end of the Tailings Trail. Here rise left and join the multiuse Cloudland Canyon Connector Trail, a hardened track forming the backbone of the Five Points trail system. Head south on a fast track.

2.0 Come to a major intersection in a gap. A plethora of pathways split from the area, but our circuit ride stays with the Cloudland Canyon Connector Trail. Descend southbound. Cross an elevated berm over a wet area.

2.3 An official signed shortcut leaves left to Shale Flats Trail. Stay with the Cloudland Canyon Connector Trail. You will join the Shale Flats Trail later. Undulate on the Cloudland Canyon Connector Trail. Ahead, pass beside mine tailings to your left.

3.0 Reach an intersection. Here a spur goes right and uphill to Caprock Trail. Stay left with the Cloudland Canyon Connector Trail and descend by switchbacks.

3.2 Head left with the singletrack Shale Flats Trail, a beginner-level mountain bike trail. Quickly pass two intersections with the short expert-level South Hogback Trail. Roll northeast through woods. Cut across small drainages with built-up berms as well as small bridges.

4.3 Come to the other end of the official shortcut with the Cloudland Canyon Connector Trail. Head right, joining the North Hogsback Trail. The trail starts out innocently then climbs to the top of the rolls along a series of mine tailings piles that make for an unusual—and fun—ride.

5.2 Meet the Bankhead Trail and stay right.

5.3 Arrive back at the trailhead.

PADDLING

Paddling is a fun and contrasting way to complement hiking and mountain biking as an adventure. The paddling possibilities in and around Chattanooga run the gamut from whitewater to stillwater and waters in between. Would we expect anything less from the Scenic City? Here you can paddle the mighty Tennessee River straight into downtown Chattanooga—viewing nearby city sights and green mountains rising in the yon. Looking for smaller waters? Try North Chickamauga Creek, with its aquamarine liquid running beneath long stone bluffs. West Chickamauga Creek offers some lively shoals while flowing past historic Chickamauga Battlefield. Perhaps you are seeking a river somewhere in between—one that is just right. Try the rural Conasauga or the sublime Sequatchie, or perhaps the large Oostanaula. Looking for a natural thrill? Paddle the fabled whitewater of the Hiwassee River, frothing forth from the regal Appalachians. Flatwater enthusiasts will find paddles on Chickamauga, Nickajack, and Parksville Lakes, all attractive impoundments with eye-pleasing scenery. Do you hear them? The paddling waters of greater Chattanooga are calling you.

Mountain rimmed Parksville Lake offers continual scenic beauty

31 Tennessee River at Chattanooga

Float the master river of the greater Chattanooga region—the mighty Tennessee. This wide-open run starts just below Chickamauga Dam. Float down the left bank of the Tennessee River, paralleling Riverwalk. Reach downtown Chattanooga, admiring the bridges and buildings before ending your adventure on the right bank at Coolidge Park. By the way, you can execute a bike shuttle using greenways nearly the entire route.

Start: Chickamauga Dam Access

End: Coolidge Park ramp under Market Street Bridge

Length: 6.3 miles

Float time: About 3.1 hours

Difficulty rating: Easy

Rapids: None

River/lake type: Big river

Current: Moderate to strong

River gradient: 1.0 feet per mile

Water gauge: Tennessee River at Chattanooga; no minimum runnable level

Season: Year-round

Land status: Some private, Riverpark along left bank in many places, Coolidge Park

Fees or permits: Parking fee at Coolidge Park

Nearest city/town: Chattanooga

Maps: USGS: Chattanooga, East Chattanooga; Tennessee River Blueway

Boats used: Kayaks, canoes, big boats, barges

Organizations: Tennessee River Blueway/Outdoor Chattanooga, 200 River St., Chattanooga, TN 37405; (423) 643-6888; outdoorchattanooga.com

Contacts/outfitters: L2 Outdoors, 131 River Street, Chattanooga, TN 37405, 423-531-7873, www.l2outside.com. These downtown folk rent boats for paddlers.

Put-in/Takeout Information

To the takeout: From exit 178 on I-24 in downtown Chattanooga, take US 27 North and follow it to cross the Tennessee River. Turn right onto Manufacturers Road and follow it for 0.4 mile. Turn right onto Cherokee Boulevard and continue for 0.1 mile, keeping straight as Cherokee Boulevard becomes Frazier Avenue. Stay with Frazier Avenue for 0.2 mile farther then turn right onto Tremont

Looking up at the historic
Walnut Street Bridge from
Coolidge Park

Tennessee River at Chattanooga

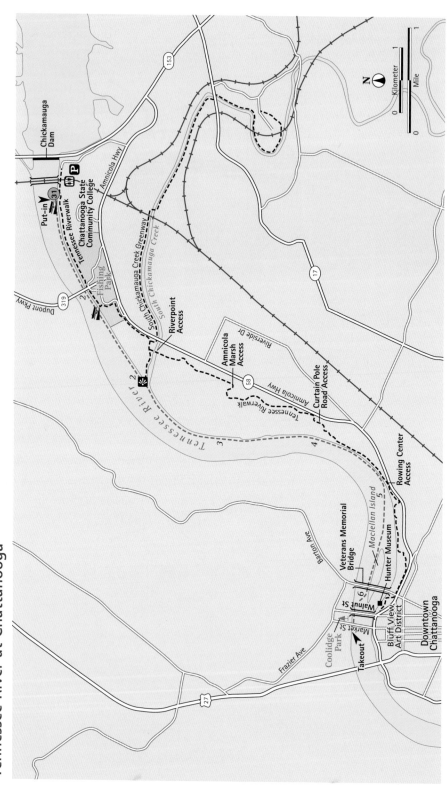

Street. Continue 1 block then turn right onto River Street, entering Coolidge Park. Follow River Street 0.1 mile then curve left with the park road to reach the ramp directly under the Market Street Bridge. Pay parking is located in the park. GPS: N35 3.599' / W85 18.568'

To the put-in from the takeout: Backtrack from Coolidge Park. Turn right on Frazier Avenue and follow it eastbound 0.2 mile to the turn for Veterans Bridge. Drive across Veterans Bridge to cross the Tennessee River then turn left on East Fourth Street. Follow East Fourth Street for 0.4 mile then veer left to join TN 58 (Amnicola Highway). Follow Amnicola Highway for 5.7 miles. Turn left at the entrance signed "Riverpark—Chickamauga Dam Segment" and follow the park road to "River Recreation." Keep going to reach the boat ramp, on your right 1 mile from Amnicola Highway. Parking is free and located near the ramp. GPS: N35 6.147' / W85 14.144'

Paddle Summary

This paddling adventure takes you down the biggest river in the region, the mighty Tennessee. Starting just below Chickamauga Dam at Riverpark, better known for its Riverwalk, you leave a boat ramp on the left (south) bank of the Tennessee and join the current. The big river presents panoramic views and parkland on your left. Bend with the river as panoramas of downtown Chattanooga and the mountains beyond open before you. The current can speed you up, and the winds can slow you down; either way, ahead lies downtown Chattanooga. Make sure to stop at Maclellan Island, a designated camping stop on the Tennessee River Blueway and a place where you can get out to explore via trail. The final part of the paddle crosses the river over to Coolidge Park, where two ramps for paddlers are available.

River/Lake Overview

The Tennessee River comes to be at Knoxville, where the Holston and French Broad Rivers converge. From there it begins a 650-mile journey, wandering southwest, picking up drainages from the Appalachian Range then turning west at Chattanooga. Here the river cuts through the Cumberland Plateau, forming the mighty gorge through the Cumberland Plateau known as the Grand Canyon of the Tennessee, just west of Chattanooga. Once freed from the gorge, the

Tennessee enters good ol' Alabama, working west to touch Mississippi. The river then turns north to reenter the Volunteer State, flowing north to reach Kentucky then feeding its mother stream, the Ohio River. During its course, the Tennessee River is dammed at several points, including Chickamauga Dam, which has spared Chattanooga from serious flooding. The river drains a little more than 40,000 square miles of land, including portions of Virginia, Tennessee, North Carolina, Georgia, Alabama, Mississippi, and Kentucky.

The Paddling

This paddling adventure will not only round out your greater Chattanooga paddling experience but also deliver a new perspective on paddling in general—the urban big-river paddle. The adventure begins at the busy eastern trailhead of Riverwalk, where bicycle adventure 23 also begins. After parking near the ramp, it is an easy departure. You are rolling down the river, the amenities of Riverpark in sight, as well as hikers and bicyclers tooling down the Riverwalk. At this point the Tennessee River is hundreds of feet across, so it is best to stick to the left bank (heading downstream). Also, the left bank offers more parkland to view. If the Tennessee Valley Authority (TVA) is generating at Chickamauga Dam (such as they do at high water), the current will be quite swift, affording you an easy float. Even at lesser flows, the current can be strong and steady.

After a mile you float under the high bridge that is DuPont Parkway. You are at Fishing Park, easy to spot by the numerous fishing piers as well as an alternate boat ramp. At 1.4 miles pass Tennessee River channel marker 469.0. This means you are 469 miles upstream of the mouth of the river. At 1.6 miles look across the river at Rivermont Park. It also a boat ramp, but it would be very difficult to cross the river and land with the current. Stay with the left bank.

At 2.0 miles you will see a trail extending into riprap banks, allowing Riverwalk users to access the confluence of South Fork Chickamauga Creek and the Tennessee River. Note which waterway is clearer, as they are both affected by upstream rains. Your cruise continues, passing occasional industrial businesses and old barge tie-offs. At 3.0 miles, float by sheer soil bluffs alternating with riprap banks.

By 3.7 miles you are across the river from the stately Chattanooga Country Club and bending to the right. Lookout Mountain rises in the distance as you turn. Pass channel marker 465.9 at 4.5 miles. Come near the Riverwalk once again. Ahead, Maclellan Island and the bridges of downtown Chattanooga come into view. Aim for the head of the island, pulling away from the left riverbank. Skirt over to the right-hand side of the island to find a landing and sign at 5.7 miles. Pull up, walk around the island, and check it out. (There is a dock on the left side of the island, but it can be busy; plus, landing at the dock makes it harder to cut across the river to Coolidge Park.)

From Maclellan Island begin cutting over and reach Coolidge Park after passing under Veterans Bridge. Once at Coolidge Park you will come to a carry-up ramp upstream of Walnut Street Bridge, but continue below the span to the easier ramp just below the Market Street Bridge, ending your paddle at 6.3 miles.

Option: A bicycle shuttle using the Walnut Street Bridge and the Riverwalk makes for an 8.0-mile one-way adventure, adding two-wheel action to this paddle.

A bald eagle perched above the Tennessee River near downtown

32 North Chickamauga Creek

Paddle this smooth, easy—and scenic—stream to enter the Tennessee River just below Chickamauga Dam. Cruise the mighty Tennessee, enjoying expansive vistas before ending at Rivermont Park.

Start: Longview Drive access

End: Rivermont Park ramp

Length: 6.7 miles

Float time: About 3.3 hours

Difficulty rating: Easy

Rapids: None

River/lake type: Creek, big river

Current: Slow; moderate to strong on Tennessee River

River gradient: 1.1 feet per mile

Water gauge: North Chickamauga Creek at Mile Straight, TN; no minimum runnable level

Season: Year-round

Land status: Private, wildlife management area, city park, TVA property

Fees or permits: No fees or permits required

Nearest city/town: Hixson, Tennessee

Maps: USGS Daisy, East Chattanooga, Chattanooga

Boats used: Kayaks, canoes; big boats on Tennessee River

Organizations: Tennessee River Blueway/Outdoor Chattanooga, 200 River St., Chattanooga, TN 37405; (423) 643-6888; outdoorchattanooga.com

Contacts/outfitters: North Chickamauga Creek Conservancy, 5051 Gann Store Road, PO Box 358, Hixson, TN 37343; (423) 842-1163; northchick.org

Put-in/Takeout Information:

To the takeout: From exit 4 on I-75, northeast of downtown Chattanooga, take TN 153 North. Follow TN 153 North for 7.1 miles to the exit signed "Access Road/ Lake Resort Drive," just after crossing the Tennessee River. Continue north on Access Road and pass through a pair of traffic circles, staying with Access Road for 2 miles to intersect Hixson Pike. Turn left on Hixson Pike then follow it for 1.3 miles. Turn left on Lupton Drive and follow it for 0.4 mile then turn right into Rivermont Park. Follow the signs for the boat ramp to the access and large parking lot on the Tennessee River, near the park's Champions Tennis Club facility. GPS: N35 5.757' / W85 15.928'

To the put-in from the takeout: Backtrack from Rivermont Park. Turn left on Lupton Drive then right on Hixson Pike. Follow Hixon Pike northeast for 4 miles and turn right onto Skillern Drive, just beyond Earth Fare. Follow Skillern Drive for 0.1 mile then turn right on Longview Drive; go just a few feet then turn left into the large parking area for the North Chickamauga Creek access. The creek access is reached via a 200-foot trail from the parking area. GPS: N35 8.438' / W85 13.732'

Paddle Summary

Begin your two-waterway adventure at a relatively new access off Longview Drive. The 200-foot portage trail will be your first adventure. Join an attractive segment of North Chickamauga Creek, winding amid a wooded corridor. The current is modest and the paddling easy as you float under Hamill Road, where houses are located above the creek. Make a big bend while passing Greenway Farms Park, with its own paddler access ramps, then cruise slowing waters before emptying into the Tennessee River near the lock just below Chickamauga Dam. Trace the north bank of the wide-open Tennessee River, enjoying hilly panoramas before

Paddling past the paddler launch at Greenway Farms Park

reaching the boat ramp at Rivermont Park. The paddle down North Chickamauga Creek is easy and straightforward. Once on the Tennessee, beware of winds and big boats, but the prospect of enjoying two such diverse waterways on one paddle outweighs any potential difficulties.

River/Lake Overview

North Chickamauga Creek is a stream of many faces. Its headwaters are found atop Walden Ridge over in Sequatchie County. Streams such as Standifer, Brimer, Frederick, McGrew, Middle, Cain and Cooper Creeks flow southeasterly before merging as North Chickamauga Creek and diving off the Walden Ridge through wild and scenic Chickamauga Gulch, a vale once mined for coal and now returned to an untamed state. Paddling crazies tackle the whitewater froth diving through the gorge at gradients up to 90 feet per mile! After emerging from the gorge and off the Cumberland Plateau, the now-calm "North Chick" meanders south toward the Tennessee River, floating through Hixson, where we pick up the stream on this paddle. The Longview Road access, along with the accesses at Greenway Farms Park, add flatwater paddling possibilities. The stream flows placidly onward to give its waters up to the Tennessee River just downstream of Chickamauga Dam, across the river from the Riverwalk.

The Paddling

The portage trail to North Chickamauga Creek is in the southeast corner of the parking lot, where you descend to an old asphalt road and keep following a clear route to the stream. The put-in can be muddy and slippery following high water, so exercise caution. Once on North Chickamauga Creek, you will be joining a 40- to 50-foot-wide cool stream running blue-green, a surprisingly clear waterway. Steep soil banks rise to overhanging ash, sycamore, and silver maple shading the sand-bottomed watercourse. The left bank of the stream is part of Chickamauga Wildlife Management Area, keeping it natural. At 0.3 mile an unnamed stream enters on river right, followed by another side stream at 0.6 mile. Save for bottoms, the banks generally rise about 20 feet or so, and rock outcrops are common.

Occasional houses are visible beyond the screen of trees, and the corridor remains wooded as the stream widens further. Fallen trees are common on the

North Chickamauga Creek

153

319

Skillern
Drive

Longview
Drive

Earth Fare ■

P 32

North Chickamauga
Creek WMA

Hixson Pike

Norfolk Southern

1

Hamill Road

2

Greenway
Farms
Park

Greenway
Farms
Main
Access

3

Trail
accessible
access

North Chickamauga Creek

Hamill Road

4

Lake Resort Drive

Hikson Pike

Azalea Drive

North Access Road

Chickamauga
Dam Lock

319

Mercer Street

5

Chickamauga
Dam

Lupton
Drive

Tennessee River

Chickamauga
Lake

Dixie Drive

Rivermont
Park

Tennessee Riverwalk

Rivermont
Park Ramp

6

Chattanooga State
Community College

Access

Takeout

Amnicola Highway

153

N

0   Kilometer   1

0   Mile   1

Low bluffs grace the shores of North Chickamauga Creek

banks, sometimes extending far enough out to make you work around them. At 0.9 mile paddle under a power line, make a bend then paddle under the Hamill Road bridge (no access) at 1.1 miles. Rock bluffs rise on river left and you soon come to the primary paddling access at Greenway Farms Park, at 1.4 miles. This park not only provides this paddling access and two others only reached by foot but also offers Chattanooga adventurers quality trails and a link to TVA's Big Ridge Small Wild Area. A hike here is detailed in adventure 2.

Though houses remain on the right bank, Greenway Farms occupies the left bank for a good distance as North Chickamauga Creeks makes a long sharp bend. Enjoy this segment of attractive stream. Turn away from Hamil Road at 2.3 miles. At 3.1 miles another Greenway Farms paddler access, along with a small stream, is on river left. Curve right (south) just beyond this landing and creek. At 3.6 miles paddle beneath a distinct 20-foot-high rock on river left that overhangs the stream.

At 4.0 miles North Chickamauga Creek comes near TN 153. Despite the noisy highway, the scenery remains attractive, a wooded corridor. Ahead on your left is the old TVA access area, now reached only by trail via Greenway Farms. You are now nearing the Tennessee River, floating under a series of bridges starting at 4.4 miles, mostly TVA land adjacent to big Chickamauga Dam and the dam lock. Emerge onto the big Tennessee River at 4.6 miles. The lock is to your left, and you can look across the river to Riverwalk Park. Though there is a boat ramp there, the swift current pushing out from below the dam makes that ramp unattainable save for the strongest of paddlers. You are much better off staying on the right (north) bank and cruising down to Rivermont Park. Ironically, the first part of your Tennessee River paddle may find you in a big eddy and going against the flow, despite paddling downriver.

Make sure to look back upstream at Chickamauga Dam and the massive infrastructure around it. Meanwhile, in the near, scope for copious birdlife—osprey, waterfowl, and herons—along a wooded shore. Views of the highlands around Chattanooga open before you and across to the Tennessee Riverwalk. Float under the high TN 319 bridge at 6.0 miles. Note the river access on the far bank just downstream of the TN 319 bridge, part of the greater Tennessee Riverwalk. From here out, just stick with the right bank of the mighty Tennessee, reaching the concrete boat ramp at Rivermont Park at 6.7 miles, ending the adventure.

33 West Chickamauga Creek

Paddle a historic stretch of the scenic "West Chick," starting at a preserved mill and alongside Chickamauga National Military Park.

Start: Lee & Gordon's Mills

End: Battlefield Parkway Access

Length: 9.8 miles

Float time: About 4.5 hours

Difficulty rating: Moderate

Rapids: Two Class II, a few Class I

River/lake type: Creek

Current: Moderate

River gradient: 2.4 feet per mile

Water gauge: West Chickamauga Creek at GA 146, Near Lakeview, Georgia; minimum runnable level 60 cfs

Season: Year-round; winter can be cold

Land status: Private, national military park

Fees or permits: No fees or permits required

Nearest city/town: Fort Oglethorpe, Georgia

Maps: USGS: Fort Oglethorpe, East Ridge; Tennessee River Blueway

Boats used: Kayaks, canoes

Organizations: Tennessee River Blueway/Outdoor Chattanooga, 200 River St., Chattanooga, TN 37405; (423) 643-6888; outdoorchattanooga.com

Contacts/outfitters: National Park Partners, PO Box 748, Chattanooga, TN 37401 (423) 648-5623; npp-ccm.org

Put-in/Takeout Information

To the takeout: From Chattanooga take I-75 south into Georgia and exit 353. Turn right onto GA 146 West/Cloud Springs Road and follow it for 0.9 mile. Turn left onto Dietz Road and follow it for 1.5 miles to GA 2/Battlefield Parkway. Turn right on Battlefield Parkway and follow it 1 mile, crossing West Chickamauga Creek. Just after crossing the creek, turn left toward Express Oil Change and veer right into the official parking area for the Fort Oglethorpe access of the Tennessee River Blueway, located between O'Charleys and Express Oil Change.

Stopping at one of the many gravel bars along West Chickamauga Creek

From the parking lot, follow the concrete trail down to the creek and a ramp that is connected to a short greenway. GPS: N34 56.490' / W85 13.381'

To the put-in from the takeout: Backtrack east on Battlefield Parkway to Dietz Road. Turn right (south) on Dietz Road and follow it for 5.1 miles (Dietz Road changes to Burning Bush Road along the way) to turn right onto Red Belt Road. Follow Red Belt Road west for 2.6 miles and turn right into Lee & Gordon's Mills, shortly after crossing West Chickamauga Creek. The put-in is on the grassy bank just downstream of the mill building. GPS: N34 53.031' / W85 15.999'

Paddle Summary

This paddle starts at restored 1836 Lee & Gordon's Mills, with its mill building and dam, then winds along West Chickamauga Creek, passing the site of the September 1863 Civil War Battle of Chickamauga. You will actually paddle under two bridges that factored into the clash along the way. The creekside scenery is surprisingly devoid of development, lining through a corridor of green dotted with bluffs before emerging at busy Battlefield Parkway. The paddle includes one straightforward Class II rapid and a few lesser shoals, as well as one old low-water road crossing that may need scouting.

River/Lake Overview

West Chickamauga Creek is a Georgia tributary of the Tennessee River. The long named stream starts in the southwestern reaches of Walker County, flowing from below the ridges of Lookout Mountain to the west and Pigeon Mountain to the east. North-flowing West Chickamauga Creek continues gathering tributaries while winding through a widening bottom before passing under US 27 near the town of Chickamauga. It soon reaches Crawfish Springs, which adds continual flow, and then West Chickamauga Creek is dammed at historic Lee & Gordon's Mills, where this paddle starts. After being freed of the old milldam, the "West Chick" winds north, becoming the boundary of Chattanooga & Chickamauga National Military Park, where the Union and the Confederacy clashed in the fall of 1863. The creek leaves the battlefield and makes its way to Tennessee, entering the Volunteer State only to soon give its waters to South Chickamauga Creek, which then heads on to the Tennessee River. West Chickamauga and South Chickamauga Creeks both offers miles of paddling pleasure, and paddling accesses continue to evolve. The towns of Chickamauga, Fort Oglethorpe, and Ringgold each have developed creek accesses on West Chickamauga Creek.

The Paddling

At Lee & Gordon's Mills, you have a short carry over grass down to West Chickamauga Creek. Before leaving, take a look at the mill, which after its construction in the 1830s doubled as the first general store in Walker County, Georgia. Upstream, Crawfish Springs provided reliable flow for West Chickamauga Creek. The mill went through different hands but remained in operation until 1967, when it was shut down. However, Frank Pierce singlehandedly restored the mill to working order, and the property later became an event venue, along with the Gordon & Lee Mansion. The landowners have graciously allowed paddler access at the mill, so be respectful of the land and goings on there.

West Chickamauga Creek is flowing swift below the milldam and you are soon pushed downstream into a wooded corridor of green. The stream is running around 20 to 25 feet wide, yet the channel is effectively narrowed by fallen logs and tan gravel bars. Normally running a translucent blue-green, the waterway will turn muddy after heavy rains. Ash and sycamore, along with nonnative privet, lord above the "West Chick" as it meanders northerly, though acute bends

West Chickamauga Creek

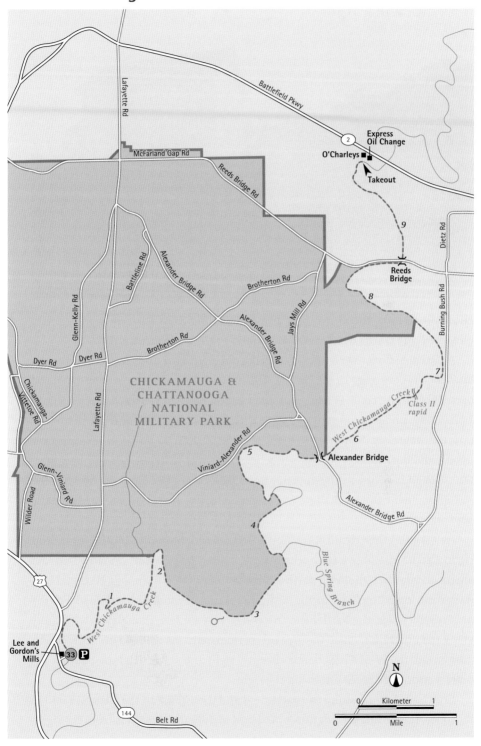

This paddle starts at historic
Lee & Gordons Mill

take it in all four directions. Low stone bluffs line the stream in places. Small, unnamed side creeks quietly add their flows to the main stream.

At 0.5 mile float over a nonthreatening old low-water bridge. It is easy to stop on West Chickamauga Creek, as the stream is often shallow as it flows by gravel bars. Though the creek is kept passable by local paddling enthusiasts, expect to squeeze by, under, or around occasional trees that have fallen from the banks into the waterway. Sometimes it will seem as if there is no passage ahead, yet upon paddling closer, you will see where previous intrepid floaters have gotten through blowdowns. Even you have to get out of your boat, chances are the stream segment will be shallow and no problem, unless a chill has blanketed the land and water.

At 1.4 miles the stream turns north (left) as a high wooded bluff rises to your right. Cedars rise above the rocks. At 1.8 miles a large, clear, unnamed stream enters on your left, draining parts of Chickamauga & Chattanooga National Military Park, including Cave Spring, as well as points beyond the battlefield. For the next several miles, the battlefield park will be on your left, though you will hardly know the difference, since the stream corridor remains wooded on both banks. Just ahead, the West Chick bends abruptly right and slows in a long pool. At 2.5 miles a spring-fed creek enters on the right.

Continue curving along the battlefield and then come to the Class II rapid at 3.6 miles. It is an angled ledge drop. The best paddling approach is from the right, the best portage on the left. Just below the ledge drop, Blue Spring Branch adds significant flow to West Chickamauga Creek as it drains lands below Boynton Ridge. At 4.2 miles the creek cuts through an old oxbow leaving right, only to quickly rejoin the current channel. At 4.6 miles navigate an easy Class I shoal. The right bank is treeless in places. Ahead, the stream splits around some islands. Float under Alexander Bridge at 5.7 miles (no paddler ingress/egress allowed per battlefield regulations).

More islands are found ahead, and the banks rise in sheer soil bluffs in places. At 6.8 miles West Chickamauga Creek cuts through an old meander. This is the site of a former and potentially hazardous low-water bridge. Placed rock here creates a Class II rapid. Stop to scout or walk your boat through, since the irregular placed rocks can cause troubles depending on water levels. Ahead, sidle along a hillside atop which runs Burning Bush Road.

At 7.2 miles float under a pair of private bridges. At 8.2 miles a clear creek enters from the left and then you curve right, floating under Reeds Bridge at 8.8 miles. Ahead, the stream slows under wooded banks. The float is lazy here, then you speed on a bend before coming to the takeout on your left, at 9.8 miles. The ramp connects to a short concrete trail, in case you want to stretch your legs.

Rapids like this keep the paddling lively

34 Graves of Nickajack Lake

The loop paddle explores mountain-rimmed Nickajack Lake. Starting at a lesser used ramp, you head into the shadow of Raccoon Mountain and Walden Ridge to find the strange, partly submerged graves of Nickajack Lake.

Start/End: Bennett Lake ramp

Length: 7.5-mile loop

Float time: About 3.8 hours

Difficulty rating: Moderate; winds could be problematic in Nickajack Lake

Rapids: None

River/lake type: Big TVA lake

Current: Very little

River gradient: None

Water gauge: Nickajack Lake; full pool 634 feet elevation, minimum winter pool 632 feet elevation

Season: March through June

Land status: Tennessee Valley Authority, private land

Fees or permits: No fees or permits required

Nearest city/town: Mineral Springs, Tennessee

Maps: USGS: Sequatchie, Wauhatchie; Nickajack Lake

Morning on the Tennessee River

Boats used: Kayaks, canoes, motorboats, fishing boats, personal watercraft, pontoon boats

Organizations: Tennessee Valley Authority, 400 West Summit Hill Dr., Knoxville TN 37902; (865) 632-2101; tva.com

Contacts/outfitters: Tennessee River Blueway/Outdoor Chattanooga, 200 River St., Chattanooga, TN 37405; (423) 643-6888; outdoorchattanooga.com

Put-in/Takeout Information

To the put-in/takeout: From exit 158 on I-24, west of Chattanooga, join TN 27 east and follow it for 4.6 miles to turn right onto Bennett Lake Road. Follow Bennett Lake Road for 0.3 mile then turn right into the signed ramp and parking area. GPS: N35 4.743' / W85 32.204'

Paddle Summary

This adventure combines a big lake, mountain views and history into one rewarding paddle. The setting is Nickajack Lake, the reservoir that backs up the Tennessee River in Chattanooga and downstream under the mantle of mountains that comprise the Tennessee River Gorge where the river cuts through the Cumberland Plateau. Start at the large but not overly busy Bennett Lake boat ramp, then head east along the north shore of Nickajack, soaking in views (as well as passing a noisy quarry). After stroking through a narrower segment, open onto Mullens Cove, where you will find three graves, rising from the waters after being inundated by the damming of the Tennessee River. Beyond the graves, swing by islands and return via the south shore of Nickajack, along a wooded shore. Finally, curve beside Pryor Island before returning to the boat ramp. The most important thing to know about this paddle is the proper time to do it—March through June; December through February if the weather is warm enough. If you go during summer, water weeds can grow so thick in Mullens Cove that they prevent access to the graves.

River/Lake Overview

Nickajack Lake is one of the two major TVA impounds of the Tennessee River in the greater Chattanooga region, the other being Chickamauga Lake.

This barge provides great contrast to a little ol' paddler

Nickajack Lake backs up all the way to Chickamauga Dam, encompassing all of Chattanooga and the incredible gorge of the Tennessee River, parts of which this paddle explores. The dam was a TVA latecomer, being completed in 1967. Nickajack Dam replaced the old Hales Bar Dam, built in 1913, the first dam on the Tennessee River. Hales Bar Dam leaked from the word go, improperly placed in porous limestone. Nickajack Dam, set 6 miles downriver, was properly placed, ending the leaking. Built to keep stable river levels for river navigation and power generation, Nickajack Dam stands 81 feet high and is 3,767 feet across. The impoundment features 179 miles of shoreline and has 10,300 water-surface acres.

The Paddling

The graves of Henry and Zilpha Long, along with a great grandson, are strange sight. In a bay of Nickajack Lake known as Mullens Cove, the three headstones rise above the water, bordered by riprap. The three residents were buried in this spot in the 1800s, well before this part of the Tennessee River was dammed, first by Hales Bar Dam then by Nickajack Dam. Back then, Mullens Cove was in the back of beyond, a rich river bottomland farmed by Henry Long and his descendants, but when Hales Bar Dam began backing up the Tennessee River, Mullens Cove turned from backwoods to backwater, isolating the graves of the Longs, surrounded by aqua.

Later, when Nickajack Lake become operational, the lake level was raised, inundating the headstones. They eventually fell over (or were tipped over). In

Graves of Nickajack Lake

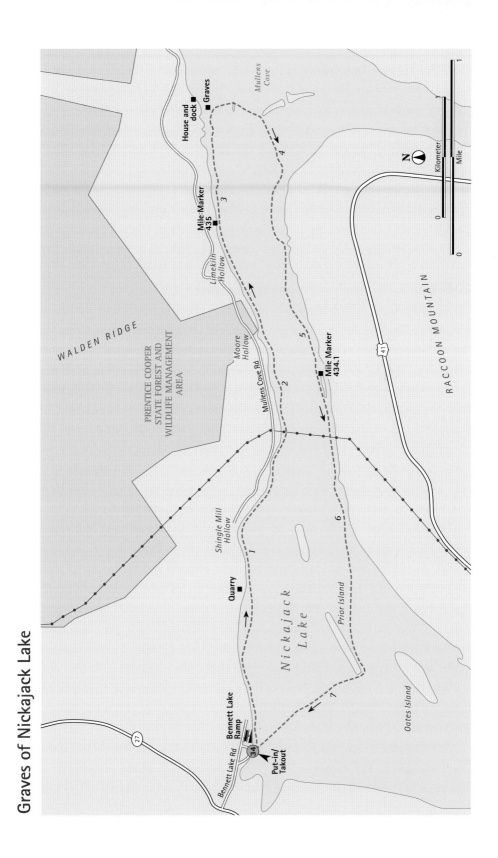

1999 TVA righted the headstones and placed riprap around the graves to prevent wave action from knocking the stones over. However, TVA made an error when righting the headstones. They were stood up facing west instead of east, as they had been before. In Christian burials, graves and headstones are faced east so that the interred can rise up and face the direction from which Jesus will rise upon resurrection, as stated in the Bible's book of Matthew.

Nevertheless, the graves stand as they are today. (TVA has moved some 550 graveyards from its lake system; however, they weren't in charge when Hales Bar Dam went up.) Therefore, we have a strange anomaly of the past that makes a worthwhile paddling destination. The graves are not hard to find, despite being just three headstones rising from the water. (There has been a buoy by the graves in the past and hopefully will continue to be there.)

You will enjoy other highlights along the way, namely views of Raccoon Mountain, flanking the south shore of the lake, and Walden Ridge, rising from the north shore. Add in a few islands to visit and you have a winner of an aquatic adventure. The TWRA Bennett Lake boat ramp, named for being in Bennett Cove, offers a steep two-lane ramp and a floating dock. Paddlers can easily launch from the floating dock. Paddle east along the north shore of Nickajack Lake. You can look south at the balance of Nickajack Lake. Raccoon Mountain rises from the far shore, Pryor Island and another unnamed island are visible in the near. Come alongside gray stone bluffs to your left. Ahead is the only downer of the trip, a noisy rock quarry with barges and docks along the river. Paddle by the quarry and its docks at 0.7 mile, leaving the reverberations behind you.

Look for barges in the main river as you paddle into Shingle Mill Hollow, where houses stand on the shore. The creek mouth in the hollow is lost in the marsh. Ahead, Nickajack Lake narrows. Float under a power line at 1.7 miles. Despite being on a lake, you will be experiencing a very mild current and heading upstream. In the distance, Walden Ridge rises more than 1,000 feet, a wooded rampart. This portion of the mountain is part of Prentice Cooper State Forest, excellent for hiking adventures, some of which are detailed in this adventure guide. At 2.3 miles you paddle by cedar-clad bluffs. More woods and bluffs occupy the left bank. You can see the bend of the river turning right now. Pass river mile marker 435 at 2.9 miles. The sign indicates you are 435 miles from the mouth of the Tennessee River where it empties into the Ohio River.

At this point, keep your eyes peeled due easterly. You will start to see a small circular island in the distance. That is your beacon to find the graves. You will also see a few more islands fronting Mullens Cove. Pass the mouth of Dry Creek

Paddler visits the graves of Mullens Creek with Walden Ridge as a backdrop

to your left at 3.4 miles. The small isle stands dead ahead, rocky at its base and topped with a few small trees. A larger isle stands to the right, and there are two bigger islands along the barge channel and former river channel, also to the right.

At 3.5 miles come to the graves, bordered by submerged riprap (GPS: N35 4.9441' / W85 28.7200'). Note that there is no land here. The small isle you have been using as a beacon stands due east, 0.1 mile deeper in Mullens Cove. You can paddle in a circle around the graves. The headstones are difficult to read, but they are a truly strange sight in the middle of a lake.

Beyond the graves, break south for a nearby small linear island you can use to stop. Otherwise, turn southwest passing a pair of islands along the old river channel then paddle for the south shore of the lake, reaching it at 4.1 miles. Obviously, watch for boat traffic when crossing the open water. You are now westbound on the south shore, with Walden Ridge rising to the north. This south shore is nothing but scenic woods.

Paddle by river marker 434.1 at 5.2 miles. Continue west, floating back under the power line at 5.6 miles. Leave the south shoreline at 6.0 miles, crossing the river channel again, aiming for Pryor Island, ragged looking, as it is subject to storms. At 6.8 miles turn north after curving around the west tip of Pryor Island. Ahead, you can see the metal floating dock of Bennett Lake ramp. Make a beeline for the ramp, reaching it at 7.5 miles, completing the paddling adventure.

35 Sequatchie River

A paddle down the Sequatchie River is the watery equivalent of sitting on the front porch—it is a relaxing endeavor that we enjoy when we get the chance and would like to do more often.

Start: Mount Calvary Road

End: Ketner's Mill

Length: 11.1 miles

Float time: About 5 hours

Difficulty rating: Moderate due to distance

Rapids: Class I

River type: Pastoral valley river

Current: Slow

River gradient: 1.8 feet per mile

River gauge: USGS gauge—Sequatchie at Whitwell; minimum runnable level 70 cfs

Season: Year-round

Land status: Private

Fees or permits: No fees or permits required

Nearest city/town: Whitwell, Tennessee

Maps: USGS Ketner Gap, Whitwell

Boats used: Kayaks, canoes, a few johnboats

Organizations: Ketner's Mill Foundation, PO Box 4426, Chattanooga, TN 37405; (423) 267-5702; ketnersmill.org

Contacts/outfitters: Willis Farm Canoe & Kayak Rental, 701 Inman Rd., Whitwell, TN 37397; (423) 827-8765; facebook.com/thewillisfarmkayakrental. These folks rent boats and operate shuttle for trips starting at Ketner's Mil l.

Put-in/Takeout Information

To takeout: From exit 158 on I-24, west of Chattanooga near Nickajack Lake, take TN 27 East for 8.4 miles. Turn left onto Ketner Mill Lane; continue for 1 mile to the mill and takeout on your left. GPS: N35 8.319' / W85 30.986'

To put-in from takeout: From Ketner's Mill, continue east on Ketner Mill Lane for 0.4 mile then turn left on Ketner Mill Road. Follow Ketner Mill Road for 2 miles then turn right onto TN 28 North. Follow TN 28 north for 6.1 miles to Mount Calvary Road, passing through the town of Whitwell along the way. Turn

The mill dam drops in uniform grace at paddle's end.

right on Mount Calvary Road, crossing the Sequatchie River. Continue for 0.1 mile beyond the bridge to an access on your right. Here a pair of rough roads lead down to a gravel bar. Scout the road first, or simply park along Mount Calvary Road and carry your boat down. GPS: N35 13.624' / W85 29.441'

Paddle Summary

Trips here are great for paddlers of all abilities. Put in at Mount Calvary Road and begin your paddle along an intimate waterway that cuts through what many argue is the most beautiful valley in the state of Tennessee, bordered by Walden Ridge to the east and the Cumberland Plateau to the west. You will gain views of these highlands from the water. The generally slow current is broken by easy riffles and shoals that keep your boat moving along but pose no hazards. Tan gravel bars are exposed along the shore in places and make for inviting stops. Hot summer days are made for a trip down the Sequatchie, as the river is mostly shaded, with plenty of deep swimming holes that beckon the paddler. Fallen trees are frequent along the river but generally do not pose an obstacle to a paddler, save for one area where the river splits around a sizable island. The Sequatchie slows the last 0.5 mile before reaching Ketner's Mill. The paddle is every bit of 11 miles, so be prepared for a full day on the water with drinks, food, and an early arrival at the put-in.

River Overview

The Sequatchie River runs through one of the most scenic valleys in America. Flowing south in the heart of the Cumberlands, the waterway is bordered on the west by the Cumberland Plateau and on the east by Walden Ridge en route to the Tennessee River. The river actually starts in Grassy Valley, high in the Cumberlands, then flows underground, springing forth in the northernmost Sequatchie Valley at the Cumberland-Bledsoe county line. The Sequatchie River meanders through the southwest-trending valley, fed by small tributaries flowing off the wooded ridges. The river becomes paddleable a few miles north of Sequatchie County, beginning nearly 60 miles of canoeing and kayaking pleasure. It passes near Dunlap and Whitwell and finally Jasper before meeting the Tennessee River near the Alabama state line. Accesses continue to change, some opening and some closing, making paddling the Sequatchie more challenging in that regard.

The Paddling

Leave the gravel bar, a local gathering spot on hot summer days, and scoot down a riffle, heading east. The Sequatchie stands 70 to 90 feet wide here, flanked by heavily wooded banks. The river's normally clear-green color reflects silver maple, box elder, and ironwood growing thickly on banks 6 to 20 feet high. Higher up the banks, oaks, hickory, and even an occasional pine overhangs the river. Since the Sequatchie is somewhat narrow, trees fallen into the river can constrict channels. Rocks and grasses line the immediate shore.

A couple more rough accesses are found on the left bank, where Mount Calvary Road parallels the Sequatchie for a short distance. The slow current speeds over shallow gravel riffles, allowing you to see the bottom of the river. Faster channels bordered by gravel bars can be as narrow as 15 feet. Occasionally, fields that occupy the rich agricultural land of the Sequatchie Valley reach the river's edge and dramatically open up the sky overhead. They also allow views of the mountains that border the Sequatchie Valley.

Mount Calvary Road soon turns away. At 0.9 mile a trickling branch enters on river left and a big bluff rises dead ahead, forcing the Sequatchie to turn right, southwest. The bluff remains on your left while bottomland stretches to your right. By 1.7 miles the bluff has given way and you float through an easy Class I rapid. This entire section of the Sequatchie has no difficult rapids.

Sequatchie River

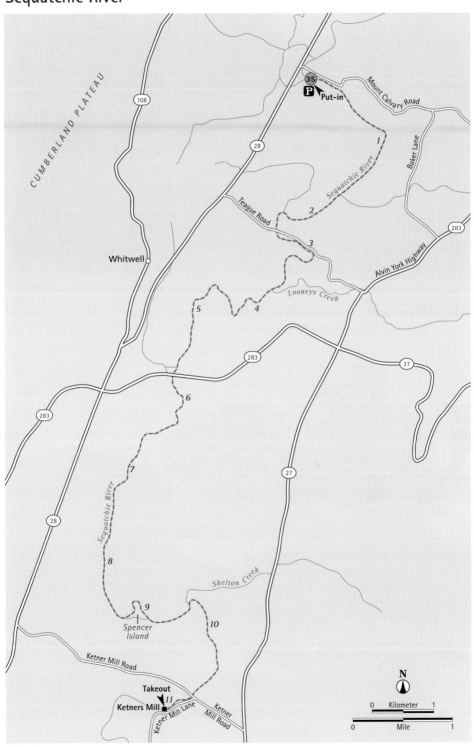

CUMBERLAND PLATEAU

108

28

283

283

27

283

27

28

Whitwell

Teague Road

Mount Calvary Road

Baker Lane

Alvin York Highway

Looneys Creek

Sequatchie River

Sequatchie River

Shelton Creek

Ketner Mill Road

Ketner Mill Lane

Ketner Mill Road

Spencer Island

Takeout
Ketners Mill

35
Put-in

1
2
3
4
5
6
7
8
9
10
11

N

0   Kilometer   1

0   Mile   1

Top: An alluring gravel bar on the Sequatchie
Bottom: Paddler eye view of Ketner's Mill

At 2.4 miles the Sequatchie bumps into a bluff on its right bank then flows under the quiet Teague Road bridge at 2.6 miles (no access). The waterway continues pinballing deep in the vale of its creation, now heading east, with Teague Road running alongside it. Ahead, views open of majestic Walden Ridge. This river segment offers more moving water and fewer slow pools. Turn away from Teague Road at 3.1 miles, bending through bottoms. At 3.8 miles big and clear Looneys Creek, draining Walden Ridge, enters on river left. The river bends at 4.0 miles and creates a gravel bar fine for stopping.

Dance over a rocky riffle at 4.3 miles. Here the Sequatchie bends sharply right, turning northwesterly, only to run headlong into a bluff at 4.7 miles. You are very close to Whitwell but cannot tell from the river, as the town is obscured by the bluff. However, ahead you will see a water intake pump on river right, serving Whitwell. At 4.9 miles the river splits around a long island with an ample gravel bar for stopping. At 5.8 miles a creek enters on river right just as you float under the TN 283 bridge.

Thus far there has been almost no development on the river, but after 7.0 miles, you see a few cabins; however, the structures do little to despoil the serenity. Relax in the slow section, or you can paddle through it. Either way, at 8.6 miles the Sequatchie bends left then splits around Spencer Island. It is a big island, and the channels around the island are correspondingly narrow. Historically, logjams have piled up here, blocking the right channel. The left channel is longer but less problematic. Hopefully, the way will be clear for you. The island ends at 9.1 miles. You are heading east, soaking in views of Walden Ridge until reaching Shelton Creek. It enters on river left at 9.6 miles, then the Sequatchie curves south. The river slows as you float under the Ketner's Mill bridge at 10.8 miles. From here, get over on river left and take out on your left at some steps just before reaching Ketner's Mill at 11.1 miles, ending the adventure. *Note:* Every autumn a fair is held at Ketner's Mill, proceeds going to maintenance and restoration of the mill. For more information visit ketnersmill.org.

36 Patten Island Circuit

Start this adventure at Tennessee's oldest state park then paddle Chickamauga Lake around a series of formerly inhabited islands, created when TVA dammed the Tennessee River.

Start/End: Harrison Bay State Park ramp

Length: 5.3-mile loop

Float time: About 2.5 hours

Difficulty rating: Easy-moderate; winds could be problematic in open-water areas.

Rapids: None

River/lake type: Big TVA lake

Current: None

River gradient: None

Water gauge: Chickamauga Lake; full pool 682 feet elevation, minimum winter pool 675 feet elevation

Season: Year-round; late summer least favorable due to water weeds in the lake

Land status: State park, TVA undeveloped property, some private land in distance

Fees or permits: No fees or permits required

Nearest city/town: Harrison, Tennessee

Maps: USGS Snow Hill, Daisy; Harrison Bay State Park

Boats used: Kayaks, canoes, motorboats, fishing boats, personal watercraft, pontoon boats

Organizations: Harrison Bay State Park, 8411 Harrison Bay Rd., Harrison, TN 37341; (423) 344-6214; tnstateparks.com. The state park marina rents canoes and kayaks by the hour.

Contacts/outfitters: Tennessee Valley Authority, 400 West Summit Hill Dr., Knoxville, TN 37902; (865) 632-2101; tva.com

Put-in/Takeout Information

To the put-in/takeout: From exit 11 on I-75 near Ooltewah, Tennessee, take US 11/US 64 West for 0.3 mile. Turn left onto Hunter Road then continue for 6.1 miles to TN 58. Turn right on TN 58 and go 1.5 miles then turn left onto Harrison Bay Road. Follow Harrison Bay Road for 1.5 miles. Enter the state park and follow the signs to the marina/boat ramp. Reach the park boat ramp at the end of the road near the park office. GPS: N35 10.068' / W85 7.287'

Waves gently lap the shore
on a summer's eve

Paddle Summary

This Chickamauga Lake paddling adventure starts at interesting-in-its-own-right Harrison Bay State Park—with picnicking, camping, and hiking trails—then wanders along the attractive state park shoreline of this big TVA impoundment, exploring quiet coves. Next, break south across the lake to Patten Island and other adjacent isles. Tour these undeveloped TVA public lands that offer camping possibilities. Wildlife is abundant on the isles, from deer to woodpeckers. Patten Island contains relics of civilization, left when the Tennessee River flooded the old town of Harrison. After circling the isles, cross open water a second time to return to the state park, where you squeeze past yet another island en route to your starting point. The waters of this paddle are popular with motorboaters; if you can time your paddle for quieter periods, you will enjoy more solitude.

River/Lake Overview

Chickamauga Lake is one of two major TVA impoundments of the Tennessee River in the greater Chattanooga region, the other being Nickajack Lake. It took four years to construct Chickamauga Dam, completed in 1940. Although it is an energy-generating dam, flood control was a major objective of this impoundment, as Chattanooga had suffered repeated terrible floods when the Tennessee River ran high. Chickamauga Lake covers 59 river miles of the Tennessee, from Chickamauga Dam east of downtown Chattanooga up to Watts Bar Dam near Spring City. The lake covers 36,000 acres of surface land, part of which inundated the old town of Harrison that this paddle explores. Chickamauga Lake features 784 miles of shoreline. It is a very popular fishing and recreational boating reservoir.

The Paddling

The boat ramp area of Harrison Bay State Park can be incredibly busy at times, with the boat slips housing large pleasure craft, a park restaurant, park office, and more, as well as anglers and other lake lovers launching from the same spot. However, there is no need for kayakers and canoers to use the double-lane launch ramp. As you look out toward the lake from the launch area, look left for a pier that you can use to load. Better yet, segments of the shoreline to the left (east)

Patten Island Circuit

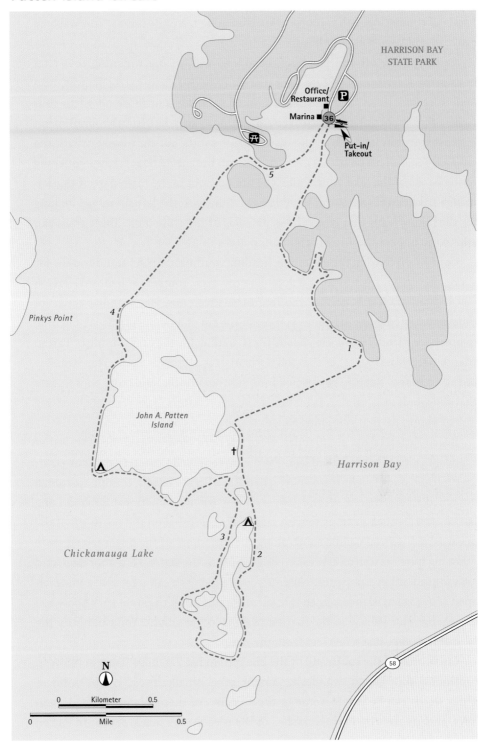

HARRISON BAY
STATE PARK

Office/
Restaurant

P

Marina ■ 36

Put-in/
Takeout

5

Pinkys Point

4

1

John A. Patten
Island

†

Harrison Bay

Chickamauga Lake

3

2

58

N

0   Kilometer   0.5

0   Mile   0.5

of the launch have been beaten down and used by paddlers like us, saving us the hassle of competing with motorboaters launching from the ramps. This way you can load and launch at your leisure.

Once you are off and paddling, head south down the widening cove that houses the Harrison Bay State Park marina. Wooded shores stretch away, covered in cedars, pines, and hardwoods. You'll soon see a little island off to your right—that is part of your return route. For now, keep left (southbound), passing coves. Patten Island is in the distance due south, but for now stay with the left shoreline, all part of the state park. You can best avoid boat traffic by sticking to the banks of the lake. At 0.4 mile you are now out in the main part of Chickamauga Lake, with open water to your right. Stay with the left shoreline, looking for the hiking trails that cover the peninsulas of the state park. These trails can add to the fun here before or after your paddle.

Continue following the shoreline, heading southeast. TN 58 stands on the far shore, and the autos traveling it look like toy cars. You are in greater Harrison Bay, created when TVA flooded the Tennessee River; now Harrison Bay is part of Chickamauga Lake. At 1.1 miles you reach the tip of a peninsula. It is now time to break for Patten Island. Head southwest, aiming for the eastern side of Patten Island, clearly the biggest isle on the horizon. It is a 0.5 mile across Harrison Bay to Patten Island. Keep an eye peeled for motorboat traffic, and cross your fingers that the winds stay calm. As you bisect the open waters, gaze west at the rising wall of mountain that is Walden Ridge.

Reach Patten Island at 1.6 miles. Head left here, aiming for some of the other islands, to circle Patten Island last. Paddle by eerie Bell Cemetery on your right, up a hill and out of sight from shore, then leave Patten Island, coming to a small unnamed island then a second longer, linear island, sometimes dubbed Long Island. At 1.9 miles a campsite with large oaks is located on the north tip of the linear island. As you paddle south along the east shore of the linear island, note other big trees, as well as cypress trees growing in the water. Listen for deer, and look for still other campsites. **Note:** if you are going to camp on these undeveloped TVA-owned islands, which is legal, make sure to let the state park know you are leaving your vehicle in the marina parking lot overnight. You can notify the park at the office just a few feet from the ramp.

Curve around the south end of the linear island at 2.4 miles. Turn northwest, continuing your circuit, wandering among other smaller isles. In late summer, water weeds can be troublesome in the shallows of these islands. Cattails, willows, and grasses rise in the marshes of the isles. At 3.2 miles, return to Patten

The wooded shore of an island in Chickamauga Lake

Island. Begin your clockwise trip around this 100 or so–acre hilly wooded preserve. When the water is at winter pool, you can see old roads and other evidence of the town of Harrison on the exposed lake bottom. When Chickamauga Lake is at full pool, you can search the island by foot for evidence of previous habitation. Landings and campsites are scattered along the shore.

At 3.7 miles turn around a point with a campsite and begin paddling north along the west side of Patten Island. You are along the main channel of the lake, the former river channel. Little gravel beaches stretch along the shore here, created by wave action from barges and other boats. Rock outcrops and soil bluffs rise along this side of the island. The land rises higher into bona fide hills. Paddle beyond the northwest tip of the island at 4.3 miles. Pinkys Point stands on the mainland to your left. Our paddle heads north northeast across open water.

It is 0.6 mile to the island of the state park and the mainland just beyond, a large picnic area. Squeeze through the shallows between the picnic area and the island. (You won't be able to get through here when Chickamauga Lake is at lower winter pool.) Ahead, open to the marina, paddling by boat slips to reach the ramp area at 5.3 miles, completing the paddling adventure. If you are looking for more waters to explore, consider paddling along the coves and points of Harrison Bay State Park north of the marina.

37 Parksville Lake

Explore two arms of this scenic mountain-rimmed impoundment in the Cherokee National Forest.

Start/End: Kings Slough ramp

Length: 8.0-mile loop

Float time: About 4.5 hours

Difficulty rating: Moderate; winds could be problematic in open-water areas.

Rapids: None

River/lake type: Mountain-rimmed lake

Current: None

River gradient: None

Water gauge: None

Season: March through Sept

Land status: Almost all national forest

Fees or permits: No fees or permits required

Nearest city/town: Cleveland, Tennessee

Maps: USGS: Parksville; National Geographic #781: Cherokee National Forest Tell-ico and Ocoee Rivers

Boats used: Kayaks, canoes, motorboats, fishing boats, personal watercraft

Organizations: Cherokee National Forest, Ocoee Whitewater Center, 4400 Hwy. 64, Copperhill, TN 37317; (423) 496-0100; fs.usda.gov/cherokee

Contacts/outfitters: Rock Creek Outfitters/Ocoee, 1690 US-64, Benton, TN 37307; (423) 338-1075; udans.com/rockcreek. This store near Parksville Lake is open seasonally and services the lake and Ocoee River, renting boats and selling outdoor equipment.

Put-in/Takeout Information

To the put-in/takeout: From exit 20 on I-75 near Cleveland, take the US 64 East Bypass for 6.4 miles. Turn right onto US 64 East and continue for 10 miles. Turn right onto Cookson Creek Road (the left turn is Hildabrand Road) and continue for 3.6 miles. Turn left onto FR 55A/Sugar Loaf Road, drive 0.4 mile, and turn right into the ramp area. GPS: N35 4.947' / W84 39.028'

Top: A morning view of Chilhowee Mountain
Bottom: Looking down on Parksville Lake from Chilhowee Mountain

Paddle Summary

This scenic paddle takes place on one of the oldest impoundments in the greater Chattanooga area—Parksville Lake, almost all of which lies within the confines of the Cherokee National Forest. You will be paddling along wooded shores sans development, save for a few cabins. Leave Kings Slough ramp then turn up slender Baker Creek Inlet, enjoying forests in the near and views of Chilhowee Mountain and Sugarloaf Mountain in the far on your way to the inflow of Baker Creek. Next, head out toward the main lake, then turn into the narrower Indian Creek Inlet, finding a marsh. Finally, return to Kings Slough via clear waters. In season, Parksville Lake can be busy with motorboats, but the two inlets explored in our adventure receive less traffic and offer the best experience for paddlers.

River/Lake Overview

Parksville Lake is an impoundment damming the Ocoee River of whitewater fame. The Ocoee's headwaters are in Georgia, where it is known as the Toccoa River. The Toccoa River begins in the North Georgia mountains, flowing off the Blue Ridge in the shadow of the Appalachian Trail. Here, much of the river flows through the Chattahoochee National Forest before being dammed near the town of Blue Ridge. The river is then freed again, continuing northwest, where it enters the state of Tennessee and changes names. In the Volunteer State, the now-named Ocoee River is one of the famed whitewater destinations in the Southeast. Here the river is also dammed in multiple places, but finally it is unleashed to meekly flow into the Tennessee River. Parksville Lake was dammed in 1911. Known as Ocoee Dam No. 1, the dam was among the first in the region. Parksville Lake has 47 miles of shoreline and stretches more than 1,930 acres of water surface.

The Paddling

Kings Slough offers a ramp, restrooms, and a large parking area. You can launch at the ramp, a gravelly shoreline, or a small dock; your choice. Leave the narrow inlet, passing a few cabins on the left. Parksville Lake is bordered by almost all national forest, but you will see some cabins on this paddle. After 0.3 mile the slender channel opens to Baker Creek Inlet, with a very narrow spit of land to your right. Paddle south around this spit.

Parksville Lake

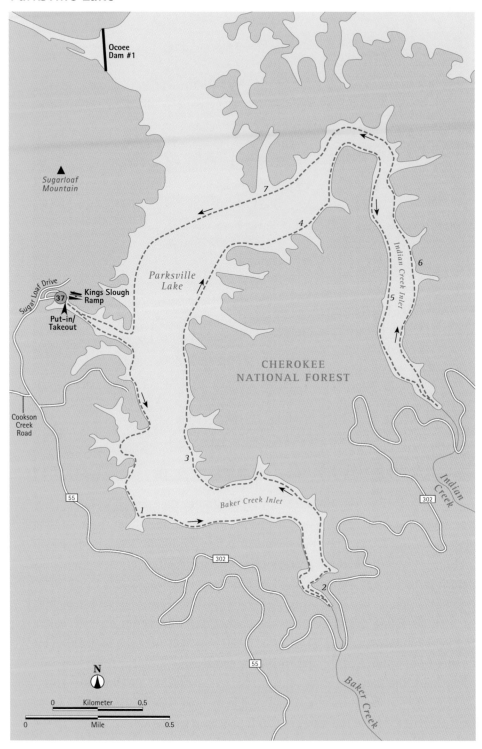

Ocoee Dam #1

Sugarloaf Mountain

Parksville Lake

Sugar Loaf Drive

37

Kings Slough Ramp

Put-in/ Takeout

Cookson Creek Road

Indian Creek Inlet

CHEROKEE NATIONAL FOREST

55

7

4

6

5

3

1

302

Indian Creek

Baker Creek Inlet

302

2

55

Baker Creek

N

0   Kilometer   0.5

0   Mile   0.5

Stopping at the mouth of crystal clear Baker Creek

Sourwood, shortleaf pines, chestnut oaks, and other dry-situation species rise along the shore. Work along the banks of Baker Creek Inlet, soon coming alongside Camp Ocoee. The YMCA retreat has been here since 1923, hosting generations of kids through the past century. Pass its facilities, scattered among a pair of watery coves while moving south in ever-narrowing Baker Creek Inlet. Additional sloughs beg exploration, depending on how much you want to paddle. At 1.0 miles follow the shoreline as the Baker Creek Inlet bends easterly. Pass a few more cabins with docks. Occasional fallen trees will force you to paddle a bit farther from shore. At 1.6 miles turn back south again, into the inner sanctum of the inlet. The watery surface continues to narrow as the shoreline closes in.

Note the campsites. Some are accessible by boat only, while others can be reached via FR 302. If the water is at full pool, you will be able to paddle all the way to the cool mountain aqua of Baker Creek, noisily contributing its flow to the stillwater lake. (By the way, Parksville Lake fluctuates 9 feet between summer pool and winter pool. Full summer pool is 838 feet elevation.) On a hot summer day, you can feel the cool air around at the creek mouth. Stopping spots are easy in this area. Leave the mouth of Baker Creek at 2.0 miles, continuing along the shoreline. The inlet is widening now, and you can look north at circular Sugarloaf Mountain, the signature peak along Parksville Lake.

At 2.9 miles, while curving north, pass exposed rock outcrops. Soon you are heading due north. Side coves break up the shoreline and offer additional paddling opportunities. At 3.3 miles paddle along a steep soil bluff, almost directly across the inlet from the Kings Slough ramp. If desiring a shorter trip, you could simply aim for Kings Slough and make the paddle a little under 4.0 miles. At 3.8 miles curve right into the greater Indian Creek Inlet as open water extends to your left. From here look northwest into the main lake and at the lake dam. The dam stretches 840 feet across between two pillar-like ridges and rises 135 feet above the lake. It was begun in 1910 and finished a year later. The hydroelectric dam features five generating units delivering 24 megawatts of power per day to the greater Chattanooga region. Two other dams are situated along the Ocoee River.

Leave the dam viewing area and paddle up the narrowing Indian Creek Inlet, with myriad pine-bordered small coves beckoning anglers and paddlers. At 4.5 miles the inlet curves sharply south and you paddle southward on the slender, almost riverine arm of Indian Creek. This is some of the best paddling on Parksville Lake, the natural tree-lined, hilly shoreline twisting snakelike. At 5.5 miles you are at the marshy mouth of Indian Creek. The water is quite shallow here, and at lower lake levels this area will be high and dry. If at full pool, however, you can sneak back to where Indian Creek adds its waters to Parksville Lake. Shoreline stopping spots can be found hereabouts.

Leave Indian Creek and work north along the inlet, enjoying new shoreline. More hill-bordered coves call you to explore, and you once again turn into the main lake. Leave the Indian Creek Inlet at 7.1 miles. This is your closest view of the lake dam. Note US 64 running along the north shore of Parksville Lake. Hopefully it isn't too windy as you cross the lake at this point, where Sugarloaf Mountain rises like a circular sentinel ahead. The paddle across the lake is a little under 0.5 mile. A few more cabins are set along the shore here. Paddle your way south, coming to the mouth of Kings Slough at 7.7 miles. From here it is a simple backtrack west to complete the paddling adventure at 8.0 miles.

38 Hiwassee River

The Hiwassee makes its way through a majestic mountainous setting, with scenery and views that make it hard to keep your eyes on the frequent attention-demanding rapids.

Start: Below Apalachia Dam powerhouse

End: Reliance

Length: 5.9 miles

Float time: 2–3 hours

Difficulty rating: Difficult for novices

Rapids: Class I–II+

River/lake type: Dam-controlled whitewater river

Current: Swift

River gradient: 14 feet per mile

River gauge: TVA water release schedule. Call (865) 632-2264 then follow the prompts to get the release schedule for Apalachia Dam, or visit tva.com.

Season: May through Oct, dam-release dependent

Land status: Public—Cherokee National Forest

Fees or permits: Launching fee at put-in and takeout

Nearest city/town: Etowah, Tennessee

Maps: USGS McFarland, Oswald Dome

Boats used: Kayaks, rafts, tubes, occasional canoes

Organizations: Cherokee National Forest, 3171 Hwy. 64, Benton, TN 37307; (423) 338-3300; fs.usda.gov/cherokee/

Contacts/outfitters: Webb Brothers Float Service, Inc./General Store, Hiwassee River, Box 61, Reliance, TN 37369; (423) 338-2373; webbbros.com

Put-in/Takeout Information

To the takeout: From exit 20 on I-75, near Cleveland, Tennessee, take US 64 East Bypass for 6.3 miles to US 64 East and continue 7.7 miles to US 411. Head north on US 411 for 12 miles and turn right on TN 30 East, just before crossing the Hiwassee River. Take TN 30 East for 6.2 miles to TN 315 in Reliance. The takeout is at the intersection here at Webb Brothers Country Store. GPS: N35 11.296' / W84 30.127'

To the put-in from the takeout: From Webb Brothers, take TN 315 across the Hiwassee River and cross the railroad tracks to turn right on Childers Creek Road. Follow Childers Creek Road for 1.3 miles, veering right to stay with Childers Creek Road at an intersection. Drive 0.3 mile farther then veer right again, now on Powerhouse Road. Travel 3.1 miles on Powerhouse Road to the powerhouse boating site. GPS: N35 10.863' / W84 26.674'

Paddle Summary

This gorgeous but challenging paddle takes place within the bounds of the Cherokee National Forest on a Tennessee state scenic river. The fun and wild ride on the Hiwassee is better done if you have whitewater experience or are paddling with those who are experienced. It is an ideal waterway for those wanting to develop/hone their whitewater skills. Having said that, thousands of neophytes go down the river each year in tubes, rafts, and rubber funyaks, using local outfitters.

Start at the powerhouse put-in and immediately enjoy the fast-moving water, which leads into some mild shoals before you begin a series of Class II–II+ rapids. Your ears will be filled with the sounds of whitewater throughout the paddle,

Kayakers prep at the put-in

either from a rapid to come, one you are on, or one you just went down. The roar echoes through the river gorge.

The Hiwassee makes its way around the Big Bend. Continue your trip over The Ledges, Bigneys Rock, and Devils Shoals, among other named rapids. Before you know it, the trip will be over and you might be tempted to do it twice in one day. The paddle is just short of 6.0 miles, but if you want to extend your adventure, you can take out at the national forest picnic area, 2.5 miles downstream of TN 315 on river left.

This paddle is dependent on water releases from TVA's Apalachia Dam. Fortunately, TVA makes daily recreational releases for the Hiwassee River from late May through August, with weekend releases in May, and the months of September and October. To find the release schedule, visit the TVA website (tva.com); look for reservoir information and then find the release schedule for Apalachia Dam. You can also do it via phone (865-632-2264). Releases generally start at 10 or 11 a.m., so be prepared to launch by noon.

River/Lake Overview

The Hiwassee is a Georgia native. The river begins near Unicoi Gap and the Appalachian Trail, where the stream is small enough to straddle, then heads north where it is impounded as Lake Chatuge. Here the watercourse enters North Carolina, curving westerly toward the town of Murphy then flows into Lake Hiwassee. Below this dam the river becomes Hiwassee by name only, minus most of its water used for power generation—that comes out below Apalachia Dam—and enters the Volunteer State. It is below Apalachia Dam that the river becomes a true river again, and where this paddle begins. The Hiwassee keeps its westerly flow, leaving the mountains and winding westward to feed the Tennessee River, ending its journey.

The Paddling

The large concrete ramp put-in is below the Apalachia Dam powerhouse. Waters rush rapidly as you paddle away. The river is perhaps 250 feet wide but very swift. Ahead you'll see rock outcrops dotting the mostly forested gorge of the river. Underwater grasses sway in the chilly, crystalline water. Small islands form here and there. The bigger ones are named. A smaller island is immediately

Hiwassee River

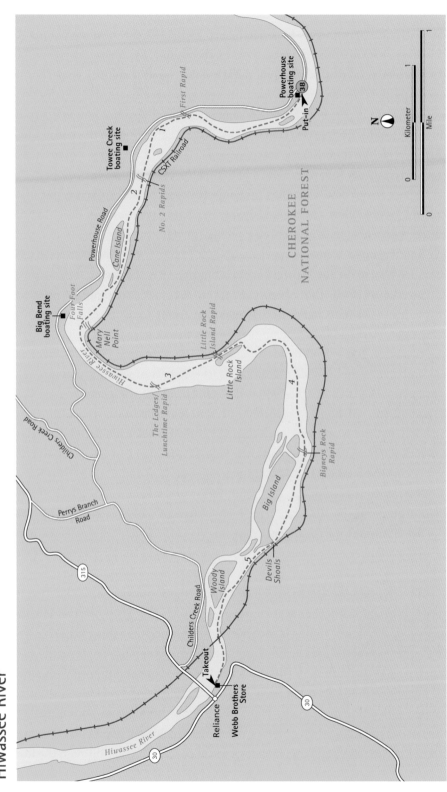

Powerhouse boating site

Put-in 38

First Rapid

Towee Creek boating site

No. 2 Rapids

CSXT Railroad

Cane Island

Powerhouse Road

Big Bend boating site

Four Foot Falls

Mary Nell Point

Little Rock Island Rapid

Little Rock Island

Hiwassee River

The Ledges/ Lunchtime Rapid

3

4

Bigneys Rock Rapid

Big Island

CHEROKEE NATIONAL FOREST

Childers Creek Road

Perrys Branch Road

315

Childers Creek Road

Woody Island

5

Devils Shoals

Takeout

Reliance

Webb Brothers Store

30

30

Hiwassee River

N

0   Kilometer   1

0   Mile   1

downstream of the put-in. In general, keep to the left side of most islands. The banks are heavily forested with river birch, walnut, sycamore, ironwood, and thick brush. A railroad stays along the left bank nearly the entire route. Fog can overhang the river as the cool water mixes with warmer air above it. The wide waterway can make route finding challenging, but it also has numerous routes on many rapids. Be apprised that the Hiwassee is often busy at the put-in immediately after the powerhouse starts generating, but if you have never been on the river, consider following someone to find the best route over the rapids. Just make sure they know what they're doing! If I were to pick someone out of the crowd, I would follow a helmeted kayaker in a hard plastic boat of his or her own rather than a neophyte in a rented a rubber funyak.

The first rapid occurs in approximately 0.7 mile as the river curves left. The main shoals are on the far right-hand side where the Hiwassee flows adjacent to Powerhouse Road. This is a good warm-up for what is to come. More islands follow just below this rapid. At 1.1 miles the Towee Creek boating access is on river right. Here paddlers load up then briefly float Towee Creek before entering the Hiwassee. The second rapid, No. 2 Rapid, is a solid drop. Then the river widens and divides and rounds more islands, the biggest of which is Cane Island. A word about the islands: Once you decide which side of the island you are going to paddle, you will find yourself committed to that side for the rest of the rapid. Stay left at Cane Island and work through Thread the Needle Rapid—watch for the rock jumbles on its lower end. Just below Cane Island, at 2.0 miles, the river comes together and Big Bend boating access is on river right.

Stay on your toes in the Big Bend. First comes Four Foot Falls/Mary Nell Point (rapids on the Hiwassee have many different names, according to whom you ask). Stay left for the biggest drops or right for smaller drops. Powerhouse Road is no longer beside the river, though the railroad tracks continue on river left.

The river widens. Downstream lies The Ledges/Lunchtime Rapid. This is a series of ledges lasting about 0.25 mile and is very fun. Start on river left then work your way down, ending up on river right, running the calmer water between the ledges to find the next viable chute. An alluring stopping spot is on the right-hand bank at the bottom of the rapid. Look for the rock cliff topped with pine.

Islands resume below The Ledges, the main one being a rocky wooded island topped with white pines rising high. This is Little Rock Island. Aim directly for the nose of the island then go left, spilling over a couple of good Class II drops at 3.4 miles. Now stay right and look for a small channel cutting through the lower end of Little Rock Island. There's no rapid in the canopied channel, just a fun flow through which to paddle. Open to an area of tiny willow-covered islands.

The river bends to the right and widens. Islands, water, and mountain scenery continue to amaze. Big Island lies ahead. Stay left there and navigate another rapid at 4.3 miles, alternately called Bigneys Rock, Three Chutes, or Funnel Rapid. Multiple chutes allow for your choice of routes. Rhododendron and mountain laurel are regular features of the islands and the riverbanks. The river is wide here, and you can gain great views of Starr and Chilhowee Mountains, which act as gates through which the Hiwassee flows and exits the highlands a few miles ahead.

Be prepared as the left channel around Big Island builds into some big train waves at the rapid known as Devils Shoals. Open boaters risk swamping here, so be prepared. A final series of easy ledges leads to flowing flatwater with beautiful mountain views. A railroad trestle is in the foreground. Once beyond the trestle stay left; the Webb Brothers takeout is on your left just before the bridge.

39 Conasauga River

This parcel of the Conasauga makes a relaxing pastoral float through rural northwest Georgia.

Start: Beaverdale canoe launch

End: Dalton Utilities canoe launch

Length: 8.4 miles

Float time: About 4.3 hours

Difficulty rating: Easy

Rapids: Class I

River/lake type: Meandering valley river

Current: Moderate

River gradient: 3.4 feet per mile

Water gauge: Conasauga River at GA 286 near Eton; minimum runnable level 85 cfs

Season: Mar through Nov

Land status: Private

Fees or permits: No fees or permits required

Nearest city/town: Chatsworth, Georgia

Maps: USGS: Beaverdale, Chatsworth; Conasauga Canoe Trail

Boats used: Kayaks, canoes, a few johnboats

Organizations: Georgia River Network, 126 South Milledge Ave., Ste. E3, Athens, GA 30605; (706) 549-4508; garivers.org

Contacts/outfitters: Georgia Department of Natural Resources, 2 Martin Luther King Jr. Dr. SE, Ste. 1252 East Tower, Atlanta, GA 30334; (404) 656-3500; gadnr.org

Put-in/Takeout Information

To the takeout: From Chattanooga, take I-75 South into Georgia and exit 341 for Tunnel Hill/Varnell. Turn left onto GA 201 North and follow it for 4.7 miles. Turn right on GA 2/Prater Mill Road and follow it 3.5 miles to Lake Francis Road. Turn right on Lake Francis Road and continue 0.7 mile then turn left onto Good Hope Road. Follow Good Hope Road for 5.4 miles (Good Hope Road changes to Boyles Mill Road along the way). Turn left into the Dalton Utilities canoe launch on the left, just before crossing the Conasauga River. GPS: N34 51.217' / W84 50.617

Author takes a break in the shallows of the Conasauga River

To the put-in from the takeout: From the Dalton Utilities canoe launch, backtrack (west) on Boyles Mill Road for 0.3 mile then turn right onto River Road. Stay on River Road for 5.2 miles. Turn right onto Beaverdale Road, continue for 0.2 mile, then turn right onto GA 2 East. Follow GA 2 for 0.4 mile to Beaverdale Grocery, on the right just before crossing the Conasauga. The Beaverdale put-in is behind the store. A parking area and trail are on the right as you face the store. GPS: N 34 55.231'/ W 84° 50.550'

Paddle Summary

The narrow, mostly shaded watercourse runs slow to moderate, with quiet sections broken by a few Class I riffles. Most of the riverside land is held in large farms, so development is virtually nonexistent. Allow plenty of time to make your trip so that you can become as laid back as the setting deserves. The addition of official river accesses on both ends by Dalton Utilities enhances the paddle.

River/Lake Overview

The Conasauga starts as a crashing mountain river, leaving the Cohutta Wilderness in the North Georgia mountains before entering the state of Tennessee. It then turns south and reenters the Peach State just upstream from the beginning of this paddle. At this point the Conasauga becomes a pastoral waterway, winding its way south to meet the Coosawattee River, together forming the Oostanaula River. The uppermost part of the river is for highly skilled whitewater experts, but after it reenters Georgia, the Conasauga offers 80 more miles of paddling that is doable by most.

The Paddling

The put-in was improved by Dalton Utilities, with a trail and ramp at the waterway. The Conasauga averages between 15 and 40 feet wide, narrowing where gravel bars force it along a bank or divide it around islands. The river is normally clear except after rains. Banks range from 10 to 20 feet high and are mud, brush, rock, and roots. A canopy of sycamore, ash, and river birch borders the Conasauga. Ironwood also abounds. Tulip trees rise on the higher banks. Grasses thicken atop the frequent gravel bars in summer.

After a few initial riffles, the river straightens out, slows down, and travels southeast. Fallen stumps and logs provide harborages for smallmouth bass and bream. Locals often float a johnboat on this stretch, fishing. While fields may come near the river, a corridor of trees nearly always provides a screen.

At 1.2 miles a bluff rises high to your right. The Conasauga makes a sharp bend to the left that culminates in a rocky Class I shoal. Watch for small creeks continually feeding the river. At 2.1 miles a channel leaves left, circling around 10-acre Hampton Island. The left channel rarely flows, save for times of flood. Where the channel renters below Hampton Island, the Conasauga widens again. At 2.6 miles the river joins an obviously man-made channel, bypassing a large bend to the right.

Here is the story as it was told to me: In 1941, with the river flowing high, two men drowned in a swimming hole on the part of the river now bypassed. This swimming hole, popular with locals, had a "swirl" when the water was up. Not wanting to wait for the water to drop, some local men dynamited a channel, bisecting the bend in order to lower the waters so they could find the victims' bodies. The blast altered the river course, but they ended up finding the bodies downstream after the water dropped. Over time the Conasauga abandoned the old meandering channel for the straight dynamited one, leaving the meander to dry up. The slough of the old river comes in on your right at 3.0 miles.

Conasauga River

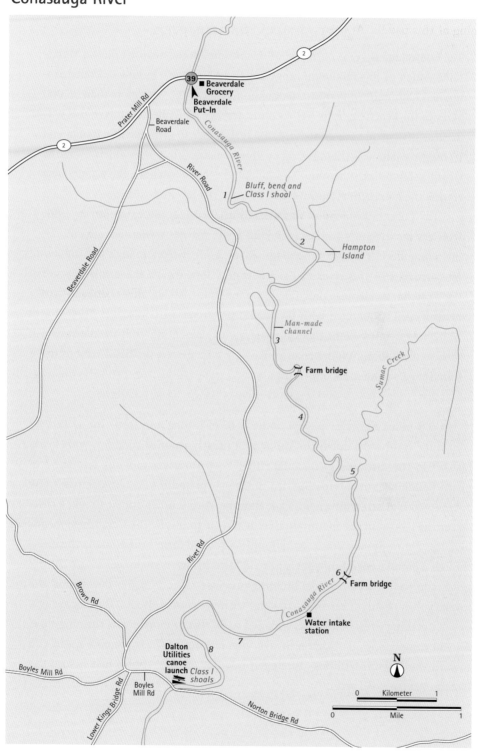

Beaverdale Grocery
39 Beaverdale Put-In
Beaverdale Road
Prater Mill Rd
2
River Road
Conasauga River
Beaverdale Road
1 — Bluff, bend and Class I shoal
2 — Hampton Island
3 — Man-made channel
Farm bridge
4
Sumac Creek
5
Brown Rd
River Rd
6 — Farm bridge
Water intake station
7
Conasauga River
8
Dalton Utilities canoe launch — Class I shoals
Boyles Mill Rd
Lower Kings Bridge Rd
Boyles Mill Rd
Norton Bridge Rd

N

0   Kilometer   1
0   Mile   1

WILDERNESS BEGINNINGS

The Conasauga River is born east of this paddle, in the nearby Cohutta Mountains. Much of this mountain range is part of Georgia's largest federally designated mountain wilderness, the Cohutta Wilderness, with more than 35,000 acres in the Peach State, as well as more acreage in Tennessee. It is in this wilderness that small springs above 4,000 feet gather to form the Conasauga and its bigger wilderness tributary, Jacks River, emerges from the wilderness at the Georgia-Tennessee state line. Even though the Jacks is bigger, the watercourse retains the name Conasauga.

The Cohutta Wilderness was established in 1984 and expanded in 1991. It offers more than 40 miles of hiking trails for the wilderness adventurer, including the 13.0-mile Conasauga River Trail, which follows the uppermost reaches of this river to its headwaters flowing off the north slope of the Cohutta Wilderness and Cowpen Mountain. Hiking this trail, you will become well acquainted with the mountain stretch of Conasauga River—the trail fords it thirty-eight times. Consider complementing your paddle with a visit to the Cohutta Wilderness. A hike here will allow a firsthand view of the Conasauga's wilderness beginnings.

At 3.5 miles the river passes under a farm bridge and ford. The waterway continues southward down the valley in a mostly wooded corridor, with fields just off in the distance. Occasional riffles keep the river moving, and the frequent bends keep it interesting. Do not be surprised if you come across a few submerged logs stretching across the flowage. At 5.0 miles Sumac Creek, a clear stream also born in the mountains, comes in on your left. The Conasauga meanders less below Sumac Creek. At 6.0 miles a second farm bridge spans the river, though a parallel road ford shows the old farm bridge is no longer in use. At 6.2 miles you pass a water intake building on river right. Not too far beyond the intake valve, the river resumes curving, with occasional shoals. The Conasauga, despite making a few bends, has widened to 80 feet or more and is running slow. As you come alongside Norton Bridge, one last set of Class I shoals speed you toward the Norton Utilities–developed takeout on river right, just before the Norton Bridge Road span.

40 Oostanaula River

Start on the Coosawattee River then join the Oostanaula as it curves through rural lands to end in the heart of Calhoun, Georgia.

Start: GA 225 ramp

End: Downtown Calhoun ramp

Length: 11.2 miles

Float time: About 5.5 hours

Difficulty rating: Moderate

Rapids: Class I

River/lake type: Medium-sized rural river entering a town

Current: Slow-moderate

River gradient: 1.5 feet per mile

Water gauge: Oostanaula River at Resaca, GA; no minimum runnable level, maximum level flood stage

Season: Year-round

Land status: Private

Fees or permits: No fees or permits required

Nearest city/town: Calhoun, Georgia

Maps: USGS Calhoun North

Boats used: Kayaks, canoes, johnboats

Organizations: Georgia River Network, 126 South Milledge Ave., Ste. E3, Athens, GA 30605; (706) 549-4508; garivers.org

Contacts/outfitters: Georgia Department of Natural Resources, 2 Martin Luther King Jr. Dr. SE, Ste. 1252 East Tower, Atlanta, GA 30334; (404) 656-3500; gadnr.org

Put-in/Takeout Information

To the takeout: From Chattanooga, take I-75 south into Georgia and exit 315 for Redbud Road/Calhoun. Head west on GA 156/Redbud Road and follow it for 1.6 miles. Turn left on US 41/Wall Street and continue for 0.7 mile. Turn right onto West Line Street in downtown Calhoun and continue for 0.3 mile. Turn right onto North River Street and stay north to quickly cross the Oostanaula River. At 0.1 mile, just after crossing the river, take the first right to enter a gravel parking lot. Follow the main road right to the river and public boat ramp. GPS: N34 30.644' / W84 57.448'

To the put-in from the takeout: From the downtown Calhoun launch, backtrack south on North River Road then backtrack on West Line Street and left again on US 41 North. Follow US 41 North for 1.8 miles; veer right onto GA 225 North then follow it for 2.5 miles. Turn right into a large parking area just before crossing the Coosawattee River. A long concrete boat ramp leads down to the river. GPS: N34 32.482' / W84 54.064'

Paddle Summary

The adventure starts on the Coosawattee River near Georgia's New Echota State Historic Site. You paddle just a short distance to meet the Conasauga River, and together they form the Oostanaula River. Therefore, in the first 0.25 mile you can paddle three different rivers. The trip from the confluence of rivers to Calhoun is relaxing, with much of the adventure on calm, languid waters flowing past farmland. Float under I-75 near Resaca, site of a Union floating bridge during the Civil War, as the river makes a giant horseshoe. Pass some stone bluffs and splashy shoals on the lower segment. The scene remains quiet and rural until trip's end in downtown Calhoun.

River/Lake Overview

The Oostanaula River drains a large portion of North Georgia and a tiny bit of East Tennessee, much of it highlands. This paddle begins where the Oostanaula's two primary tributaries converge—the Coosawattee and the Conasauga. From there the Oostanaula winds southwesterly for nearly 50 miles, where it meets the Etowah River in Rome, Georgia. Those two streams together form the Coosa River.

The Paddling

Leave the long boat ramp on the Coosawattee River to immediately float under the GA 225 bridge. At 0.1 mile, your float on the Coosawattee is over and it merges with the Conasauga River. Paddle a bit on the Conasauga just to say you were on three rivers in one day. Note the different colorations displayed by the waters of the Coosawattee and the Conasauga. Though they both drain forested mountains then rural farmlands, the Conasauga is generally regarded as the more pristine and usually clearer river, though the Coosawattee is stilled at

Oostanaula River

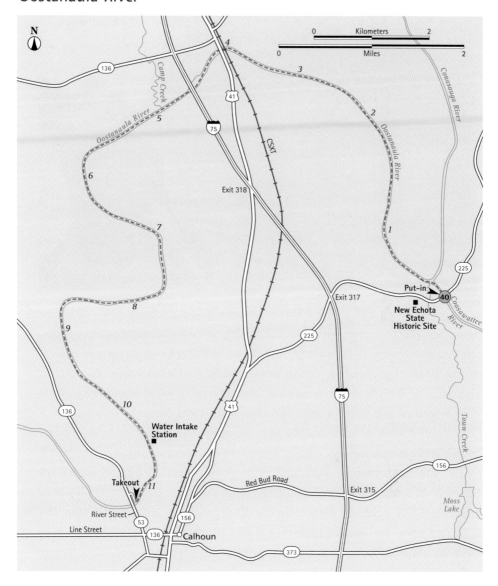

Carter's Lake. The colorations on the day of your paddle may be due to other factors, such as a fresh thunderstorm hitting one or another waterway. No matter the color scheme of the day, it is fascinating to watch the two waters meld into the Oostanaula River.

In just a few feet on the Oostanaula, Town Creek enters on river left. This stream is named for the Cherokee capital of New Echota, which was established

A faster section of the Oostanaula

here (see sidebar). Below Town Creek, the newly formed Oostanaula stretches more than 180 feet wide, with little in the way of obstructions or other hazards, just straightforward river floating. That is one of the reasons this is a near-ideal outing, albeit a little long for inexperienced paddlers—no fallen tree strainers, no big rapids, no fast maneuvering needed. Just get in your kayak or canoe and float.

A screen of ash, silver maple, and river birch trees lines the riverway, with fields beyond. Next to no development exists above the soil banks, save for a few houses and a couple of river camps. Some farmers use the river as an irrigation source. You are paddling northbound but beginning to make a grand arc toward Calhoun. At 2.4 miles an unnamed creek enters on river left. At 4.0 miles float under the CSXT Railroad bridge then the US 41 bridge. A gravel bar for stopping is located here. The hamlet of Resaca is just north of the river. Here, in May 1864, as General Sherman was on his ruthless March to Sea, the Confederates and Union clashed. At the end of the three-day battle, the Union pushed south through Resaca, using pontoon bridges to cross the Oostanaula River, continuing toward Atlanta.

Our paddle continues past some cedar-clad bluffs to reach the unmistakable roar of I-75. Float under the busy road at 4.5 miles. The noise soon recedes into the background as clear Camp Creek enters on river right at 4.9 miles. The Oostanaula continues its grand arc, and you turn fully south at 5.9 miles, where a wooded bluff rises on your right. The banks remain wooded. At 6.6 miles float down a light and easy shoal. Find another little rapid at 7.1 miles. The river seems to speed up as a whole down here in riffles. Occasional partly wooded bluffs rise on river left.

The floating remains easy, and soon you are passing a water intake station on river left at 10.6 miles. Funny thing, it still doesn't seem like a town is just 0.5 mile ahead. An unnamed creek enters on river left at 10.9 miles. You are almost there. When you see the North River Road bridge ahead, get over to river right, where the ramp is. A shoal is located just downstream of the ramp; if you are on the wrong side of the river, it may be difficult to cross the river in the shoal. At 11.2 miles, just before the bridge, you reach the ramp, ending this paddling adventure.

NEW ECHOTA

New Echota State Historic Site is located just 0.5 mile from this paddle's put-in. You will drive directly by the site of the Cherokee's last capital city, where the aboriginals attempted to govern not by their ways but by the ways of the United States, with representative governments, written laws, and courts. The Cherokee first met here—near where the Conasauga, Coosawattee, and Oostanaula Rivers meet—in 1819 to resolve problems using what was called a National Council, the representative body that also worked with Cherokee leadership, which included a principal chief. In 1825 the National Council voted to make their capital at this spot, replacing the old capital of Chota, in East Tennessee, that had been lost to the white man. The National Council named their capital New Echota, memorializing the former seat of governance.

New Echota was plotted and inhabited, even included a river ferry. Although an average of sixty or so Cherokee resided here year-round, the capital would flood with people during meeting season. Alas, the Cherokee governmental experiment was not to last, as a young United States determined to reserve all the land east of the Mississippi River for themselves. The Cherokee were unceremoniously removed in 1838 during the infamous Trail of Tears.

New Echota was used as an assembly site for the removal to what became Oklahoma, with Fort Wool built to house the Cherokee before they were forced west. After that, New Echota was no more. However, today you can visit the site and learn about the history that took place near this paddle.

Climbing is big in
greater Chattanooga
COURTESY TENNESSEE
BOULDERING AUTHORITY

ROCK CLIMBING ADVENTURES NEAR CHATTANOOGA

While hiking, paddling, and bicycling are activities undertaken by both casual and dedicated outdoor adventurers, there is a group of devoted men and women who revel in rock climbing opportunities here in the Scenic City. From crags on the Cumberland Plateau to in-town climbing gyms, Chattanooga is nationally known for its rock climbing adventure destinations, and is often hailed as the kingpin of climbing east of the Mississippi River as well as the best urban climbing locale in the country—and that is saying a lot.

A bona fide climbing community has grown out of the wealth of rock climbing venues in the region, such as the famed Tennessee Wall, Foster Falls, the Stone Fort, and Sunset Park, with more climbers being introduced to the sport via climbing gyms. Among these areas you can undertake traditional climbing, sport climbing, free climbing, or bouldering. Whether you are a novice or an old hat, rock climbing can add one more Chattanooga outdoor activity to your adventure possibilities.

Moreover, rock climbing can be high adventure—clinging to the stone face of a mountainside, hanging by the tips of your fingers, muscles tightened, beads of sweat popping from your forehead as you plot your route skyward. Fear and a dry throat. A moment in life vividly etched in your mind. Then you drift back to your office desk, remembering you have a job, a family, and responsibilities too great to endeavor in such a pursuit.

Not so fast, my friend. Rock climbing is an activity that no matter how good you are, or how bad you are, there is going to be something available at your level. A main attraction is "the rush." It's when your hands are starting to ache—you can barely hang on. Your friends are encouraging you on with yells of "Go! Go! Go!" and you manage to make that next handhold, and the next, finishing your route.

Rock climbing engages you both mentally and physically. You must incorporate your brain and your body to climb fluidly. Climbing requires a great deal of problem solving, yet it is similar to a dance where the wall is your partner and the different holds and features dictate the moves you have to make.

The Yosemite Decimal System is used for rating climbs. Degrees of difficulty in climbing are rated Class 4 and Class 5. Class 4 is essentially climbing without a rope, with the potential of injury if you fall. Class 5 is climbing with a rope, with potentially fatal consequences if you fall. Each class has incremental degrees of difficulty.

Safety note: This is one outdoor adventure that you do not want to begin on your own. Purposefully learn with experienced climbers, or use the available climbing gyms for instruction.

If you decide to climb, here is some terminology to help you at least sound like you know what you are doing:

Harness: Device that goes around a climber's midsection to which a rope attaches.

Anchor: Metal screws bolted into a rock wall for attaching a rope.

Carabiner: Small metal device with a clip that holds rope to an anchor.

Lead climber: The person at the top of the rope leading the climb. Generally places anchor points while climbing.

Traditional climbing: Born of mountaineering, often known as "trad climbing." This is when climbers place all their bolts and ropes to protect against falls, then remove them after the climb is complete

Free climbing: Climbing using natural rocks features without using a rope for assistance. Can be roped in case of falls, yet the rope cannot be used to aid the climb.

Sport climbing: Climbing that relies on preplaced, permanent anchors used for protection.

Bouldering: Rock climbing on natural or artificial walls without ropes or harnesses.

Pitch: Length of a section of wall being climbed.

Belay: Derived from a sailing term meaning "hold fast." That is what the person holding the climbing rope does for the person climbing.

Top rope: Climbing where the rope leads from the climber to an anchor above him/her and back down to the belayer. The safest form of roped climbing and the standard method at commercial climbing walls.

The following five climbing Chattanooga destinations can scratch your climbing itch.

Climbing Gyms

A climbing gym is arguably the best way to break into the sport of climbing. High Point in downtown Chattanooga has an iconic and eye-catching outside climbing wall, probably the best advertisement for climbing in town. It also features inside climbing walls, a bouldering room, training walls, even a kids' climbing area. It really does have it all when it comes to indoor climbing. If you are new to the sport, you can take climbing classes; they also offer American Mountain Guides Association–certified outdoor climbing guides. High Point also has a Riverside facility in Chattanooga. For more information, check out highpointclimbing.com.

Tennessee Bouldering Authority, located in the St. Elmo area of Chattanooga, also offers a fine place for beginners to engage in rock climbing or for veterans to stay sharp. Bouldering specialists, their gym covers in excess of 3,000 square feet. For more information visit www.tbagym.com.

Climbing gyms can form a quick fix for bouldering junkies COURTESY TENNESSEE BOULDERING AUTHORITY

Rock walls like
this attract
climbers of all
stripes. MARIO
MORANTE

Tennessee Wall

This premier climbing destination put Chattanooga on the national climbing map. To this day, the Tennessee Wall, or T-Wall as it is dubbed in climbing circles, attracts climbers from all over the country. In fact, the T-Wall has lured climbing fanatics to move to the Scenic City. Located in the Grand Canyon of the Tennessee River within the public confines of Prentice Cooper State Forest, the Tennessee Wall rose to prominence in the 1980s. Extending nearly 2 miles in length, the wall offers hundreds of routes and has about every type of challenge and climb you could possibly want. Guides have been written that are solely devoted to climbing the Tennessee Wall. If there is a downside, the Tennessee Wall faces south and can be blistering hot much of the summer; thus it is a favored cool-weather destination. Also, since the Tennessee Wall is within the bounds of the state forest, the area is closed during hunts, no exceptions. Find out hunt dates on the Prentice Cooper website: tn.gov/agriculture/forests/state-forests/prentice-cooper.html.

Sunset Rock

Sunset Rock is located along the northwest side of Lookout Mountain in Tennessee, near the northernmost point of the mountain. This public land is part of Chickamauga & Chattanooga National Military Park. A traditional climbing destination, Sunset Rock has been attracting climbers since the 1960s, possibly even earlier. Bouldering is done here as well. Plenty of routes are available. The high-quality sandstone rock and incredible views on mostly single-pitch routes, along with its close proximity to downtown Chattanooga, attract climbers for quick adrenaline fixes. Parking can be a problem; contact the National Park Service at Point Park (706) 866-9241 for the latest parking allowances.

Foster Falls

Despite being better known as a hiking, backpacking, and car-camping destination, Foster Falls draws rock climbers from not only greater Chattanooga but also around the country. The climbing area is set on the gorge walls of Little Gizzard Creek and is accessible by trail. (By the way, you'll get a good look at 60-foot Foster Falls en route to the climbing destination, a fine example of the superlative

The Stone Fort is a boulderer's nirvana. MARIO MORANTE

scenery found here.) The vertical sandstone walls and overhanging walls of rockhouses create a wealth of climbing opportunities, including nearly 200 routes along a nearly 2-mile section of climbable wall.

Stone Fort

Also known as Little Rock City, the bouldering mecca is located on the edge of Montlake Golf Course on Mowbray Mountain where the Cumberland Plateau drops off. It all started when climbers snuck onto the golf course to climb; eventually an agreement was worked out with course management. Tackle some of the 700 or so boulder problems at a place that also has its own guidebook. The Stone Fort is quite popular, partly due to its excellent climbing lines, and becomes an almost-festive atmosphere, with climbers working together and urging one another on. Today climbing is officially sanctioned at the golf course, as long as you purchase a climbing pass and sign a waiver. You actually park in the same lot as the golfers! *Note:* Dogs are strictly forbidden.

These are just some of the many rock climbing locales in the greater Chattanooga area. As you grow in the sport of rock climbing, you may find yourself at other Chattanooga area destinations, such as Rocktown, Suck Creek Canyon, Deep Creek, and Castle Rock. Go for it!

Mountain view near The Pocket Campground

Camping Adventures Near Chattanooga

C amping is a wonderful way to enhance a paddling, hiking, bicycling, or rock climbing adventure—or it can simply be an adventure unto itself. The Chattanooga region has a variety of drive-up, auto-accessible campgrounds that serve as a quick getaway for you and your family or a group of friends wanting to enjoy the great outdoors.

Some enduring scenes come to mind when I think of camping: morning rays of sunlight piercing the trees; wood smoke gently curling upward from the flickering fire; riding bikes over gravel roads; the folly of erecting a brand-new tent; friends and families having supper together, all hands running for cover as an afternoon thunderstorm breaks loose; the smell of hamburgers wafting through the trees; an angler proudly displaying freshly caught fish while returning to camp; autumn's golden leaves drifting onto a well-worn, initial-carved picnic table.

To get you started on your camping adventures, here are five recommended frontcountry drive-up campgrounds for you to consider. All are within an hour's drive of Chattanooga and close to the hiking, bicycling, and paddling adventures detailed in this guide.

The Pocket Campground

Nearest town: Villanow, Georgia

Open: Apr through Oct

Individual sites: 27

Each site has: Picnic table, fire grate, tent pad, lantern post

Site assignment: First-come, first-served; no reservations

Facilities: Water spigots, flush toilets

Fee: Yes

Contact info: fs.usda.gov/conf

The Pocket offers quiet wooded camping in the valley of a clear cool spring. The unusual name reflects the campground's being encircled by Mill and Horn Mountains, forming a horseshoe. The Chattahoochee National Forest recreation area was developed by the Civilian Conservation Corps in the late 1930s and presents a relaxing venue with adventures nearby.

The campsites are laid out along a loop road, with a couple of spur loops off the main loop. The first few sites are along the outflow of The Pocket spring. The campsites—like the entire campground—are well maintained. Oaks, pines, maples, and dogwoods shade the well-separated sites.

A restroom building with flush toilets is located inside the loop. Water spigots are located throughout the campground. The Pocket Campground will fill on summer holiday weekends and nice-weather weekends in late spring and early fall. At other times, you should be able to get one of the first-come, first-served campsites.

Adventurous campers like to explore the spring here or make the 2.5-mile Pocket Loop hike that starts at the campground. The Pocket Nature Trail makes a 1.0-mile loop and offers interpretive signage along the way. Anglers will toss a line into nearby Johns Creek.

Just a short drive away is the Keown Falls trailhead, from where you can hike to the 40-foot cataract of Keown Falls on the way to Johns Mountain Overlook. You could also enjoy a scenic drive through these parts of the Chattahoochee National Forest using the Ridge and Valley Scenic Byway. The drive begins at GA 136 and GA 201 then heads south on Armuchee Road to GA 27. It then heads south on GA 27, turns left on GA 156, and turns left on Floyd Springs Road to Johns Creek Road to Pocket Road, right by The Pocket Campground.

Access: From exit 336 on I-75 near Dalton, southeast of downtown Chattanooga, take US 41 North/US 76 West for 2.6 miles to GA 201. Turn left on GA 201 South and follow it for 10 miles to the intersection with GA 136/East Armuchee Road at Villanow. Turn left on GA 136/East Armuchee Road and follow it 0.3 mile to Pocket Road. Turn right on Pocket Road and follow it 7 miles to the signed left turn for The Pocket Recreation Area. GPS: N34 35.065' / W85 5.147'

Foster Falls Campground

Nearest town: Jasper, Tennessee

Open: Year-round

Individual sites: 26

Each site has: Picnic table, fire grate, lantern post

Site assignment: Reservations required

Facilities: Water spigots, flush toilets, hot showers

Fee: Yes

Contact Info: tnstateparks.com

Foster Falls Campground, located by famed Foster Falls and the adjacent trails and rock climbing opportunities therein, is part of South Cumberland State Park and makes an ideal base camp for exploring the adjacent activities. The twenty-six sites are laid out in a simple loop under level, wooded land. The campsites are large and well dispersed if you like to spread your gear out—or bring a lot of it.

The bathhouse has been renovated since the state park took over the campground. Water spigots are easily accessible. With reservations required, you will never have to worry about getting a campsite on a nice weekend. Additionally, you can pick out your site online, though nothing beats seeing a site in person.

Climbers flock to Foster Falls Campground.

The campground will feature a mix of people relaxing in the great outdoors, along with ambitious hikers and rock climbers. Foster Falls is a place where you won't run out of outdoor activities, whether it is going to see waterfalls, swimming in the pool at the base of Foster Falls, tackling the sheer walls of the Little Fiery Gizzard Creek gorge, or executing a loop hike at one of the many nearby units of South Cumberland State Park, including Grundy Lakes, on the National Historic Register. See the Lone Rock Coal Ovens here, as well as interpretive history. It all starts here at Foster Falls Campground.

Access: From exit 155 on I-24, west of Chattanooga, take TN 28 North for 1.5 miles. Join US 41 North and continue through Jasper, for a total of 9.5 miles on US 41, to reach Foster Falls Road; turn left into the park. The campground entrance is on the left, before your reach the hiking trailhead. Address: 498 Foster Falls Rd./Tracy Hwy. 41, Sequatchie, TN 37374. GPS: N35 10.893' / W85 40.297'

Chilhowee Campground

Nearest town: Cleveland, TN

Open: Apr through Oct

Individual sites: 88

Each site has: Picnic table, fire grate, lantern post; some have electricity

Site assignment: By reservation and first-come, first-served

Facilities: Water spigots, flush toilets, hot showers

Fee: Yes

Contact info: fs.usda.gov/cherokee

Enjoy mountaintop camping here at Chilhowee, in the Cherokee National Forest amid land and water recreation galore. Not only do you have a wealth of activities from which to choose—hiking, mountain biking, paddling, rafting, swimming, and more—but you also have a wide array of campsites from which to choose, whether with or without electricity or walk-in tent sites. The campground is well maintained and large enough to accommodate all sorts of campers, including you.

Rightfully popular in all seasons, with loyal campers who return yearly, the campground is laid out in several loops with restrooms and water spigots convenient for all. A campground host keeps the campground secure, safe, and clean.

The lake—with swimming beach—at Chickamauga Campground

You can walk to 7-acre McKamy Lake from your campsite. It offers fishing, paddling, and swimming in season. Looking for bigger water? Undertake a hair-raising ride on the famed Ocoee River with its wild rapids. Nearby outfitters are ready to guide you down the waterway that was the paddling site of the 1996 Summer Olympic Games. Nearby Parksville Lake presents stillwater paddling, swimming, and boating activities you can undertake on your own.

A network of 25 miles of hiking and mountain biking trails lace Chilhowee Mountain, where you can make loops or view 65-foot Benton Falls or two-stage Rock Creek Falls, part of the Rock Creek Gorge Scenic Area. There is truly a lot to do here at Chilhowee Mountain Campground, a fine place unto its own.

Access: From exit 20 on I-75 near Cleveland, take the US 64 East Bypass for 6.4 miles. Turn right onto US 64 East and continue for 15 miles. Turn left on FR 77, just after the Ocoee District Ranger Station, and drive for 7.3 miles. Chilhowee Campground will be on your right. Turn right toward the campground and travel 0.4 mile to reach the camp. GPS: N35 9.0139' / W84 36.4545'

Davis Pond

Nearest town: Signal Mountain, Tennessee
Open: Year-round
Individual sites: 4
Each site has: Picnic table
Site assignment: First-come, first-served; no reservations
Facilities: Vault toilets
Fee: No
Contact: tn.gov/agriculture/forests

Prentice Cooper State Forest is an important recreational resource for greater Chattanooga residents and visitors. Perched atop the Cumberland Plateau overlooking the Grand Canyon of the Tennessee River, the state forest is home to copious flora, fauna, incredible geological features, and a fine system of paths featuring the Cumberland Trail. The forest is also managed for hunting and forestry—please check the state forest website for hunt dates, when only hunters are allowed in the forest. ***Note:*** When staying at Davis Pond, you are expected to be at your campsite by sunset. The access road is gated until sunrise to discourage poachers.

Davis Pond has only a few developed sites, but you can pitch your tent by a small, man-made pond. The grassy, partly forested camping area is roped off, keeping autos in one area and campers in another. A vault toilet is the only amenity, but the price is right—free. The forest has another camping area at the forest entrance—Hunter Check Station Campground. This camping area is somewhat rough and heavily used, with no picnic tables. It is on sloped woods with plenty of barren spots but will do in a pinch.

The hiking at Prentice Cooper is superlative. More than 40 miles of trails take you past waterfalls, overlooks, and natural arches and among grand forests. Some of my favorite destinations are Natural Bridge, a massive arch; Lawsons Rock, with a stellar vista you reach after passing a waterfall; and Ransom Hollow, a remote stone perch with a westerly view of the gorge of the Tennessee River. Though the trails are closed to bicyclers, cyclists can ply the forest roads. Speaking of the roads, you will pass cemeteries and homesites, relics of when this land was home to hardscrabble farmers who were eventually bought out to create the preserve we enjoy today.

Access trails of Prentice Cooper State Forest from Davis Pond

Access: From the junction of US 27 and US 127 northwest of Chattanooga, take US 127 North for 1.6 miles to TN 27 West. Turn left on TN 27 West and follow it for 8 miles to Choctaw Trail and a sign for Prentice Cooper WMA. Turn left on Choctaw Trail and follow it for 0.2 mile to Game Reserve Road. Turn left on Game Reserve Road and enter Prentice Cooper State Forest, where it becomes Tower Road. Keep straight on gravel Tower Road for 6.5 miles then turn left on Davis Pond Road and follow it for 0.6 mile to the campground on your left. GPS: N35 10.034' / W85 25.122'

Cloudland Canyon Campground

Nearest town: Trenton, Georgia

Open: Year-round

Individual sites: 30 walk-in tent-only sites; 73 tent and trailer sites

Each site has: Picnic table, tent pad, fire ring; tent and trailer sites have electricity and water hookups

Site assignment: Reservations required

Facilities: Water spigots, flush toilets, hot showers

Fee: Yes

Contact info: gastateparks.org

Sitton Gulch is a beautiful place with clear waters and wildflowers